MW01068917

BECOMING THE PASTOR'S WIFE

BECOMING THE PASTOR'S WIFE

HOW MARRIAGE REPLACED ORDINATION AS A WOMAN'S PATH TO MINISTRY

Beth Allison Barr

BrazosPress

a division of Baker Publishing Group
Grand Rapids, Michigan

© 2025 by Beth Allison Barr

Published by Brazos Press
a division of Baker Publishing Group
Grand Rapids, Michigan
BrazosPress.com

Printed in the United States of America

All rights reserved. No part of this publication may be reproduced, stored in a retrieval system, or transmitted in any form or by any means—for example, electronic, photocopy, recording—without the prior written permission of the publisher. The only exception is brief quotations in printed reviews.

Library of Congress Cataloging-in-Publication Data
Names: Barr, Beth Allison, author.
Title: Becoming the pastor's wife : how marriage replaced ordination as a woman's path to ministry / Beth Allison Barr.
Description: Grand Rapids, Michigan : Brazos Press, a division of Baker Publishing Group, [2025] | Includes bibliographical references and index.
Identifiers: LCCN 2024036206 | ISBN 9781587435898 (cloth) | ISBN 9781493447848 (ebook)
Subjects: LCSH: Spouses of clergy. | Women in church work—Baptists. | Christian leadership—Baptists. | Women—Biblical teaching. | Sex role—Biblical teaching.
Classification: LCC BV4395 .B37 2025 | DDC 253/.22—dc23/eng/20241002
LC record available at https://lccn.loc.gov/2024036206

Scripture quotations are from the New Revised Standard Version Bible, copyright © 1989 National Council of the Churches of Christ in the United States of America. Used by permission. All rights reserved worldwide.

Scripture quotations labeled KJV are from the King James Version of the Bible.

Scripture quotations labeled NASB are taken from the (NASB®) New American Standard Bible®, Copyright © 1960, 1971, 1977, 1995, 2020 by The Lockman Foundation. Used by permission. All rights reserved. www.lockman.org

Scripture quotations labeled NIV are taken from the Holy Bible, New International Version®, NIV®. Copyright © 1973, 1978, 1984, 2011 by Biblica, Inc.® Used by permission of Zondervan. All rights reserved worldwide. www.zondervan.com. The "NIV" and "New International Version" are trademarks registered in the United States Patent and Trademark Office by Biblica, Inc.®

Cover art © Heather Landis, IllustrationX

Jacket design by Paula Gibson

Baker Publishing Group publications use paper produced from sustainable forestry practices and postconsumer waste whenever possible.

25 26 27 28 29 30 31   7 6 5 4 3 2 1

This is for my husband, Jeb.
If more pastors had your integrity, courage, and faith,
the church would be a much better place.

Contents

Introduction

"I still do the bulletin."

She was the wife of a retired small-town pastor. We stood next to the booth sponsored by her church, watching as volunteers served hot dogs to children and firefighters at the summer festival. "Our new preacher is good, but he isn't married. I'll do the bulletin until he gets a wife," she said.

My husband was standing close behind me. I heard a muffled sound of laughter as he turned and walked away. The young preacher wasn't even married, but his future wife already had a job.

"Oh," I said. "That is kind of you."

Unlike my husband, I can keep a straight face. It is a ministry survival skill. Part of me wanted to laugh with him, but the other part was just bemused. Never mind who this pastor's future wife would be; never mind that she might have a career of her own; never mind that she might hate administrative tasks. It was assumed her high calling was to serve alongside her husband; her high privilege was to do what the church needed her to do.

She would become the pastor's wife. This meant, among other things, that she would do the bulletin.

My daughter chose that moment to interrupt, tugging on my sleeve. She wanted a hot dog and needed me to hold her winnings (melted candy tangled with pencils and wristbands in a plastic firefighter hat). Fulfilling my role as mother was an acceptable excuse to leave a conversation—well, to leave almost any situation—in the world of white evangelical Christianity.[1]

Years have passed since I walked away from that conversation, following the short legs of my child as she ran toward her dad. I can't remember what happened next. I can't even remember the name of the retired pastor's wife.

But I have never forgotten her words.

The matter-of-fact assumption about what the pastor's future wife would do and who she should be is familiar to me. Maybe this is why I've never stopped wondering about her. I knew she was destined to do the bulletin, but what else would she face in her new life as a pastor's wife?

Would she be interrogated, as I often had been, while her husband was being interviewed for a pastor's job? Would she sit in a separate room at that time answering questions from staff wives about when she would have kids and whether she would prioritize her husband's job over her career? Would she be asked to quantify how many hours a week her job "outside the home" would take her away from her family? Such questions in any other professional setting would be off the table, yet they are *de rigueur* in some churches today.

Or maybe, as I experienced at a different church, the candidate's wife would stand on the stage and introduce herself to the male deacons sitting with their wives two-by-two in the pews below, assuring them that writing a dissertation would not hinder her ministry. Would she have to explain that even though she could play piano and teach children, she didn't want to do either?

Or maybe, as I saw once in a job ad, she would be required to submit a glossy photo of herself and résumé to go with her husband's application. Mary O. Ross, the third president of the Woman's Auxiliary for the National Baptist Convention, USA—and a pastor's wife for thirty-nine years—writes that a pastor's wife "at all times and under all circumstances" should look "her best." "A little makeup properly applied, may help the personal appearance of even the minister's wife," she encourages. In an earlier retelling of Proverbs 31, Ross emphasizes the importance of dress too, writing that the "Black Minister's Wife" should wear "some of the best and most beautiful clothing" because "her husband's profession bids the family to look well and act well."[2]

Appearances shouldn't matter, but they often do.

Once I met the wife of a pastoral candidate who was significantly taller than her husband. He had applied for a job at the church we served. Many commented about their height difference at the candidate dinner, and soon thereafter he was removed from consideration. While no one at the church was explicit about it, I suspect the size disparity between the pastor and his wife factored into his removal from the job pool.

Dorothy Pentecost—wife of J. Dwight Pentecost, a longtime professor of Bible exposition at Dallas Theological Seminary and pastor at Grace Bible Church in Dallas—had written a book for pastors' wives that was recommended to me. In words reminiscent of Ross's, she explains that a pastor's wife is the "church hostess" and should "appear as attractively dressed as possible all the time." But she goes further than Ross, addressing not only wardrobe but also the body—dedicating a chapter titled "Do Calories Count?" to weight management. "Overweight is a sign of a spiritual lack," Pentecost contends. The "easiest way" to maintain healthy weight is to "live constantly under the control of the Spirit."[3] Her book, like Ross's, is dated, but given the number of chapters on appearance in more recent books by pastors' wives, this kind of advice still resonates.

Take, for example, Dorothy Kelley Patterson's 2021 edition of *A Handbook for Ministers' Wives* (first published in 2002). Patterson—together with her husband, Paige Patterson—has been instrumental in the resurgence of conservative theology within the Southern Baptist Convention. She writes that true beauty is found in a woman's heart rather than in a mirror reflection. Yet, even in the recent edition, she dedicates a section within the second chapter to appearance.

"Your hair, makeup, and clothing work together to frame your testimony," she writes. "A pleasing presence is enhanced by an attractive appearance, happy disposition, poised demeanor, friendly nature, and gracious manner." Like Ross, Patterson invokes the Proverbs 31 woman, explaining how this woman enhanced her husband's reputation with beautiful (and probably expensive) clothing. "Any husband needs a wife of whom he can be proud, and preachers are no exception."[4] A beautiful outside might not be required for the pastor's wife role, but it was certainly something to work toward.

Again, I couldn't help but wonder how prepared the young pastor's hypothetical bride would have been for her new role, to have her appearance, career goals, and administrative skills considered a part of her husband's qualifications for the job.

Would she—could she—fully understand what she was getting herself into?

Because I did not.

Just consider how Marilyn Brown Oden, a guidance counselor and wife of a Methodist minister, explained the role of pastor's wife in her 1966 book *The Minister's Wife: Person or Position?*:

> With this ring also comes the one unique complexity in the ministry by marriage, that of our traditional involvement in our husbands' profession. We like to compare ourselves with those who share the law by marriage or medicine by marriage. These women also must accept the complexity of long schooling. But when hubby's graduation day rolls around (finally!), the wives are not expected to cure ills and try cases. On the other hand, as our husbands receive their diplomas . . . we find that we receive an invisible but traditionally enforced contract of total partnership in this role.[5]

"Ministry by marriage" is an interesting phrase, isn't it?

Oden sees similarities between the role of a pastor's wife and that of any other wife who supports the career of her husband (especially when the career requires additional years of training, as with a doctor, lawyer, or professor). It was common in the post–World

War II era for wives to be lumped into the jobs of their husbands. But Oden argues that the pastor's wife role is different because only the pastor's wife is expected to do the work of her husband too.

Becoming a pastor's wife is not just marrying a pastor.

It is not just supporting a spouse with a demanding job.

It is not just living up to expectations to cook dinner for your husband's coworkers or to accompany him to work-related occasions.

Becoming a pastor's wife is becoming a "total partner" with your husband in his job.

Not every wife of a pastor will resonate with this description.[6] As one of my Baylor colleagues said, "My mom would have stared in utter disbelief" at someone who told her she was the "church hostess." My colleague is the son of a northeastern Methodist minister and grew up mostly in the Boston area. That said, my research assistants (Katie Heatherly and Brooke LeFevre) and I analyzed 150 books published by and for ministers' wives, ranging in date from 1923 to 2023 and including Protestant denominations from mainline to evangelical to historically Black. We examined ninety of these books closely, comparing the language they use to describe the pastor's wife role. Our study suggests that, for many Protestant women in the United States, the expectation to become a "total partner" with a pastoral husband is common. As one 2013 book explains, "a minister's wife needs to know how to minister alongside her husband as a fellow soldier of Jesus Christ." Rather than always fighting on the "front lines," her ministry is often behind the scenes—"supplying her husband with fresh resources, whether by praying for him or by preparing a meal or getting his suit cleaned."[7]

In a 2011 analysis of a study that surveyed more than three thousand United Methodist clergy spouses, sociologist Gail E. Murphy-Geiss confirms Oden's perception that the expectation persists for pastors' wives to participate in their husbands' work. The idea that a pastor and his wife are in a "two-person single career" is "alive and well among married, Protestant clergy, especially male clergy and their wives," she writes. "Hiring a Protestant minister has long been a two-for-one deal, which does not seem to be changing,"[8] even while the husbands of female clergy do not get subsumed into their wives' ministries. Tamika Ledbetter (also a pastor's wife) took this 2011 description one step further in her 2018 dissertation, showing that, despite resistance from pastors' wives, churches still perceive a pastor's wife as a "*no-choice* volunteer leader" expected to "serve as an extension of the husband's ministry."[9]

After considering all this, I better understood an episode from my childhood.

It was the time my church rejected the youth pastor application of a man they had previously chosen to serve as interim. The rejection shocked me. The leaders had chosen him once, and he had done a good job. He met the educational qualifications. He was fun, goofy, smart, and a natural leader for teenagers. What's more, I noticed even then how he put the girls on equal footing with the boys. He seemed like what we needed.

But he wasn't married, and church leaders didn't seem interested in hiring a single man for a full-time pastoral role. I'm not sure whether it was because they feared the sexual risk of hiring a single man to work with teenagers. I'm not sure whether they considered a single man to be less mature than a married man, or whether they simply understood the role of a pastor as including the labor of his wife. What I do know is that I heard one of the adult committee members say that it was time for the candidate to marry. I'm sure there is more to the story (there always is), but I am also sure that he lost the job, at least in part, because he lacked a wife.

I don't think this stance of my childhood church was unusual. Murphy-Geiss quotes the aphorism that "marriage is as much a requirement for the Protestant ministry as celibacy is for the Catholic priesthood." She also cites a 2008 finding that 94 percent of "all Protestant clergy in the United States are married, and, unlike most other professions, the pastor's family is often involved in his/her work."[10] And marriage seems to be on the rise for Protestant clergy, as a 2017 Barna Group study found that 96 percent were married.[11]

These trends and persistent attitudes mean that the pastor's role is *by design* a two-person job in which only one person receives a salary, title, and official position. For a pastor's wife, especially one in the American evangelical tradition, the very nature of her husband's calling presumes her supportive and unpaid labor. He literally can't do it without her.

This is why that retired pastor's wife I talked to so long ago assumed that the new pastor's eventual wife would do the bulletin. Her labor was just part of his job.

Except ministry isn't *just* a job.

It is perceived as a calling.

A calling by God to be a minister.

A calling by God to be a minister's wife.

A calling by God to marry *into* ministry, not just to marry a minister.

Do you see the difference?

This is why the pastor's wife is often expected to become a "total partner" in her husband's job. This is why Dorothy Patterson started a program to equip wives for ministry, complete with classes teaching them how to pack their husbands' suitcases and even how to exit a vehicle modestly. This is why a church hiring committee asked me to quantify the hours I spent on my academic career and assure them that it wouldn't distract me from ministry. This is why even pastors' wives who view themselves as detached from their husbands' jobs can still feel social and spiritual pressure to be actively involved—and guilty when they opt out.

It's because the calling of the husband includes the calling of the wife.

While Black churches conceive of the role of pastor's wife somewhat differently than white churches, there is agreement on this issue. Weptanomah W. Carter, wife of the late Harold A. Carter, prominent former pastor of New Shiloh Baptist Church in Baltimore, explains, "One of the first questions the Black congregation usually asks about a prospective minister after 'knowing he can preach' is, 'Is he married?'"

"Black churches," she continues, "feel that their pastors can be more effective if he has a cooperative mate. Thus, the call of the Black minister means also the call of the minister's wife."[12] The First Lady, as the pastor's wife is often called in Black churches, often carries more authority than her white counterpart. In some churches she is recognized as a co-pastor who preaches and provides pastoral care in an official capacity. Even so, she is sometimes reminded that her calling is to help her husband while submitting to his pastoral authority. "He may be your husband," writes Yolanda G. Butler, an ordained Pentecostal minister and wife of Bishop Donald H. Butler, "but when he steps into the role of the shepherd, he is your pastor."[13]

The pastor is the head of ministry, in his church and in his marriage.

A Historically Anomalous Role

More than twenty-five years ago, I chose to marry a man I knew was called to ministry. He told me early in our friendship that he had chosen social work as his major to better prepare him for ministry. He told me that he felt called to be a pastor and planned to attend a Baptist seminary. I knew this when I said yes to his first dinner invitation. (Should I confess we went to the Cracker Barrel?)

He was licensed and ordained in a Southern Baptist church a few months before our wedding, and I was an eyewitness. I remember how my red dress stood out against the blue fabric of the pew as the ordained men walked forward to lay their hands on him. My father, a longtime ordained deacon, joined the group of men praying over him. My then-fiancé wore the tie I picked out. I remember how his Catholic grandmother cried with joy to watch her Baptist grandson take the vows that were next-best to becoming a priest, vows that meant she could still have great-grandchildren. I was so proud of him (I still am).

I made my choice to become a pastor's wife with eyes wide open.

I made my choice to join with my husband in ministry.

I have never regretted that choice.

I do not regret making pancakes at 2 a.m. for teenage girls laughing in my living room. I do not regret hosting small groups, baby showers, Bible studies, and even game nights for junior high boys who left Dr Pepper cans and spilled M&M's all over my house. I do not regret the hard conversations with hurting young people, the late-night assembly lines putting together binders for student retreats, the early mornings spent driving boxes of doughnuts to hungry kids and coffee to their sleep-deprived leaders, the long afternoons of teaching summer Bible studies. I do not regret trying to sleep in a lumpy bunk bed with muffled snores and talking all around me, or even the time I had to deal with bleary-eyed and drenched teenage girls after our tent flooded in the middle of the night (although that was the last time I agreed to go camping with a youth group).

I do not regret sharing my life and my faith with so many people, not even after experiencing—as I tell in *The Making of Biblical Womanhood: How the Subjugation of Women Became Gospel Truth*—the painful firing of my husband from his youth pastor job.

I do not regret my life as a pastor's wife.

But that doesn't mean I don't have regrets.

When I first got married, I didn't realize how strange the pastor's wife role is. For me, these expectations were normative. It hadn't occurred to me how inappropriate it was to interview the wives of pastoral candidates as participants in their husbands' jobs. Or that it was wrong that these women had to endure questions about their fertility (or lack thereof) and personal careers (for those who had them). Or what it meant that my childhood church would encourage the pastors' wives to hold friendly holiday competitions showcasing their homemaking skills within their parsonages. I would just put on my velvet dress and help serve punch, because this was what we did.

It wasn't until near the end of my PhD program that I began to understand how unusual the expectations placed on pastors' wives really are.

I mean, how common is it for your husband's former boss to greet you by leaning over and shouting at your stomach, "Anyone in there?" on the eve of your dissertation defense?

How usual is it to be chastised by another pastor on staff for not making the childcare arrangements for a church conference, despite you being one of the speakers and never having been on the children's ministry staff?

How usual is it to find that the requirements of your job application had become the subject of an elders' meeting, prompting a discussion about whether pastors' wives should be allowed to work outside the home? As my vocation transformed from "Beth is in school" to "Beth is a professor," I found that the expectations that my job take a back seat to my husband's job became more pronounced.

How usual is it for some of the duties of a husband's paid job, for which he has been trained, to be separated out and reserved for his unpaid wife, regardless of her individual calling, gifts, and vocation?[14]

As my research for *The Making of Biblical Womanhood* progressed, I saw more clearly how anomalous the pastor's wife role is. Unlike other authoritative roles in church history, the role of pastor's wife is not based on leadership skills, ecclesiastical office, or spiritual gifting. It is a role based on a human relationship—marriage. The calling of a husband assumes the calling of his wife. While some women who marry pastors feel called to vocational ministry (as I do), other women do not. Yet the general parameters often are the same. She will do the bulletin, play piano, teach children's Sunday school, organize Vacation Bible School, lead the fellowship committee, maybe even share the pulpit, and—always—behave the way she is expected.

I saw more clearly, too, how the Southern Baptist Convention (SBC), the largest and most powerful white evangelical denomination in North America, has both informed and exemplified this version of the pastor's wife role during the last half of the twentieth century. The SBC, peaking at over 16 million members in 2006, comprises the largest percentage of US evangelical churches, which in turn form the largest percentage of Protestant churches in the US. While the SBC has worked to maintain a distinctive identity, even refusing to join the National Association of Evangelicals, it nonetheless embodies the full range of evangelical characteristics. These include David Bebbington's classic evangelical quadrilateral (a focus on the Bible, the atoning work of Christ, evangelism, and activism), an emphasis on revival over reformation—both extremes of Wesleyan and Reformed theology—and the conservative white culture that historian Kristin Du Mez describes as centered on "patriarchal authority, gender difference, and Christian nationalism."[15] The SBC, whether it wants to or not, epitomizes evangelicalism. Given its sheer size and power (both political and economic), it is not surprising that the SBC also casts a long shadow on the evangelical world. "The major players in Southern Baptist conservative life more frequently overlapped with those of the religious right, and disproportionate numbers in the religious right were also from the South," writes historian Elizabeth Flowers. "To fully understand American evangelicalism in the postwar period . . . it is essential to cast our gaze on Southern Baptists."[16] In the same way, to fully understand the pastor's wife role within American evangelicalism, we must "cast our gaze" on the conservative white culture of the SBC.

The role of pastor's wife was born in the Reformation era, but it wasn't until the second half of the twentieth century that it was elevated as the highest calling for many Protestant women, waxing in importance as more independently authoritative roles for women waned. The 1970s, for example, saw an explosion in the number of denominations supporting women's ordination, leading to more women attending seminaries and becoming ordained.[17] Southern Baptists initially expanded opportunities for women too, ordaining Addie Davis in 1964 (the first SBC woman ordained into ministry) and witnessing an increase in women studying theology at the SBC's six seminaries. Remarking on this trend, Baptist historian H. Leon McBeth wrote in 1977, "One may no longer assume that women seminarians are preparing for the traditionally 'feminine' church jobs. Many of them are preparing and planning to be *ministers*; some are frankly aiming at the pastorate." By 1984, twenty years after the ordination of Davis, the number of ordained women in the SBC had increased to around 200—a "twenty-fold increase in less than a decade," which placed the SBC "on the same trajectory as the mainline, liberal denominations."[18]

By 1984 the SBC was taking steps to reverse this trend. The resolution—passed June 13, 1984, at the national convention in Kansas City—asked "local Baptist churches to cease ordaining women ministers since 'the Bible excludes women from pastoral leadership because the man was first in creation and the woman was first in the Edenic fall.'"[19] It was also in the 1980s that published books for pastors' wives, including those that emphasized male headship and female submission, became more common.[20] In 1981, for example, Betty J. Coble—a well-known SBC pastor's wife and educator—published *The Private Life of the Minister's Wife* with an SBC press. "In marriage the man is assigned leadership," she stated. "The husband's God-given assignment is to make the final decision, which becomes the marriage decision." Submission, which she described as a "followship role," is God's assignment for wives, including the minister's wife.[21]

While people have hotly debated female ordination, historians and lay leaders have overlooked the connection between the decline of female ordination and the attendant rise of the pastor's wife role.[22] Moreover, a hyperfocus on the historical continuity of women's exclusion from church leadership roles has pushed out a more nuanced understanding of why women have been excluded from these roles. Barring women from institutional leadership may be everywhere in church history, but it is not everywhere the same.[23]

I argue that these are critical oversights. As historian Kate Bowler recently affirmed, "The long history of women's struggle for ordination and an institutional expression of spiritual equality had left most women in the precarious position of seeking permission for the authority to teach."[24] The role of pastor's wife authorized ministry opportunities for women. It offered ways for women to exercise leadership. It legitimized the spiritual significance of women's roles as wives and mothers.

But what if the role of pastor's wife came at a cost for women too?

What if, even as it authorized opportunities for women in the local church, it simultaneously deauthorized women's independent leadership, especially within the white evangelical movement? Could it be that the gradual aligning of the pastor's wife role with the conservative ideal of biblical womanhood (as happened within the Southern Baptist tradition) helped to obscure women's independent leadership in some Protestant spaces? Could the exclusion felt by single women within white evangelical spaces be linked to the erosion of independent leadership opportunities for women? Are white evangelical ideas about women beginning to seep into the Black church, constraining what has historically been a more welcoming space for women leaders?[25]

As one young woman recently said to me, "When I told my youth pastor I felt called into ministry, he said it meant I would marry a pastor."[26]

Unlike *The Making of Biblical Womanhood*, this book isn't my confession.

It isn't even my story, although it does tell some of my story.

Becoming the Pastor's Wife is the history of how Christian women gained a new and important leadership role.

But it is also the history of how this gain came at a cost for women too.

Both the cost and the gain are bigger than we have yet realized.

1

Where Is Peter's Wife?

"I think that church has a female pastor."

Our pastor was sitting across the room, his wife next to him. Together they were a mirror image of me next to my husband. I don't remember if it was a scheduled conversation or the aftermath of dinner. I do remember it was early in our tenure at the church. I also remember how the pastor didn't break eye contact with me.

The pastor used the occasion to learn more about me and my family. He had been asking me about my brother, then a graduate student at Baylor University. Had my brother made a profession of faith? Yes. Did he have a girlfriend? Yes. What church did he attend?

My answer to this last question prompted the pastor's response: "*I think that church has a female pastor.*"

I dropped my gaze.

I'm not a good liar. I knew the church my brother was attending ordained women and supported them as preachers and pastors. I knew this church would support a woman as senior pastor.

And now I knew our complementarian pastor knew this too.

Complementarianism, for those unfamiliar with the term, is a patriarchal system born in white evangelicalism that uses the

Bible to justify privileging male authority. Complementarians claim to support the spiritual equality of women and men even as they argue that God ordained a gender hierarchy and assigned a permanently subordinate role to women. Variation exists among complementarians (some enforcing it more strictly than others), but women in the complementarian church must yield at some level to masculine authority—which means complementarianism rejects the independent leadership of female pastors.

Waco, Texas, where my family and I live, is a hot spot for the debate about Baptist women pastors. Only a small number of Baptist churches in Waco fully support women in church leadership, but several of these supportive churches have played prominent roles in Waco history. Several have direct ties with Baylor University, including having tenured professors and alumni serving on their pastoral staffs. Sitting on the banks of the Brazos River, Baylor is the oldest continually operating university in Texas and the largest Baptist university in the world. In 1994, three years after freeing itself from potential denominational control by the Southern Baptist Convention, Baylor launched George W. Truett Theological Seminary—a Baptist seminary that affirms women in ministry.[1] One year after Truett graduated its first class, Waco's Calvary Baptist Church hired Julie Pennington-Russell as the first female senior pastor of a church affiliated with the Baptist General Convention of Texas.

Waco, then, is home to a Baptist seminary that supports women's ordination. It is also home to the church that hired Texas Baptists' first female senior pastor.[2]

I don't know exactly how much the pastor who was questioning me knew of this history. He knew that, at the time, I agreed with him about complementarian theology, otherwise he wouldn't have hired my husband. What he didn't know was that I didn't find female pastors as problematic as he seemed to. He was concerned about my brother attending a church with a female pastor. I wasn't.

How could I be? I had spent the past few years earning a PhD in medieval history. How could I perceive a woman preaching in my twenty-first-century town as wrong when I knew that medieval Christians perceived Mary Magdalene as the first preacher to the disciples, the "apostle to the apostles"? How could I believe that the push for women in church leadership was a product of the 1960s feminist movement when I knew that the fourteenth-century pope Gregory XI turned regularly to a preaching woman for spiritual advice and counsel?[3] I might have (at that moment) believed that the best interpretation of 1 Timothy 2 excluded women from exercising authority over men, but that didn't mean I could simply forget the long history of Christian men accepting women's spiritual authority.[4] Even while maintaining my complementarian stance, I understood that centuries of church teaching and practice ran counter to it. Because of my academic training, I knew that both the acceptance and rejection of women's ministry leadership had historical precedence within orthodox Christianity.[5]

That conversation clued me in, maybe for the first time, on the prevailing perspective in much of contemporary evangelicalism: that support for women in church leadership didn't just signal a difference of opinion; it signaled the slippery slope leading to apostasy.

It was an uncomfortable realization.

That discomfort stayed with me as I was mentored into leadership roles considered appropriate for a pastor's wife, such as teaching Bible study to teenage girls and co-leading, alongside my husband, parenting classes that did not include biblical content. It stayed with me when a pastor's wife I respected cautioned me that my career should take a back seat to my husband's. "He doesn't follow you, even if your job has better pay and benefits," she said. "You follow him." I was encouraged to be a leader, but one who submitted to male headship. Be a Titus 2 woman, I was told. I was even offered a pink T-shirt with the words WORKER AT HOME emblazoned across the front.

I'm not sure when the strangeness of my position first became clear to me, but it soon did. I was being mentored as a leader, but it was a carefully controlled type of leadership designed to emphasize the godliness of female dependency and of male headship. I was being taught that women's independent leadership (i.e., female pastors) was nonbiblical while women's dependent leadership (i.e., pastors' wives) epitomized biblical womanhood.

At the time, I hadn't read Nancy Wilson's *True Companion: Thoughts on Being a Pastor's Wife*, as it was not published until 2013. But I think my then-church-world would have agreed with her lumping women's ordination with topics she believed should be "renounced," such as abortion and infanticide. Married to Doug Wilson, the religiously and politically conservative evangelical pastor of Christ Church in Moscow, Idaho, Wilson perceived her pastor's wife role as "a unique calling and a great honor," in contrast to the danger presented by ordained women.[6]

The problem was that I knew only one of these positions was emphasized in the Bible.

And it wasn't the role of the pastor's wife.

"I Choose to Be a Minister and Not a 'Minister's Wife'"

In 1983 North Hill Baptist Church in Minot, North Dakota, extended a call to Sarah Wood Lee and her husband Sean, who was a church planter apprentice appointed by the Southern Baptist Convention Home Mission Board. The church in Minot agreed to ordain Sarah to "gospel ministry" to join her husband after she completed her seminary degree (a master of divinity). Sarah and Sean saw themselves as a "ministry team" called together to do the work of God. Sarah's ordination would follow the previous ordination of another church planter apprentice's wife, Kathy Hoppe. Ordained in 1982 at First Baptist Church in Sonoma, California, Kathy planned to become a chaplain while her husband, Merlin (known as Jeff), pastored. Like the Lees, the Hoppes were serving in North Dakota as church planters appointed by the SBC Home Mission Board.[7]

Local SBC pastors did not agree. Ron Rogers, pastor of First Southern Baptist Church in Roundup, Montana, voiced his concern in a letter dated December 14, 1983.

> Dear Dr. Tanner,
>
> I am expressing my extreme displeasure concerning the appointment of Sean and Sarah Lee and Merlin and Kathy Hoppe, as Church Planter Apprentices. I object to the ordination of Mrs. Hoppe and the planned ordination of Mrs. Lee. I believe they have the right to believe any way they want, but since these ladies' husbands are being paid with Cooperative Program money, I urge you to discontinue any financial support. I believe that the ordination of women is in direct violation of the Bible and Southern Baptist beliefs. Their husbands undoubtedly have the same beliefs.[8]

Rogers sent the letter to Bill Tanner, the director of the Home Mission Board, and copied other SBC leaders, including Paige Patterson. Even though the Home Mission Board had categorized Lee as "church and family" instead of as a ministry partner, it did not pacify SBC pastors like Rogers who continued to express their outrage.

Her categorization as "church and family" (also described as "family and church" or "home and church") did not pacify Sarah Lee either.

She voiced her objection in a letter to Irvin Dawson, director of missionary personnel for the Home Mission Board, on September 28, 1983:

> I am writing to you in response per your letter per August 13. In it you said you were appointing me to the "church and family" category. I must insist that you do not categorize me this way. . . . Please "categorize" me as <u>ministry team partner</u> or something to that. If you can't, then don't categorize me as anything. . . . I choose to be a minister and not a "minister's wife."[9]

Her request was ignored.

The Home Mission Board responded to her that "our official action will be in keeping with our guidelines." They classified Lee as she had requested to *not* be classified. Dawson responded to Lee on October 11, 1983, "The family and church category indicates the spouse's support of the ministry of the primary worker, but allows her/him to work at a secular job and/or to become involved in the ministry to the extent desired. There are many spouses in the family and church category who are quite actively involved in mission work."[10]

It was okay for Sarah Lee to do work alongside her husband, but she could not be given the ministry title of her husband. When her husband did the work, it was as a church planter apprentice officially called by the SBC. When she did the work, it was to support his official calling.

Unlike Sarah Lee, I have never felt called to ordination. I have always seen my ministry as supporting the ministry of my husband. I guess, to reverse her words, I would rather be a minister's wife than a minister.

Yet I sympathize with her frustrations.

I understand what it is like to feel categorized as support staff for male pastors.

Once, for example, a church member emailed me a question about childcare. I wasn't on staff and had no official position at the church. Since I couldn't help, I sent the question to someone who could: a male pastor who oversaw family ministry.

I remember being shocked by his response: take care of it myself. While it wasn't as outrageous as the Home Mission Board informing Sarah Lee that she wouldn't be recognized as a ministry partner alongside her husband, I felt belittled. From what I recollect, his email made it clear this childcare concern wasn't his job—despite the fact that he was a full-time paid pastor overseeing family ministry. As a pastor's wife, I apparently had the right qualifications to handle childcare.

Sarah Lee, despite her qualifications and calling, was deemed unfit to be categorized as a ministry partner with her husband, whereas I, as an unpaid volunteer who didn't work in childcare (I primarily volunteered in youth ministry), was deemed fit to handle a job that a male pastor declined to do. Do you see what we have in common? These different incidents reduced us, as pastors' wives, to similar unwanted positions: as support staff to pastors.

Churches may claim that women's ministry is of equal value to men's ministry; they may claim that the "family and church" category is just as significant as the "church planter apprentice" category. But when women's work comes with lower (or no) pay and the women doing it are given lower status as employees or volunteers and they are assigned the tasks that men do not want to do, these claims ring hollow.

One recent example came in spring 2023, when Lifeway Research, part of the SBC's publishing arm, prepared a report called "State of Ministry to Women." The researchers "surveyed 1,001 evangelical and Black Protestant female churchgoers and 842 women's ministry leaders in the U.S." and included "respondents or their churches who have interacted with Lifeway in some way in the last 3 years." It's likely that many of the women who participated in the study are in churches that uphold the formal SBC belief that women are called to supportive roles and men are called to leadership roles. The report revealed that 83 percent of women's ministry leaders are volunteers or unpaid staff. Put another way, of the 842 women working in ministry in Black Protestant and evangelical (predominantly Southern Baptist) churches, only 17 percent receive any sort of remuneration. Of the women in this survey, 466 identified as SBC members. The survey was conducted in April and May 2023, ending three weeks before the 2023 Southern Baptist Convention annual meeting began in New Orleans.[11]

Do you know what this reveals?

It reveals that the same convention that voted in a landslide to disfellowship churches with female pastors depends on female labor that is not financially compensated. Writing for *Christianity Today*, Jen Wilkin summarized the implications for female ministry leaders: "They often serve without recognition, without compensation, and without resources."[12]

But what does this have to do with the pastor's wife role?

Wilkin's description of unpaid female ministry leaders applies just as readily to pastors' wives. However important Sarah Lee's work in planting churches was, it wasn't deemed worthy enough for her to be recognized as a "ministry partner" with her husband. Despite her ordination, training, and calling, Lee found her ministry demoted and financial support for her husband's ministry threatened.

Sarah Lee chose to be called a "minister and not a 'minister's wife.'"

The SBC called her something less.

Prisca and Junia

But is this the Bible's attitude toward ministry wives?

Let's look at the evidence, starting with Prisca and Aquila. They were a married couple named in the New Testament who were both involved in teaching ministry. They are intriguing because Prisca's name, in contrast to the social mores of their Greco-Roman world, is usually referenced first. Nijay Gupta suggests that this could be because she "was the more active (and therefore more widely known) ministry leader." Far from a modern argument, Gupta notes that the early church theologian John Chrysostom made a similar suggestion. "He claimed that in Romans 16:3 Paul names Prisca before her husband 'in recognition of the fact that her piety was superior to her husband's.' It is unclear what Chrysostom meant here by 'piety,' but it seems reasonable that this prior mention identified her as more prominent in gospel activity." If this is so, and Prisca is the more prominent minister of the pair, then Aquila might be the first example of a minister's husband.[13]

It is possible.

It is just as possible that social status (rather than ministry prominence) explains why Prisca's name is listed first. I confess, it is more fun to think about Aquila as the first known pastor's husband rather than as an ex-enslaved person married to someone freeborn. We can't tell from the text. We just know that her name comes first four out of six times. We also know, based on historical evidence, that this is significant. Even if Prisca did not exercise more authority than Aquila, she certainly did not exercise less. Luke and Paul portray her as a teacher, house church leader, and evangelist who worked alongside Paul, as did her husband. They were a ministry team.

Could it be that the SBC refused Sarah Lee what both the apostle Paul and the gospel writer Luke bestowed on Prisca: recognition that God calls women to do the same ministry work as men?

Not everyone at the Home Mission Board was happy with Sarah Lee's treatment. Bill Tanner, the director, in his proposed statement in 1985 regarding women's ordination, made this comment: "To be perfectly honest, I would have some personal problems about an ordained woman being pastor of the church I attend." Directly above the end of this sentence he added a handwritten note: "I think this is at least partly culture and tradition." The statement then continues as typed: "But I am not willing to impose my own feelings on some other autonomous church. I sincerely believe in the autonomy of the local church, and if a church believes a woman is called of God and wants to ordain that woman, I cannot and will not impose my own personal views on that church."[14]

Tanner was uncomfortable with ordained women (at least as pastors) but wasn't convinced his view was biblical. His comment that "culture and tradition" partly led to his discomfort fits with his affirmation that "there are valid scriptural arguments for either position." Tanner perceived the Bible as unclear on this issue, which explains why he refused to let his objections stand in the way of local SBC churches choosing to ordain women. He might have been wrong, and he recognized that.

Can you imagine how different the SBC would be if Tanner's posture had prevailed?

I wonder which texts gave Tanner pause enough to admit he might be wrong. Maybe he was thinking about Prisca and Aquila as a "valid scriptural argument" for women's ordination. Or maybe he was thinking about our second ministry couple, Andronicus and Junia.

Junia is one of the greatest challenges to complementarian theology. Unlike Sarah Lee, Junia is given the same titular recognition as Andronicus. In Acts 16, Paul references the pair as "prominent among the apostles." While this phrase has driven some scholars to gender-bending textual contortions as well as imaginative prepositional interpretations in their attempts to erase the biblical reference to a female apostle, Junia is nevertheless called an apostle by Paul. Luis Josué Salés, a scholar of early Christianity, describes the attempt to render Junia as "well known to the apostles" instead of "prominent among the apostles" as "symptomatic of Anglo/European Orientalizing tendencies and epistemological positionalities in New Testament Studies." Or, put more simply, symptomatic of Western scholars' tendency to view Scripture through a Western lens and with a Western patriarchal axe to grind. Salés writes that these scholars "have taken a different road to absurdity by contesting the identification of Andronikos and Iounia as apostles." Their interpretations are "tendentious, even misleading."[15] I can't help but think about Black preachers such as Julia Foote who—rather than trying to diminish women like Junia and Prisca or alter the biblical text to support a claim about female subjugation (as white evangelicals are prone to do)—instead recognized the significance of Paul using the same term to describe both women and men in ministry.[16]

Paul, meanwhile, was oblivious to the controversy that his praise of Junia would one day stir. He describes Junia and Andronicus as having ministered alongside him, risking their lives for him. Nowhere does he suggest that Junia's ministry was dependent on that of Andronicus. In modern terminology, Junia was a missionary, perhaps even a church planter.

The apostle Paul recognized the ministry of Junia with the same terminology he used for Andronicus.

The SBC refused to recognize the ministry of Sarah Lee with the same terminology it used for her husband.

As I sat in the archives reading the 1983 SBC response to Sarah Lee, I couldn't help thinking about Al Mohler's claim that "for nearly 2,000 years, the Christian church has limited the office of pastor to men." He has reiterated this claim several times over the years, including in a May 2021 essay responding to the ordination of three female pastors at Saddleback Community Church (an SBC megachurch founded by Rick Warren).[17] Mohler declares that "the Christian church in virtually every tradition through nearly two millennia in almost every place on earth has understood these texts clearly. In most churches around the world, there is no question about these texts even now." Mohler claims that his argument is rooted in the Bible, saying that "the real issue in this debate—and the only issue worth debating—is the authority and interpretation of the Bible."[18] However, Mohler continually substantiates this claim from "nearly 2,000 years" of Christian history, which includes the medieval Christian world. I will return to this claim, because it is central to the debate about women's roles in the SBC. For now, let's look at the root of his claim: that the Bible limits the "preaching office" or "office of pastor" to men. Mohler, speaking for the SBC, defines the pastoral role as centered on preaching and teaching as well as providing "spiritual leadership and oversight for the congregation."[19]

I wonder what he thinks women like Prisca and Junia were doing. Does he really think they were not preaching, teaching, and providing spiritual leadership within the early church? After all, the biblical text shows us that Prisca was teaching authoritatively and, as demonstrated by her encounter with Apollos in Acts 18, providing spiritual leadership and oversight. Junia is specifically called an apostle, one of the leadership gifts mentioned in Ephesians 4:11: "The gifts he gave were that some would be apostles, some prophets, some evangelists, some pastors and teachers." Whereas *apostle* appears multiple times in the New Testament, Ephesians 4:11 is one of the few mentions of *pastor*.[20] Although I personally don't think hierarchy is embedded in this list of leadership gifts, I would think those who do see hierarchy embedded in the order of a series (such as Adam and Eve) overlook the fact that "apostles" are mentioned first and "pastors and teachers" are mentioned last.[21] From the hierarchical point of view, one could argue that "apostle" is a more authoritative position than "pastor." That would mean Junia was given the most authoritative title in the early church.

So, again, what does Mohler think Prisca (called a coworker alongside Paul who exercises pastoral oversight) and Junia (who is labeled with the same title Paul claims for himself) were doing?

Does he think they would have needed the kind of "gender-specific" ministry equipping provided by The Southern Baptist Theological Seminary to address their "issues and giftedness" as women?[22] Or that either of them would have described herself as "first and foremost a homemaker" who supported the ministry of her husband? This is how Dorothy Kelley Patterson describes her role as a pastor's wife.[23]

I confess I was surprised when Brooke LeFevre, a PhD candidate assisting me with research, drew my attention to how Patterson frames Prisca and Aquila's ministry. "Priscilla was very much a part of her husband's ministry," Patterson writes in *A Handbook for Ministers' Wives*. "Every minister needs a soulmate as Priscilla was to Aquila." Straying from the biblical pattern, Patterson places Aquila's name before Prisca's. "The pattern of Aquila and Priscilla is one of partnership by design. They work together and comple-ment each other, but clearly they follow the biblical guidelines for Christian marriage." The description is jaw-dropping. Patterson offers no evidence that this couple abided by male headship and female submission, nor that Prisca was merely a part of Aquila's ministry instead of the other way around. Patterson doesn't use the phrase "pastor's wife" for Prisca, but that seems to be how she envisions her: as a partner to her husband's ministry instead of a minister in her own right.[24]

Indeed, given the biblical evidence of Prisca and Junia, I do not understand how Patterson can state confidently that "examples of women in Scripture overwhelmingly place wives and mothers in the home."[25] I find myself thinking along the same lines as Julia Foote, the daughter of former slaves who became the first woman ordained a deacon in the African Methodist Episcopal Zion Church. Foote proclaims, "When Paul said, 'Help those women who labor with me in the Gospel [Phil. 4:3],' he certainly meant that they did more than to pour out tea."[26]

Patterson's language about Prisca and Aquila may not accurately reflect the biblical text, but it does accurately reflect the 1984 Kansas City Southern Baptist Convention resolution that her husband, Paige Patterson, assisted by Paul Pressler and W. A. Criswell, supported for adoption. Along with stating that women are excluded from pastoral leadership because "the man was first in creation and the woman was first in the Edenic fall," the resolution also states that "Priscilla joined her husband in teaching Apollos, and women fulfilled special church service-ministries as exemplified by Phoebe whose work Paul attributes as that of a servant of the church." According to the SBC resolution, Prisca supported the ministry of her husband and Phoebe supported the ministry of Paul. They were not called to the same ministry roles as men.[27]

To bring us full circle, Mohler's claim at the 2023 Southern Baptist Convention meeting that female pastors "violate" biblical authority reflects a certainty absent from the biblical texts.

It also reflects a certainty absent from SBC history. James (Jimmy) Draper, former SBC president, wrote in a letter on March 16, 1983, that he "personally" did not believe it "is scriptural for us to ordain women to the ministry or to the deaconship." Yet, he continued, "there are Southern Baptist churches, on the east coast particularly, who have ordained women for over 100 years.

While I personally disagree, each local congregation has a right to determine its own policy."[28]

Could it be that what Mohler argues is a position of biblical authority—indeed, the entire basis for the SBC's 2023 decision to disfellowship churches with female pastors—is only one possible biblical interpretation, and a rather weak one at that?

Where Is Peter's Wife?

"Oh, so you belong to the youth pastor?"

The woman stood at the end of the pew, waiting for me to answer. I was young, new to the church, and not yet accustomed to questions like this.

"I don't belong to him," I corrected. "We are engaged to be married."

"Oh, honey, you belong to him," she said, patting my arm. Then she looked over at my twenty-two-year-old fiancé as he stood talking to a congregant. "He's a fine one to belong to. You are lucky."

I stared at the woman. Had she just ogled my husband-to-be, then described me as belonging to him, which sounded to me like I was his property? Before I could reply, the woman said, "It is good he's getting married soon," giving me a knowing look. Then she walked away.

I knew at the time that marriage was expected for clergy in my conservative evangelical world. I knew that a wife was often considered a participant in the pastoral job description. I *knew* this, yet it was hard to process that my person was now an expected component of my husband's job.

Not only did it seem weird, it also didn't seem very biblical.

We know very little about the wives of Jesus's disciples. It is safe to assume that most (if not all) of the disciples had them, as most men in the biblical world did. The disciples would have been no different, needing women to mother their children, to meet social and religious expectations, to be economic partners.[29] So, if the disciples were married and Jesus called them into ministry, what role did their wives play? Off the top of your head, can you name their wives? Do you know whether Paul was married? How about Peter or James or John?

Of the twelve disciples, we have only one mention of possible wives. In 1 Corinthians 9:5 Paul states, "Do we not have the right to be accompanied by a believing wife [sister], as do the other apostles and the brothers of the Lord, and Cephas?" In the case of Peter (Cephas), we know that he had a wife. While Paul might be referencing the wives of other apostles, he might also be referencing female coworkers like Phoebe and Euodia. It is possible he is even referencing his own wife. This is what Clement of Alexandria thought, writing in the late second or early third century: "Even Paul did not hesitate in one letter to address his consort. The only reason why he did not take [his wife] about with him was that it would have been an inconvenience for his ministry. . . . But the latter [apostles], in accordance with their particular ministry, devoted themselves to preaching without any distraction, and took their wives with them not as women with whom they had marriage relations, but as sisters, that they might be their fellow-ministers in dealing with housewives."[30] Paul's reference is so brief that it is hard to know for sure who these women were. While it might refer to ministry wives working alongside their husbands, it might also refer to female coworkers. It is true that Peter is a clear example of a married apostle with a believing wife. It is also true that Paul was most likely not married at this time (or ever), so it is unlikely he was asking to bring a "believing wife" along with him. From this perspective it is possible, as contemporary Bible teacher Marg Mowczko suggests, that Paul's rhetorical question included female coworkers too.[31]

This means that while 1 Corinthians 9:5 might indicate wives partnering with their apostle husbands (probably as close as we get in the New Testament to pastors' wives), that isn't the only interpretation.

What about other church leaders? Stephen? James the brother of Jesus? Jude?

We assume they were married, but the biblical text provides no evidence of their marital status.

Let's expand to the Pauline epistles. Paul doesn't seem to have been married when he became a Jesus follower, but it is possible he had been married previously given his status as a Jewish leader. If he had been, we know nothing about his wife. What about those in his circle? Barnabas? Timothy (we know about his mom)? Silas? Apollos? Luke? Epaphras? Titus?

The reality is that we know little about the spouses of early church leaders—either the spouses of men or of women. Indeed, aside from Prisca and Junia, the only other New Testament reference we have to a ministry wife in the early church is Peter's wife.[32]

Who was she?

Peter was about as ordinary a Galilean man as one could find. He was a fisherman who worked alongside members of his family, including his brother. I imagine his family life was ordinary too. We know Peter had a wife, because Matthew describes how Jesus healed his mother-in-law (Matt. 8:14–15). New Testament scholar Lynn Cohick suggests that Peter's wife worked as a fishmonger in Capernaum, selling what her husband caught.[33] She probably helped run the family business as Peter began his travels with Jesus (somebody had to feed the kids). Meeting Jesus would have been the most extraordinary thing that had happened to Peter. We know it radically changed his life. We also know, from 1 Corinthians 9:5, that Peter's wife was a part of this change, traveling with him during the earliest days of the Jesus movement. As Paul asked, "Do we not have the right to be accompanied by a believing wife, as do the other apostles and the brothers of the Lord and Cephas?"

And that's it.[34]

Peter's wife, a wife of one of the disciples in the inner circle of Jesus, the wife of one of the primary leaders in the Jesus movement, a wife who traveled with her husband and was known to other apostles like Paul, and all we know about her is that she existed. We know more about Peter's relationship with women like Tabitha (Acts 9:36–42) than we know about Peter's relationship with his own wife. More to the point, we know far more about the ministry of Tabitha, an independent woman, than we know about the ministry of Peter's wife.

"Where is Peter's wife?" asks New Testament scholar Jaime Clark-Soles in *Women in the Bible: Interpretation Resources for the Use of Scripture in the Church.* "We see his mother-in-law, but never his wife. Paul and the Gospels mention that he has a wife. In fact, where are any of the male disciples' wives?" Clark-Soles notes that we know other apostles had wives because of 1 Corinthians 9:5. So "what does it mean," Clark-Soles asks, "that while we hear that other apostles have wives, we never meet these wives?"[35]

If ministry wives are uniquely called by God, just as Jesus called Peter and John on the Galilean shores and Paul on the road to Damascus, if Scripture expects "some pastors will be married" (as Gloria Furman surmises from 1 Tim. 3:2 and Titus 1:5–9), then why are there few (if any) biblical examples of "women who serve the church as partners with their ministering husbands"?[36] Of course, it could be that these women were just overlooked. The equivalents of pastors' wives may have served vitally in the early church. Their work, like the work of so many other women throughout history, may have been masked by patriarchal structures. This is plausible. The silence of the biblical text about women married to "ministering husbands" cannot be read as either support for or rejection of the pastor's wife role.

But the silence of the biblical text still creates an awkward situation.

Given the amount of emphasis placed on "biblical" womanhood in complementarian spaces (what women did or didn't do in the biblical text dictates what women should or shouldn't do in the modern church), it strikes me as odd that a role with such tenuous biblical evidence has become the primary role highlighted for women.

Simply put, Peter's wife isn't there.

And that is my point.

The Women Who Are There

My students are often struck when I show them video clips of the Olympic flame ceremony in Greece that signals the beginning of a new Olympic season. Women dressed as ancient priestesses reenact a ceremonial lighting of the torch by the sun god (helped by a concave mirror). The ceremony owes more to modern choreography than ancient reality—except for the female priestesses. The sight of so many women officiating a replica of a religious ceremony provokes a lot of student questions—the most common of which (along with Karen Jo Torjesen's book *When Women Were Priests*) helped inspire the title of my next chapter.[37]

"Dr. Barr," someone in my class often asks, "were women really priests?"

Yes, I tell my students, there were female priests in the ancient (including biblical) world.[38]

Not much else may be historically accurate about the Olympic flame ceremony, but they got the female priestesses right. "The ancient evidence suggests that official religious service was the one area of public life in which Roman women assumed roles of equal legitimacy and comparable status to those of men," writes historian Meghan DiLuzio in *A Place at the Altar: Priestesses in Republican Rome*.[39] Christianity was born into a religious space familiar with women serving in religiously authoritative roles. After reading a draft of this chapter, Nijay Gupta reminded me about both the Vestal Virgins and the Oracle of Delphi—two of the most powerful religious positions in the Greco-Roman world that were both occupied by women. The Vestals, for example, were "legally isolated" from their families so that they could function independently, advising both religious and political leaders as well as teaching initiates. "Women were not simply tools of their male priestly hierarchy, but rather ritual agents in their own right," DiLuzio concludes.[40] Female priests and prophets functioned as autonomous leaders who did not need the supervision of men.

Biblical womanist scholar Wilda C. Gafney, a professor of Hebrew at Brite Divinity School, captures the irony of restrictions against women preaching and leading in modern churches and synagogues in her introduction to *Daughters of Miriam: Women Prophets in Ancient Israel*:

> More than three thousand years after the prophet Miriam led the Israelites dancing and drumming across the Sea of Reeds, some Jewish and Christian communities still restrict the role of women in proclamation, leadership, and presence in the pulpit on what they call biblical and traditional grounds. However, the biblical text presents female prophets leading the people of God and proclaiming the word of God unremarkably, as part of the natural order of things.[41]

New Testament scholar Scot McKnight urged me to talk about what women were actually doing, such as prophesying. Female prophets like Philip's daughters are present in the text, and their presence is a formidable opposition to those who claim women cannot serve in pastoral offices. Did you know Paul lists the spiritual gift of prophecy alongside that of apostle and teacher? We've already seen one woman named as an apostle by Paul. Did you know that several women are named and shown to be prophets in the New Testament? From Mary the mother of Jesus who proclaimed the Magnificat in Luke 1:46–55, to Anna the prophet who lived in the temple and held the infant Jesus in her arms, to the four daughters of Philip who "prophesied," to Paul's assumptions in 1 Corinthians 11 that women are prophesying and praying in church just like men, female prophets are visible and active in Scripture—unlike Peter's wife. As theologian Susan Hylen writes,

"Although prayer is a more familiar form of speech for us today, we should not overlook the importance of prophecy in Paul's experience and teaching. Women were some of those with prophetic gifts, and they were expected to speak for the group when they had a message from God."[42]

Alongside Gafney's *Daughters of Miriam*, one of the most important books I assign in my graduate seminar on women's religious authority is by Sarah Coakley, the Norris-Hulse Professor of Divinity Emerita at the University of Cambridge and previously the Mallinckrodt Professor of Divinity at Harvard University. My students agree that it is one of the most difficult books I assign. But they also agree that *Powers and Submissions: Spirituality, Philosophy and Gender* is game-changing. What Coakley argues is what both Scot McKnight and Nijay Gupta urged me to consider: the centrality of prophecy and prayer (and hence the centrality of the Holy Spirit) to the early church.[43] Prayer embodies female religious experience and empowers women. That is why, Coakley argues, "the Church had politico-ecclesiastical reasons for preventing this vision of God, with its prioritization and highlighting of the Spirit, from getting too close to center stage."[44] Honestly, if you are reading the Bible, you'll see that preaching is not the primary authoritative medium. It is prophecy and prayer—what women like Mary the mother of God and Philip's daughters are doing. It is what Paul tells us women are doing too. Can you imagine what would happen to arguments excluding women from pastoral authority if we recentered our definition of pastoral authority from preaching to praying?[45]

I can.

I can also tell you that, as Sarah Coakley's book has done, it would change the game.

Our (Wo)Man-Made Problem

What are we to say, then? Should we regard the pastor's wife role as unbiblical and get rid of it? By no means!

Scripture needn't explicitly spell out every church position for it to be legitimate in modern Christian practice. The historical world that birthed first-century house churches differed dramatically from the post-Reformation world that birthed Protestant ministers. It isn't surprising that the modern role of pastor (especially senior pastor or preaching pastor) has no direct correlation in the New Testament. The fact that we don't know more about Peter's wife, nor about wives of the other male leaders in the New Testament, shouldn't be a problem. The absence of Peter's wife doesn't invalidate the role.

The absence of Peter's wife shouldn't matter.

The problem is that we have *made* it matter.

We have taken a position never mentioned directly in Scripture and turned it into the highest ministry calling for contemporary evangelical women, allowing it to supplant other ministry roles. We have pressured women who do not feel called to ministry into ministry service because of their husbands' vocations. We have told women that their best path to ministry is literally to follow behind men.

Consider the following quote from the wife of Norman Vincent Peale, used by H. B. London Jr., a fourth-generation minister who worked for Focus on the Family, in his foreword to Joyce Williams's 2005 book, *She Can't Even Play the Piano! Insights for Ministry Wives*. London states that he used this quote previously in a book he coauthored for pastors' wives: "I agree that any woman might have other stimulating jobs, but none is so difficult and demanding, so exciting and potentially rewarding as the job of living with a man, studying him, supporting him, liberating his strength, compensating for his weaknesses, making his whole being sing and soar the way it was designed to do."[46] Sure, women can flourish in separate vocations, but their "maximum flourishing" (to use John Piper's words) comes from supporting a man.[47]

Let me pause for a moment.

I am a pastor's wife. I have loved being a pastor's wife. My goal is not to discredit the role or the women who faithfully serve in this role. My goal is not to write an exhaustive history of every itera-tion of the pastor's wife role, either. My goal is to think about the role of pastor's wife historically—especially how the evolution of the role within US evangelicalism more broadly and the Southern Baptist Convention more specifically has intersected with changing attitudes toward women in ministry. Both American evangelical-ism and the SBC are majority-white movements, so the evidence I draw from mostly reflects a white perspective.

Yet I am aware that the experience of the Black pastor's wife is a critical part of the story that needs more attention. Don't you think that, instead of arranging a pulpit swap or another coffee talk, it is time for the white church to sit down and learn from its Black sisters and brothers on their terms, in their space?[48] While it is true that white evangelical culture has shifted the trajectory of the role of the Black pastor's wife, at least in more conserva-tive churches, it is also true that the distinctiveness of the Black experience underscores how much the role is shaped by culture as opposed to the Bible. And as we will see in the final chapter, I think the Black pastor's wife role offers hope for the future.

So, let's look at some evidence about how the pastor's wife role is understood by pastors' wives themselves.

A Divine Calling

High Call, High Privilege: A Pastor's Wife Speaks to Every Woman in a Place of Responsibility was one of the first books handed to me as a young pastor's wife. In her memoir of being a pastor's wife for more than forty years, Gail MacDonald reinforced the idea that my marriage to a minster meant I was called to ministry.

But MacDonald gave me something new to think about too.

Listen to what she writes: "I believe that the majority of women for whom ministry has been an unhappy experience share a com-mon dilemma. They have perceived neither the principle of the inner fire nor its potential. They have consigned themselves to trying to make life work according to structures and external standards. . . . They find themselves facing the lot of fishbowl lives and saying, 'We've learned to hate it.' Be assured that ministry is far too draining to be sustained without the experience of the inner fire."[49]

In other words, says MacDonald, the problem with many disillusioned pastors' wives is their failure to recognize their role as a calling. They don't experience the "inner fire" of God's calling to be a pastor's wife. And, because of this, ministry becomes drudgery, draining their joy, so MacDonald writes to help them catch this inner fire.

I appreciate that MacDonald recognizes that women can be called to ministry without being married to a pastor (although her book is geared more toward women who, like herself, married into ministry). Yet her argument that not recognizing a calling can lead to disillusionment underscores her belief that the role of pastor's wife *is* a specific calling—a privileged ministry role. Ministry women, she writes, should share "the joy that erupts from knowing that God has privileged each of us to be a part of a life marked by serving."[50] If a pastor's wife lacks that joy, it is because she has either forgotten the privilege of her calling or "never found it" to begin with. I don't think MacDonald meant to say that pastors' wives who find their lives more bitter than sweet have themselves to blame, but—whether she meant it or not—that is what her argument implies.

Gail MacDonald isn't alone in her assessment of the role of the pastor's wife as a God-ordained calling.

In 1976 Weptanomah W. Carter wrote one of the first books directed to the wives of Black ministers, titled *The Black Minister's Wife*. Like MacDonald, Carter explains marriage to a minister as a divine calling. "The effective minister's wife feels a sense of the divine call of God. She does not select her role. She rather finds herself called into it." Whatever her background or career may have been before, Carter explains, becoming a minister's wife changes her life trajectory: "A force of power is placed upon her that calls her to the task of redemptive service," and "without the sense of this divine call that strategically places one in the heart of the gospel ministry, healing and redemptive service will not be forthcoming."[51] In perhaps the most intriguing part, Carter writes that if the pastor's wife takes the marriage vow to be sacred and binding, "then the wife should inevitably share some sense of the divine call."[52] By tying the calling of the pastor's wife to the marriage vow, Carter sacramentalizes the role. Ordination for the pastor's wife occurs in the marriage ceremony.

Dorothy Kelley Patterson's *A Handbook for Ministers' Wives* was published almost thirty years after *The Black Minister's Wife*. She does not use language reminiscent of ordination, but she does agree with Carter about the divine nature of the role. Marrying a minister means accepting a call to ministry: "When a woman marries a minister, she not only chooses a life partner, she also accepts a life's work."[53] The understanding in Patterson's world is that God calls women to the role of pastor's wife in the same way that God calls men to the role of pastor. Like Carter, she emphasizes that the wife's calling comes through marriage. "Most women who become pastors' wives never hear a divine call to ministry; rather, they marry men who have had such a call." Patterson promises her readers that their calling will be confirmed through "a slow unfolding of God's will through the working of the Holy Spirit in [their] heart" because "God never has separate plans for a husband and wife."[54] Patterson is more emphatic than Carter about the dependent nature of the pastor's wife, even describing a pastor's wife as she "who held the ladder while he [the pastor husband] climbed to success."[55]

Based on this model of a ministry wife divinely called to support her husband's job, Southern Baptist pastor Tommy French, a close friend of the Pattersons, donated $100,000 in 2008 to Southwestern Baptist Theological Seminary to create a scholarship endowment for the wives of students preparing for ministry. "A pastor's wife is called to complement her husband in ministry," said French. "As a helper you have to be theologically sound and *know your husband's craft.* This scholarship will give the needed tools and training to best assist their husbands."[56]

"Know your husband's craft." Do you see the significance of those words? So many women who marry pastors are taught that they are specifically called into their husbands' ministries, that marriage to a minister literally means accepting a call into ministry. That their job is to do their husband's job too.

It's easy to explain Patterson's views as the product of a bygone era. Yet as I was beginning research for this project, another PhD student at Baylor, Anna Beaudry, drew my attention to a woman much younger than Patterson named Christine Hoover. Hoover runs a ministry for pastors' wives and is the author of *The Church Planting Wife: Help and Hope for Her Heart.* Writing in 2013, she describes the calling of a pastor's wife with words similar to Patterson's: "The Lord called me to ministry just as he did my husband. It's not as if he called Kyle and I'm just a tagalong through his life. It's just that my ministry looks different. My ministry is often in the background."[57] For Hoover, the calling of her husband to ministry included her calling to support his ministry.

Her position is the same as Patterson's: the pastor's wife has a ministry role in which she is specifically called and gifted by God to support the ministry of her husband.[58]

But this isn't a role that the Bible expressly spells out.

The types of roles the Bible *does* describe for women are those of collaboration alongside male colleagues, not those contingent on being a wife. While some authors of pastor's wife books recognize the biblical absence of the role, most still characterize it as a calling necessary for the success of the pastorate.

Gloria Furman, a graduate of Dallas Theological Seminary and wife of Dave Furman, pastor of Redeemer Church of Dubai, provides a case in point. She acknowledges the biblical absence of the role in her book, *The Pastor's Wife: Strengthened by Grace for a Life of Love.*[59] Yet she also describes the pastor's wife as "handpicked" by God and claims that she has a "practical, direct, and strategic role in her husband's potential to shepherd the flock of God." The role of the pastor's wife has no clear guidelines or model in Scripture, yet it is crucial to successful pastoral ministry. "Because you are 'one flesh' with your husband, you can consider your ministry to your husband as part of a joint effort with him in ministering to the body of Christ," Furman continues.[60] Despite the "smorgasbord of ministries" available, "wives of men in ministry have a God-given calling and enablement to serve their husband."[61] It is worth noting that Furman regularly writes for The Gospel Coalition and her book is listed as a text for a 2022 Seminary Wives Institute course at The Southern Baptist Theological Seminary.[62]

Furman recognizes that the "office" of pastor's wife does not exist in the Bible and that it is fundamentally no different from the role of wife. Relying on passages like Titus 2:3–5, she emphasizes women's ministry primarily through the lens of marriage.

Nor is she an outlier, at least among white evangelical pastors' wives.

Dorothy Patterson, who uses the term "First Lady," acknowledges that "a pastor's First Lady has no job description, yet she walks into a role with amazing expectations and sometimes overwhelming responsibilities." It is a dependent role. "She is her husband's wife and thus, according to biblical mandate, *his helper*."[63] In the same way, Christine Hoover explains, "there is no job description or checklist for how to be a church planting wife."[64] Yet she is positive that the wife is specifically called to support her husband's ministry: "God has called both of you to plant a church: one to lead and the other to help. To be clear, you are the helper, not the leader."[65]

Do you find it unsettling that they have so much certainty about the ministry calling of a role that is so unclear in biblical texts—especially the confident claims that it is a subordinate role?

I do.

Shevalle Kimber provides a different perspective. She is married to Boise Kimber, pastor of First Calvary Baptist Church in New Haven, Connecticut. She describes herself as "a called and ordained woman of God" who has served as a pastor and chaplain. In the introduction to her 2023 book *First Ladydom in the Black Church*, Kimber recognizes that "a First Lady is not a biblical office. It is not mentioned or outlined in scripture, nor is it inferred." Rather, it's a cultural role that has acquired specific "rules, regulations, and expectations."[66] History made the pastor's wife role, and the specific culture of the Black church tradition imbues it with authority and significance.

Do you see the difference between Kimber's perception of the pastor's wife role and that of Patterson, Furman, and Hoover? Between portraying the pastor's wife role as a subordinate helper role grounded in the biblical text (biblical womanhood, if you will) and recognizing it as an extrabiblical role shaped by church culture?

Is it possible that, while championing the need to take the Bible seriously, some of us have undermined the "plain and literal" ministry of women in the Bible?

Is it possible that white evangelicals like Patterson, Furman, and Hoover have obscured the independent leadership roles held so prominently by biblical women like Prisca and Junia, promoting instead a dependent leadership role for women that lacks a biblical model? Is the problem with Peter's wife not her biblical absence but rather how we have imagined her legacy?

I think we have worked so hard to promote biblical women as we imagine them to be that we have forgotten how to see biblical women as they are.

We have been taught this so well that when Al Mohler declares that "for nearly 2,000 years" churches have limited the office of pastor to men, we believe him.

We have internalized these teachings so much that we believe a woman's place is not in the pulpit but behind it, supporting her husband. Or, in the words of Dorothy Patterson, holding the ladder for him to climb.

And we believe it has always been this way.

But it hasn't.

2

When Women Were Priests

My childhood Southern Baptist Convention church had a Wall of Pastors. Lining one of the hallways in our church was picture after picture of pastors in historical order of their service. Some of the pictures included the deacons too. My preteen friends and I whispered about the "headless man" whose ghostly image was reportedly captured in an early photograph. No one had ever seen this apparition, but we were certain photographic proof existed. A few of us spent one all-night lock-in searching the church library shelves for proof, only to decide the picture had probably been spirited away to the church gym which, conveniently, was also hidden—walled up, we believed, because a ghost haunted the old basketball court. It made sense to our preteen brains that a haunted photograph would be hidden in a haunted room.

We never found the picture.

I can't remember now whether the headless man was believed to be an early pastor of the church or just a deacon. What I do remember is that every person on the Wall of Pastors was a white man. It never occurred to us that the headless specter, whether deacon or pastor, could be anything other than a white man.

But let's imagine that, growing up, I had been able to recall photographs of a more diverse set of leaders. What if, say, there were twenty photos on that wall, and twelve of them depicted women as both pastors and deacons? If some of those leaders, both male and female, were brown as well as white? If the women depicted, just like the men, stood alone—their leadership independent from that of a spouse?

Can you imagine how a hall of pastors with male, female, white, and brown faces could have taught generations of churchgoers to believe that the pastoral office belongs to the people whom God calls?

I can.

I can also tell you that you don't need to imagine it. Because it isn't imaginary.

J. Ligon Duncan III, a member of the Council on Biblical Manhood and Womanhood and chancellor at Reformed Theological Seminary, has claimed that "historic Christianity speaks with one voice on . . . an all-male pastoral ministry."[1]

But it hasn't.

Historical evidence shows female leaders existed in the early church. Rather than holding the ladder for a pastor husband to climb, these women climbed the ladder themselves.

The Priscilla Catacombs

In March 2023, I traveled with my son's senior class to Italy. I had been to Rome once before for a short trip, but this trip was for ten days and took us from Orvieto to Assisi, Florence, Rome, Pompeii, and the island of Capri. Most of the trip followed a preplanned itinerary without much flex time. But we had one morning free in Rome.

I knew exactly where I wanted to go: the Catacombs of Priscilla.

The Priscilla Catacombs are one of the largest burial spaces that we know of for Christians living in Rome in the second and third centuries. The catacombs were the site of more than 3,500 burials before Christianity was legally recognized by Rome in the fourth century. According to medieval guidebooks, the bones of at least six popes and more than three hundred martyrs once rested here.

I wanted to see the Priscilla Catacombs because of what it suggests about women's leadership in the early church. With fifteen high schoolers and sponsors in tow, I made my way to one of the most ancient addresses in Rome: 430 Via Salaria.

It was an eye-opening experience.

Everywhere around us was evidence that cast doubt on modern church leaders' claims that female pastors violate biblical teaching. That's because I was standing in an ancient Christian cemetery founded by a female patron at a time when female house church leaders proliferated.[2] Some scholars think Prisca and Aquila, the married couple who founded several house churches and ministered alongside Paul, might have been buried here.[3] Nicola Denzey suggests in *The Bone Gatherers* that Prisca's ossuary may have been kept in the oldest part of the Priscilla Catacombs—the highly decorated Greek chapel that contains a striking number of female images.[4]

Like the nearby catacombs of Domitilla, Commodilla, Lucina, and Balbina, the Priscilla Catacombs are believed to have been donated by a wealthy female patron—in this case, a member of the senatorial Acilii family. Christine Schenk reminds us that "many ancient churches and catacombs in Rome began as private house churches and cemeteries owned by women patrons." Since twelve of the twenty "pre-Constantinian titular churches" in Rome are named for women, Schenk writes, "there is good reason to surmise that over half of Rome's early house churches were founded and hosted by female patrons."[5]

Admittedly, founding a house church doesn't necessarily mean having a teaching role. Yet Carolyn Osiek and Margaret Mac-Donald argue that it's reasonable to conclude that these women did: "It is safe to say that those texts that seem to indicate women hosting Christian house churches mean just that."[6]

Remember that hall of male pastors and deacons in my Southern Baptist church?

Evidence suggests that a hall of pictures depicting leaders of the earliest Christian communities in Rome would have been much more diverse.

Evidence suggests that churches in Rome that Paul was closely connected to followed female leaders.

Some may disagree with the implications of the evidence; some may dismiss Phoebe, called a deacon in Romans 16:1, as less authoritative than a male deacon; some may argue that the house churches were named for wealthy women who supported them rather than women who led them. But they cannot refute the reasonable (and arguably more likely) possibility that women *led*, not just "hosted." After all, in Romans 16:3 and 1 Corinthians 16:19, Paul greets Prisca and Aquila and "the church at their house."[7] This doesn't guarantee Prisca led the church, but it is likely that it does, since the custom would have been to identify a house by the male head (the church at Aquila's house) instead of by "the church at their house."[8] At the least, it's reasonable to assume that Phoebe (who is never identified with a husband) held the office of deacon, just as the biblical text suggests; it is also fair to assume that Prisca led a house church, just as the biblical text suggests, where she likely taught, perhaps with a husband beside her.

Could it be that a plain and literal reading of New Testament texts shows some instances in which women are leading in the early church, and in other circumstances the text sanctions silence and submission for women?

I love the reflection Susan Hylen makes at the end of *Finding Phoebe: What New Testament Women Were Really Like*. She doesn't argue that the New Testament is egalitarian (because it isn't). Instead, she argues that ideas about female inferiority existed alongside "ideals that allowed and even encouraged women's active participation in their communities." Women led in civic and religious offices in the first century; they "used their influence and resources in powerful ways to benefit their families and communities"; they exhibited the virtues upheld for both male and female leaders (civic and religious), which would have included silence in some circumstances and authoritative advocacy in others.[9] Prisca co-leading a house church was not only possible in first century Rome, it was also in keeping with what her female contemporaries were doing.

It seems disingenuous to argue that female leadership violates "fundamental biblical authority" when there is strong evidence that female leadership was recognized and accepted by New Testament authors, just like female leadership was recognized and accepted in the New Testament world. As my Baylor colleague David Whitford teaches freshmen every semester in his introductory religion course, the evidence for women's leadership roles in the early church is all around us. We have textual evidence, archaeological evidence, and hostile evidence—such as Pliny's early second-century letter to the emperor Trajan complaining about Christians and identifying two female deacons.[10]

The evidence is there.

We just need to learn to see it.

Dorothy Patterson's View of Women

I didn't know about the Priscilla Catacombs when my husband was a seminary student at Southeastern Baptist Theological Seminary. I suspect most of the students as well as their wives didn't either, since Dorothy Patterson oversaw their curriculum.

I want to impress upon you the significance of Dorothy Patterson within the white evangelical pastor's wife story. Elizabeth Flowers argues that she was a key leader not only in shaping complementarian theology but in forging "strong links to the larger evangelical world."[11] She was the architect of women's programs at Southeastern Baptist Theological Seminary that focused on equipping female seminary students, women's ministry directors, and pastors' wives. She partnered with SBC institutions, such as Lifeway

Christian Resources and the Women's Enrichment Ministry, and more broadly with conservative evangelicals, such as the Council for Biblical Manhood and Womanhood (CBMW). If you follow the primary source evidence marking the growth of complementarian theology—from the creation of the International Council on Biblical Inerrancy in the late 1970s to the 1984 SBC resolution on women in ministry to the founding of the CBMW and writing of the Danvers Statement in the 1980s to debates within the Evangelical Theological Society to the Baptist Faith and Message 2000—you will find Dorothy and Paige Patterson at every turn.[12] Through the leadership of this husband-wife team, the SBC established complementarianism as the leading understanding of gender roles. I would argue that the evangelical networks built by Dorothy Patterson established complementarianism even more broadly as well.

Patterson's views on biblical womanhood show she either didn't know or deliberately downplayed the truth about women in early Christianity.

For example, in one 1998 paper, she describes Mary, the mother of Jesus, as embodying a "gentle and quiet spirit" when she "let the miracle of incarnation happen to her." She describes the women in the Bible "who followed Jesus during His earthly sojourn" (like Mary Magdalene and the sisters in Bethany) as working "quietly in the background to minister to the Lord and in His name (Luke 8:2–3). Their behind-the-scenes service to the Lord must have made His public ministries easier and more effective." She argues that Jesus limited the sphere of women's activities while elevating "the domestic responsibilities they used in ministering to Him to a new importance."[13] In another paper, dating from 1988, Patterson states that there's no biblical evidence for women serving as "bishops, elders, or pastors and very little that they were accepted as deacons."[14] Her argument is consistent: women in the early church did not hold ecclesiastical office—they instead had a quiet spirit, choosing to be submissive workers at home as well as behind-the-scenes supporters of their husbands.

There's one particularly concerning way that Patterson writes about Mary, the mother of Jesus. Patterson says that Mary "let" the incarnation "happen to her" with "a quiet spirit"—the same "quiet spirit" that Patterson argues is the correct posture of a godly woman in submission to her husband.[15] New Testament scholar Amy Peeler, in her book *Women and the Gender of God*, argues that this framing of Mary casts the mother of Jesus as the "Total Rape Victim." Peeler argues it's dangerous to sexualize the annunciation with male and female characteristics (i.e., arguing that the submissive stance of Mary is akin to the posture of a woman with her husband). "The only interchange between men and women in which men must initiate and women must receive is forcible genital intercourse. Rape by a man of a woman is the only time when initiation must be from the male," she says.[16] In this light, Patterson's description of Mary is haunting.

What Patterson taught the women in her classes haunts me too. I declined to take her classes, but I have since corresponded and talked with women who did. Patterson taught women in her class for ministers' wives that their highest calling was to support their husbands as wives, mothers, keepers of the home, and sexual partners. She taught her students how to pack a suitcase for their husbands, stating it was their "job" to have it ready for him before he left and to unpack it when he returned home. She taught students how to modestly exit vehicles, which they would practice during class. She privileged married women over single women in the course, even directly facing the married women without looking at the single women when discussing marital intimacy. She taught that sex itself demonstrates the God-given design to privilege the needs of men over women. Why? Orgasm is required for men to release sperm (and hence "create a child"—as if that's the only thing needed), whereas the wife may become pregnant without orgasm. In this way, one former student told me, the class learned that women's sexual enjoyment mattered less than men's. She also required students to demonstrate a talent that could be used to support their husband's ministry. This lesson may have encouraged some students, as they learned to value whatever they could offer—from twirling a baton to singing to playing the piano to demonstrating how to apply makeup. But the talent lesson also reinforced Patterson's overarching message: that the best a woman could offer was to center her life on her husband's ministry.[17]

In short, Dorothy Patterson taught women that their primary ministry was to support their husbands and submit to male leadership. She argued that women in early Christianity never served in leadership roles and that Jesus himself had "elevated" the ministerial value of women's domestic labor that supported the work of men.

And she taught this to class after class, year after year.

An Office of Her Own

Let's return to the Priscilla Catacombs.

They have a striking number of images of women and contain the earliest frescoes depicting women in church history.

In fact, the catacombs contain so many images of women that, in trying to make sense of them, some scholars have postulated that the catacombs were a site of women's worship. Nicola Denzey, for one, has suggested that the so-called Greek Chapel in the Priscilla Catacombs was a privileged space "geared toward use by and for Christian women," as it contains images of the sisters from Bethany, Mary and Martha, standing with Jesus at the resurrection of Lazarus; Mary the mother of God holding Jesus and receiving the magi; the stories of Thecla and Susanna; and even a communal meal depiction (the *Fractio Panis*) that shows a veiled woman presiding.[18] Carolyn Osiek comes to a different conjecture, saying that there are so many women in the Greek Chapel because "a powerful female patron owned and was buried at the site and she decided what would be painted on the walls."[19]

There was only one image I had in mind when I planned the last-minute field trip to the catacombs: the image of the woman in the Cubiculum of the Velata, or Room of the Veiled Woman.

She did not disappoint.

The woman is wearing what could be liturgical garb (including a veil on her head). She stands in a position that would have been understood as religiously authoritative in the Greco-Roman world: the *orans* position. In this position, a figure stands with eyes elevated and arms raised on either side and palms lifted upward. Religious scholar Karen Jo Torjesen associates the *orans* position "with women's liturgical praying and prophesying," and as such, it is "evidence of the earliest tradition of women preachers," and with the possible institutionalization of the "office of widow."[20]

Torjesen's assessment is strengthened by the evidence gathered by Christine Schenk. Schenk statistically analyzes depictions of women and men in early Christian art—especially art found in catacomb frescoes and sarcophagi.

What she finds is striking and is outlined in her book *Crispina and Her Sisters*. For example:

1. Women comprised 76.8 percent of individual adult Christian sarcophagus portraits. Schenk writes, "This finding coincides with opinions from other scholars that women were of higher status and more influential within the early Christian subculture than commonly recognized."[21]

2. Of the solo portraits that are *orans* and also have positive gender identifications (159 total), women comprise 115 and men 44. Schenk concludes, "Solo female portraits were 2.3 times as likely as solo male portraits to be depicted in an *orans* position."[22]

3. Of greatest note, "solo portraits of Christian women with authoritative iconography such as scroll and speech gestures occur in similar proportions to solo portraits of men with this iconography." Schenk writes that this is especially

surprising because, given that passages like 1 Timothy 2 and
1 Corinthians 14 are often used to silence women in many
modern churches (whose leaders claim the restrictions reflect
the early church), one would expect early Christian images
to depict mostly male leaders with "these iconic 'power and
status' motifs." Instead, women with "authoritative iconography" are depicted "in similar proportions" to men.[23]

Since these findings about early portraits of Christian women
link the *orans* position with religious authority—liturgical praying,
prophesying, and, Torjesen suggests, preaching—at the time of the
Priscilla Catacombs' creation, we have reason to wonder whether the
prominent female figure in the Room of the Veiled Woman represents
one of the earliest depictions of a woman with religious authority.

Scholars such as Sandra Glahn have postulated a separate office
for women in the early church—a possibility reasonable enough
for a 2024 article from Vatican News (the official news site for the
Roman Catholic Church) to suggest that the woman portrayed in
the Cubiculum of the Velata was "enrolled in the order of widows."[24] Most people in my world recognize the office of elder,
but fewer know about a potential office of widow. Just consider
the implications of 1 Timothy 5:9–10: "Let a widow be put on
the list if she is not less than sixty years old and has been married only once; she must be well attested for her good works, as
one who has brought up children, shown hospitality, washed the
saints' feet, helped the afflicted, and devoted herself to doing good
in every way." Multiple scholars have examined textual evidence
for the order of widows, including the writings of Clement I and
Origen, early church texts like *Didascalia Apostolorum* and *Tes-
tamentum Domini*, conciliar texts, and evidence from the New
Testament (1 Timothy, Acts, and the Gospels). They've reasoned
that historical evidence for an office of widow extends beyond images of women painted on Roman catacombs.[25] Osiek and Kevin
Madigan describe these women as "the service organization of

the early church, especially for works of charity to needy women and hospitality to visitors."[26] By the third century, the order of widows is "consistently listed with the clergy" and was even given instructions "similar to those in the pastoral epistles" by Clement of Alexandria and Origen.[27] The later prohibitions against widows teaching and baptizing could suggest that widows had taken on these pastoral responsibilities too.

Which brings us back to the image of the veiled woman at the catacombs.

Regardless of whether she is preaching or enrolled in the order of widows, it's likely that she represents a woman fulfilling a leadership role. The first reason, as we have discussed, is that she is depicted in an *orans* position, which signifies prayer, prophecy, or preaching. A second reason is because of the images flanking the veiled woman. On the left, the woman is depicted in a ceremony with a man seated in a high-backed chair who is laying his hand on her shoulder. The woman holds a scroll and another man stands behind her. The seated man (the seat is a sign of authority) appears to wear a liturgical robe (the dalmatic) with a cloak (a pallium) around his shoulders. The scene on the right mirrors the scene on the left as the woman is now seated in a high-backed chair (again, a symbol of authority). Instead of a scroll, she holds a baby.

It is possible, as our tour guide in Rome suggested, that the threefold image represents scenes from the deceased woman's life—that the center image is her praying in paradise, the left image is her wedding, and the right image is her as a mother.

It is also possible that the threefold image represents an entirely different range of events from her life—that the center image portrays the woman in a religiously authoritative position, the left image depicts a consecration ceremony, and the right image depicts her fulfilling the function of her office, caring for unwanted babies.

Schenk thinks the latter interpretation is reasonable. As she writes, "The beautiful fresco in the *Velata* cubiculum may well commemorate an ecclesiastical widow who . . . was a woman of stature who ministered in the third century church at Rome." While the scene on her left represents her ordination, the scene on the right represents her ministry, which was the same as that of other "wealthy Christian widows in ancient Rome . . . to care for unwanted newborns exposed to die."[28]

Denzey provides some caution, wondering if the images simply represent a learned woman with enough wealth to depict herself in publicly authoritative ways. "Rather than just assume that she belonged, submissively, to the church and/or her husband," wonders Denzey, what if we recognized this woman's agency? "The images above her grave are bold, costly, and rare." They center a woman taking action as an "expert practitioner" who publicly learns, reads, and prays—"perhaps even of prophecy or public learning."[29]

Regardless of their differences, both Schenk's and Denzey's interpretations of these scenes reveal an independently authoritative woman, which makes a lot of historical sense.

But upon finishing the tour that day in Rome, I didn't get any hint from our tour guide or the official guidebook that the veiled woman might have been a literate woman, much less an authoritative leader. Indeed, this scene was described as scenes from a dead woman's life who followed traditional expectations for womanhood. She married, gave birth, and prayed.[30]

Think about what that means for the many travelers who come to see the catacombs.

Instead of seeing the possibility of an independent woman in the early church, whose authority is legitimized as a public intellectual or even by an ordination ceremony—they see only a woman defined by her dependent relationship as a wife.

What I Can Say

I want to pause here and write even more frankly to you, reader.

I know what's assumed about the images of women in the Priscilla Catacombs.

I heard all the assumptions on the tour that day.

I heard that these images do not depict women in authoritative positions.

I heard the veiled woman is a wealthy female patron praying, and that the images flanking her represent marriage and motherhood.

I'm not going to overstate the evidence presented by Schenk. I cannot guarantee that she is right that the Priscilla Catacombs depict women serving in ordained clerical roles.

What I can say is that the veiled woman suggests a woman of influence in the early church, and that the depiction in the two flanking images show her agency and independence, perhaps even recognizing her as a religious authority.[31]

What I can say is that the Priscilla Catacombs present an abundance of depictions from the early centuries of Christianity representing women, many of whom are in authoritative positions. Gary Macy has described Schenk's research as "the most important analysis of new evidence in decades."[32] Her research also fits with a growing body of archaeological evidence documented by scholars like Joan Taylor that indicates female leadership. For example, a fifth-century image on the catacomb walls of Naples depicts two women, Cerula and Bitalia, in the orans position wearing liturgical garb with the Alpha and Omega symbolizing Christ's victory above their heads. "Most striking of all," writes Taylor and her coauthor Helen Bond, "is that they are shown with open books containing the four Gospels and emitting tongues of fire (probably to indicate the Spirit, which comes from the texts). Cerula is grey-haired, and perhaps a little older than Bitalia; the figures of Peter and Paul stand on either side of her in separate panels." Art historian Ally Kateusz argues that, given the iconography, these women represent bishops.[33]

This suggests that the ordination of women in early Christianity is not as controversial as many modern Christians might think. Luis Josué Salés argues the "unrestricted ordination" of second-century women in the Phrygian church could indicate an "original Pauline custom," even as Osiek and Madigan find that "evidence for women presbyters is greater in the West than in the East," evidence that "cannot be confined to fringe or 'heretical' groups."[34]

The evidence from the Priscilla Catacombs does not conclusively prove female leadership in the earliest centuries of the church. But it casts enough doubt to undermine the claim that male-only leadership is a matter of "fundamental biblical authority."

Ministers by Choice

In his 1983 book, *The Minister's Wife: Her Role in Nineteenth-Century American Evangelicalism*, historian Leonard Sweet notes that "the minister's wife is not the child of the Reformation. She is the child of the early church, when married men were regularly ordained."[35] The first time I read this, I wrote in my notes that there's a difference between a "minister's wife" and a woman who is married to a minister. Just because early clergy members were married doesn't mean their wives were expected to join the ministry team.

Evidence from the first few centuries of church history shows women in ministry who were not married, women in ministry who were married to ministers, women in ministry married to nonministers, and women who married ministers but did not seem to serve in ministry with their spouses.

Let me restate that because it is important.

Evidence from the first few centuries of church history shows that marriage to a minister did not automatically presume a vocational calling for the spouse (remember Peter's wife?). In addition, women, even married women, could serve in ministry without a spouse in ministry.

If you haven't read Gary Macy's *The Hidden History of Medieval Women's Ordination*, you should. Macy is professor emeritus of religious studies at Santa Clara University and has served as the

Herodotus Fellow at the Institute for Advanced Study in Princeton (1991–92) and the Senior Luce Fellow at the National Humanities Center (2005–6). Jane Tibbetts Schulenburg's review of his book in *Speculum*, the medieval history flagship journal, sums up the significance of his research. Macy, she writes, shows that "historically there is no question that women in the early period were considered ordained clergy and shared the status with men."[36]

Macy provides the historical framework that the 2023 SBC messengers lacked to be able to properly evaluate Al Mohler's claim that for two thousand years the church has limited the office of pastor to men.[37] Reading Macy would have shown them that women throughout church history have served in ecclesiastical offices, received ordination, officiated at the altar, and exercised authority over men. The messengers would have learned that the reason they don't know about these women is because this history "has been deliberately forgotten, intentionally marginalized, and, not infrequently, creatively explained away." It is a fact, Macy shows, that "women were ordained for the first twelve hundred years of Christianity."[38]

Before we continue, let's clarify some terms.

First, let's talk about ordination. What we understand as ordination today was slow to develop. Also, the meaning of ordination shifted during the medieval era, from merely recognizing leadership function to a ritual bestowing of clerical identity. I will talk more about this shift in the next chapter. For now, just know that the word *ordination* references a person who is recognized as fulfilling a clerical function.

Second, let's define the terms used for female office holders. The primary offices recognized in the early church (excluding the possible existence of the order of widows) are those of *presbyteros* (senior leader, elder, priest), *diakonos* (servant, deacon, ministry provider), and *episkopos* (overseer, manager, bishop).[39] Historical evidence exists for women described by all three of these titles. Madigan and Osiek have cataloged around one hundred potential references to women as deacons, ten women as presbyters, and one reference to a female bishop in the early Western church.[40] The historical evidence shows such women existed; the challenge is determining what these titles indicate about a given woman's status. Are the female presbyters the wives of presbyters? Or as Madigan has argued, could they be clergywomen who had "authority in local communities, or performed quasi-diaconal service at the altar, assisted itinerant priests, and, possibly, engaged in other, routine, if unspecified presbyteral activities"?[41] Context helps determine the different meanings of *elder*: an older person, the wife of an office holder, or a female holder of a clerical office. The terms are the same, yet the meaning can be different.

So, let's talk about women as clergy wives, compared with female presbyters, deacons, and bishops.

Between the fourth and sixth centuries, several references to female presbyters exist in legislation and funerary inscriptions. Conventional wisdom, including what I remember being told as a student, often supposes female presbyters (as well as female deacons and even bishops) as akin to pastors' wives: they carried the title of their husbands. Take the sixth-century legislation from the Second Council of Tours and the Council of Auxerre that forbade sexual relationships between a presbyter and his "presbytera," or the church councils between 441 and 583 that specifically reference the wives of presbyters and deacons as "wife" (*uxor*) or "spouse" (*conjux/conjunx*).[42]

This certainly sounds like a pastor's wife! Yet there are differences.

First, some women carrying the titles of presbyter, deacon, and bishop are serving in ministry roles without the involvement of a spouse. Take, for example, Leta in Calabria whose husband (not referenced as a presbyter) erected a funerary inscription to his wife the "presbytera." The "presbytera" Martia, who officiated the Eucharist alongside two men in Poitiers, serves as another example (there is no indication that she is married). "Women, it would seem," writes Macy, "were still ministering at the altar in the late eighth century," even as some legislation tried to outlaw their ministry.[43]

Second, some women with these same titles were married to clergy, but they carried the titles because they were ordained and served in ministry roles—not because of their marriage. Macy argues that the words "*episcopa, presbytera*, and deaconess" are not used for all ministry spouses. This is different from the title pastor's wife (or minister's wife), which is often applied to any woman married to a minister. Not so for ministry spouses in the early church. As Macy explains, "The orders of *episcopa, presbytera*, and deaconess then were clerical orders to which the wives of bishops, priests, and deacons could aspire, but they did not always do so."[44]

Did you hear that?

The wives of clergy in the early church could serve in ministry—and were ordained specifically to ministry roles—but did not have to serve. Marriage to a minister did not automatically enroll them in church service.

What a difference it would make for a ministry wife called to ministry to be able to serve as a ministry partner alongside her spouse instead of subsumed under his role!

Macy's evidence suggests that women in the early centuries of Christianity did not carry clerical titles simply because they had married clergymen. Women carrying the title of presbyter, deacon, or bishop might have been married to clergy, but that wasn't necessary. Likewise, women married to clergy were not automatically presbyter, deacon, or bishop. They only carried these titles if they fulfilled the clerical roles.

Let me say that another way.

Women received clerical titles because they served in clerical roles, not simply because they were married to ordained men. Do you see the difference that makes? Instead of marriage being the triggering factor, a ministry calling was the triggering factor, and marital status was less relevant. Driving this point home, Macy writes that "ordination was to a particular function rather than to a particular metaphysical or personal state. It was what they did, not who they were, that made women *episcopae*, *presbyterae*, and deaconesses. Any woman who performed that ministry and was ordained to it, married or single, could be an *episcopa*, *presbytera*, or deaconess."[45]

It was what they did, not who they were.

The veiled woman in the Priscilla Catacombs stands alone because she could; her identity was separate from the identity of a husband. One of my academic friends noted that if the veiled woman had been a man, there would be no controversy about what the images represent. We would assume he was a leader in the early church, and we wouldn't worry about his wife.

Married or single; married to a clergy spouse; or married to a lay spouse.

Ministry was what women chose to do, not simply an extension of a husband's job.

In Memory of Her

I had traveled with students on day trips to Canterbury for years.

This year was different.

Andrew Bartlett, author of *Men and Women in Christ: Fresh Light from the Biblical Texts*, met me and my class of seventeen undergraduates at the Canterbury West train station.[46] He had volunteered to host my students at his house for tea and scones and had arranged a guided tour of St. Martin's Church.

I watched my students gather around his table, debating how best to eat their scones—with cream or jam added first. I watched as they carefully poured tea, stirred in sugar, and laughed as they drank together. The breeze blew through open windows and doors, bringing fresh scents of flowers and the buzzing of conversations from students in the garden.

My favorite moment of that day happened inside St. Martin's Church, one of the most significant sites in the history of English Christianity. It is the place where a young bride from a dysfunctional yet powerful French family maintained her worship of the triune God even after being married to a non-Christian king. This young bride insisted that she be allowed to keep her faith and be given the means to continue her worship—namely, a church and a priest. From where we sat in the church nave, we could just see the outline of a door leading into the oldest part of the church.

The door is called Bertha's door.

It's unknown whether Bertha would have used the door, but the name is bestowed in her memory (as is a statue placed in a walled-up niche in 1997). The plaque on the front step leading into the modern entrance memorializes her too, designating "Queen Bertha's Walk." St. Martin's Church, along with Canterbury Cathedral and St. Augustine's Abbey, are part of a UNESCO World Heritage site.[47]

Why is Bertha of Kent so important?

Because Bertha was the woman whose steadfast faith created a path for Gregory the Great, the bishop of Rome at the end of the sixth century, to send a reluctant Benedictine monk across the channel to convert the Angles into angels (as Gregory's dream had foretold).[48]

Because of Bertha, her husband Ethelbert of Kent met with this monk named Augustine under a tree just down the road from Bertha's church.

Because of Bertha, Ethelbert was baptized, officially bringing Roman Christianity to England.

Because of Bertha, Canterbury became the most authoritative seat in the English church (think the archbishop of Canterbury) instead of London becoming the primary site.

Bertha's door opened into an unimpressive Roman building repurposed as a sixth-century church; it also opened England to the establishment of Roman Christianity as the dominant faith.

It is fitting for the door to be named in memory of her.

After the guide had finished her talk, a student tapped me on the shoulder.

"Dr. Barr, who are those other women?"

I looked up, noticing for the first time a stained-glass window divided into four sections. Each section depicted a different woman: the top left "BERTHA REGINA," the bottom left "S DOROTHEA," the top right "S ETHELBURGA," and the bottom right "S MARGARITA." The window, in other words, depicts Queen Bertha, St. Dorothea (a virgin martyr), St. Ethelburga (daughter of Bertha who spread Christianity in England through her marriage to King Edwin of Northumbria and who served as an abbess), and St. Margaret (another virgin martyr who defeated a dragon and whose deathbed preaching converted hundreds to the faith).[49]

A window in memory of Bertha, Dorothea, Ethelburga, and Margaret.

After the student walked away, I stayed, looking up. It was then that I realized two of the women were depicted with croziers—Ethelburga and Margaret.

Croziers are symbols of ecclesiastical authority, usually wielded by bishops. I can't say why the Victorian artist put croziers in the hands of these women. I'd like to think that the artist realized how appropriate it was to do so. Ethelburga, after all, served as an ordained cleric in the role of abbess (more about this in the next chapter). Margaret was alleged to have been a shepherd, tending flocks in the field before she was imprisoned for her faith and became known for her preaching—which she continued even as she was being executed.

I'm sure you see now why St. Martin's Church is so memorable to me.

From its walls to its windows, St. Martin's Church remembers women.

As I stood there in the church that day, I was reminded again that the problem isn't a lack of evidence for the significant roles played by women in early Christian leadership.

Nor is the problem that we have simply forgotten.

The problem is what we have chosen to remember instead.

Instead of remembering women like Bertha, who gave directions to both her husband and a priest that resulted in the conversion of England to Roman Christianity, or instead of remembering the *orans* position as indicative of authoritative religious speech (prophecy, prayer, and preaching), we remember John Piper's warning that a woman who gives directions—even traffic directions—to a man should do so in a way that does not offend his God-given responsibility to lead.[50]

3

The Not-So-Hidden History of Medieval Women's Ordination

My husband does the laundry.

He always has. I can't imagine life without his neat piles of perfectly folded towels and stacks of underwear.

I mow the lawn.

I always have. I find it therapeutic. Chaos may reign throughout the rest of life, but no Dallis grass mars the front yard. Plus, it gives me a good dose of sunshine, counts as exercise, and gives me time to think.

Once, when my husband had his first full-time job and after we had bought our first home, a church member saw me mowing the lawn. My husband got an earful the next Sunday for slacking in his manly responsibilities. He and I laughed about it, but I remember feeling awkward. Why did a church member feel they could criticize how my husband and I divvied up household chores? My husband was less surprised. He had once been reprimanded at an Exxon station when I had pumped the gas while he went inside to pay. "Just let me pump the gas," he said afterward.

I did. It was easier.

When I relayed the lawn-mowing and gas-pumping stories to one of our longtime friends who was also a pastor's wife, she nodded. Her husband was the cook in their family, but she would take the credit when they had guests for dinner or brought food to church events. It was easier to pretend than to explain to church members that their pastor wore the apron.

Cooking is a gendered task I did and still do. After a couple of awkward months at our new church, I found that when I asked other women for recipes and cooking advice, it made them relax and talk more comfortably with me. One woman offered to give me lessons about how to cook large meals for gatherings, as that was a skill I would need in ministry. I joined the hospitality committee and was added to the kitchen and meal-train rotations.

I started coteaching youth Sunday school (this is ironic, as a woman coteaching Sunday school is what led to my husband's firing at a different church) and helping with the children, but I still only had one friend at church. The rest of the women had started warming up to me, but they didn't invite me to their get-togethers. It could have just been an oversight, or maybe they thought I was too busy with school, or maybe they were waiting for me to ask to be included. I honestly don't know. But it was discouraging.

Things changed after the pastor publicly praised what he perceived as my modesty. I had been helping with a children's performance, and most of the church was in the audience. When I bent down to walk under a stage prop, I was facing the congregation, and I held my blouse to my chest with my hand. After the performance, as I stood with a group of church leaders (the pastor, some deacons and their wives, and my husband), the pastor praised me for not allowing my neckline to gape open, remarking that other women should learn from my example.

Shortly after, I was invited to a girls' night out.

I felt like I had finally passed the pastor's wife test.

But it had come at a cost.

I had spent the previous few months de-emphasizing my PhD work (I worked part-time for the Department of Women's and Gender Studies at the University of North Carolina at Chapel Hill) and minimizing my chores in the division of labor at home. Instead, I had been emphasizing my cooking and hospitality skills and my willingness to teach and volunteer with children and youth.

I also kept my mouth shut a lot.

This strategy had led to greater acceptance, but I felt like I was walking on eggshells. I couldn't say what I really thought.

And I had thoughts.

I had thoughts about the number of church members proclaiming the King James translation of the Bible to be the only acceptable English Bible translation. Some argued it was "double inspired," meaning the text was inspired by God not only in its "original manuscripts" but likewise in the English translation of 1611.

I ordered a KJV 1611 as a form of passive resistance. You see, most people in the church were using the modern iteration of the KJV even as they claimed the 1611 text was divinely inspired. What they didn't realize was that what they were reading wasn't the same as the 1611 version, not least because the 1611 translation included the Apocrypha. The Apocrypha comprised texts that the Southern Baptist world of rural North Carolina would not have considered canonical and would have dismissed as "popish."

I also had thoughts about the annual "Mother of the Year" award. I put forward the name of a woman who faithfully brought her children to church every Sunday and Wednesday despite her husband refusing to come. Other women told me that he was known to drink and cuss. The deacons rejected her name because they didn't feel that a woman could win the award if her husband wouldn't be eligible for the "Father of the Year" award, given on Father's Day. A deacon's wife won the award.

I was frustrated, to say the least.

One night as I was multitasking—working on a dissertation chapter while trying to stuff tortillas for a church meal the next day—I got so frustrated I decided I wasn't going. They didn't need me at another event; they certainly didn't need more food. My dissertation chapter did need me; it was already a few days overdue. I told my husband, expecting him to be irritated or to try to talk me into going. "It is your choice," he said.

He was right. It was my choice—the job was his, not mine. I had forgotten that over the past few months. I had been so eager to be an asset to my husband in his new job, to prove that working on my PhD would not hinder his ministry, that I had lost some of myself in the role. Instead of being who I really was and using the gifts God had given me, I had been trying to be the pastor's wife I thought the church community wanted. I was exhausted, and all I had seemed to achieve was gaining the (temporary, as I would soon learn) acceptance of a handful of people.

Three things happened after that.

1. I said no to a local job that many at church were encouraging me to accept because they thought it would be a good job for a pastor's wife. It offered a stable income but would have put my PhD work on the back burner. My husband fully supported my decision and defended my choice. When I told one of the only women in the community whom I felt I could be honest with (she too was a pastor's wife and worked with the local Baptist association), she just smiled. "You married a good man," she said.

2. I received a tentative query from the chair of the history department at Baylor University, asking whether I would be interested in taking a temporary lecturer position for the next year as I was finishing my dissertation.

3. I delved headlong into my dissertation. That email from Baylor had triggered a desire in both my husband and me to go back to Texas. We had been living in North Carolina for several years, and the thought of being near family again—especially as we were beginning to think about children—was

enticing. So, I dredged up my notes on the more than forty manuscripts of *Festial*, John Mirk's late fourteenth-century sermon collection, which I had spent several months studying in archives throughout England. I also began to map out the monastic establishments connected to Lilleshall Abbey, Mirk's home base near Shrewsbury, Shropshire, to try to trace potential influences on his work.

It was my dissertation research on Mirk that introduced me to a woman named Milburga.[1]

Why Milburga Matters

The name Milburga may not catch your medieval fancy the way "Marian" or "Katherine" or even "Julian" does. My daughter informed me "Milburga" sounds more like a disease than a woman.

But I promise that you want to hear her story.

Milburga was born to rule, politically and religiously.

Her lineage, as recorded by an eleventh-century text preserved in the twelfth-century record book of St. Augustine's Abbey (yes, the abbey founded by the Benedictine monk greeted by Queen Bertha in the previous chapter), indicates that Milburga was the great-great-granddaughter of King Ethelbert and Queen Bertha of Kent—which means she was related to the most significant royal family in early medieval Britain. Her father was a minor king (more like a prince), while her uncle was the more well-known king of the Mercians.

Although Milburga was a woman born in the mid-seventh century, we know quite a bit about her. Most of the evidence comes from documents composed between the eighth and thirteenth centuries: the thirteenth-century *The Life of Milburg* (British Library Additional MS 34633), which is a copy of an early twelfth-century text written by Goscelin of St. Bertin; a twelfth-century copy of *Mildburg's Testament* (included by Goscelin in his *Life*);

an eleventh-century list of saints (*Secgan B*); the eleventh-century *Mildrith Legend*; the twelfth-century *The Miracula Inventionis Beate Mylburge Virginis* (Lincoln Cathedral Library MS 149); and one letter written during Milburga's lifetime by St. Boniface referencing an event at Wimnicas. Wimnicas is "among twenty-three . . . religious institutions mentioned in pre-[Norman] Conquest sources between 871 and 1066."[2]

A long-running joke among scholars of premodern periods—given the sparseness of sources for premodern women, especially ancient and early medieval—is that one piece of evidence is a theory and two pieces of evidence is proof. From this perspective, Milburga's historical reality is about as rock-solid as you can get.

The terms *legend* and *hagiography*, the types of historical records that tell much of Milburga's story, are often misunderstood. Neither means a made-up story like a tall-tale or a sketchy account based on more degrees than between me and Kevin Bacon. A legend in medieval Christianity is a type of sacred text, often the life of a saint, read aloud during a church service; a "legenda" was a collection of stories of the lives of saints, organized to follow the liturgical calendar. The word *hagiography* denotes a genre of religious texts written to make known the sanctity of men and women considered to be holy by their local communities. Hagiography is thus a type of religious biography.

To be sure, these texts are not objective, as they were intended to teach lessons and confirm sanctity. Neither were they composed by authors adhering to modern standards of evidentiary proof. Even so, medieval saints' lives are rooted in history. David W. Rollason concludes that hagiography is "a living genre which in some cases may have as much claim to have been in touch with the society in which it was written or read as medieval historical writing itself."[3] Rollason does caution that while hagiography can be used as a reputable historical source for the life of a saint as well as the historical context of the saint's following, its reliability does depend on how much of a time gap exists between the written account of the life and the actual life of a saint. In the case of Milburga, the gap between the composition of her legends and the reality of her life can be filled in (at least to some degree) from other historical sources.

In other words: You might doubt the early twelfth-century stories imbuing Milburga's eighth-century life with supernatural power over birds, but that doesn't mean you should doubt that Milburga was the abbess of one of the most powerful monasteries in the most powerful kingdom of early medieval England.[4]

Milburga's position casts doubt on claims from Christian leaders today that women have never exercised the pastoral role. Her story shows a time when women's independent leadership in the church was more normative; it shows a woman whose ministry derived from her social status as an elite woman *and* from her ordination by a bishop rather than from her dependent status as a wife; most important, it shows how our understanding of terms like *pastor* and *ordination* stem more from historical context than the Bible.

Was Milburga a Pastor?

Milburga was a Benedictine nun.

How could she be equivalent to a Southern Baptist (or any other modern Protestant) pastor?

On the one hand, she can't be—if only because our modern evangelical understanding of the pastoral office did not exist in the early medieval world (ditto for ordination, but that is for the next section).

On the other hand, there are similarities between Milburga's ecclesiastical office of abbess and the modern office of pastor. Let's start with the Southern Baptist Convention's current definition of a pastor: "'Central to the pastor's role is the responsibility to preach and teach.' Pastors also provide spiritual leadership and oversight for the congregation."[5]

Pastors preach, teach, and provide spiritual leadership to a congregation.

Milburga served as abbess over the monastic community of Wimnicas (now known as Wenlock Priory) in the Mercian sub-kingdom known as Magonsaete. Wimnicas was founded as a "double monastery" around 670.[6] A double monastery is how medieval scholars reference the "peculiar" monastic communities that emerged in France and England (roughly from the seventh to the tenth century) in which a female superior ruled over a community of both monks and nuns.[7] When Milburga became the abbess of Wimnicas (around 680), she was charged with providing spiritual leadership to men and women.[8] Rose Lagram-Taylor summarizes that "under her rule Wenlock flourished, receiving benefactions from her brothers Merchelm and Milfred and holding lands across Shropshire, Herefordshire, and Wales."[9]

It is important to note that some scholars argue that double monasteries were either houses where female communities were attached to preexisting male communities or primarily female communities with the necessary male clergy for performing sacraments. These interpretations emphasize that medieval women were spiritually dependent on male clergy, but that isn't necessarily accurate. Some scholars charge that some historians have been "too quick to assume women's total dependency on male priests, especially for the early medieval period."[10] Evidence suggests some female communities could perform liturgies, including celebrating the Eucharist, and provide their own pastoral care without male clergy.[11] When Sarah Foot describes a double house, she is referencing communities that lived under the authority of an abbess or prioress.[12] At least eighteen such houses existed in early medieval England, and it's possible there were twenty-four more. Some of these houses, like Wimnicas, were likely segregated between the sexes regarding worship and dormitories; other houses show no evidence of segregation. The power in these houses "lay firmly in female hands."[13]

Overall, evidence from these double monasteries shows that women imbued with ecclesiastical oversight fulfilled the function of their office, including providing spiritual instruction and performing pastoral duties. This fits early medieval church expectations, as Foot writes, "that women could fulfil spiritual functions."[14] Gary Macy agrees with Foot, writing that "abbots and abbesses in earlier centuries preached, heard confessions, and baptized, all powers that would be reserved to the priest in the twelfth and thirteenth centuries."[15]

If you are thinking, *Milburga was an abbess, but that isn't like the pastor of a local church*—

You are right.

An abbess is a *more* authoritative role than pastor.

Milburga was more like a bishop, which is why depictions of her include a crozier. Did you know the primary word from which we derive *pastor* (*poimainō*) is mentioned only three times in the New Testament, most notably in Ephesians 4:11 but also in Acts 20:28 and 1 Peter 5:2? It also references a function (shepherding) rather than an office. New Testament scholar Nijay Gupta reminds us that "if you turned up to a first-century church gathering and asked to meet *the* pastor, the people would look around trying to figure out which one person you were inquiring after."[16] The word from which we derive bishop, *episkopos*, is one of the three terms appearing in the New Testament to demarcate church leadership roles (*diakonos* and *presbyteros* are the other two). It is the most formal "leadership title," indicating its bearer was charged with providing oversight of a Christian community. As Gupta explains, "*Episkopoi* played more of an oversight or advisory function, and the *diakonoi* carried out the ministry initiatives and activity."[17] This is exactly the type of function the medieval office of bishop fulfilled: providing oversight and pastoral care to laity and clergy.

I use the word *bishop* intentionally to describe Milburga's role as abbess for two reasons. First, I have found that when my students hear a feminine office (such as deaconess or abbess), they often presume the position is less authoritative than a male office (such as deacon or abbot). I suspect some of you might have thought the same thing: *Oh, she is an abbess; that means she was a woman who taught other women.* This is an incorrect and anachronistic presumption, applying to the early church a modern complementarian understanding of women's ministry that says women are only qualified to teach women and children (which, for some reason, makes them less authoritative because women and children are less important than men?).

The second reason I use the term *bishop* is that the early medieval world equated the roles of abbesses and abbots with the role of bishops. The organized ecclesiastical world of Western medieval Catholicism, where priests oversaw parishes and bishops oversaw priests and archbishops oversaw bishops and the bishop of Rome (a.k.a. the pope), along with his cardinals, oversaw them all, was still developing in the early medieval world. It wouldn't be fully formed until after reforms spanning the eleventh through thirteenth centuries. Until then, boundaries blurred, with the ecclesiastical office of monastic superiors (abbots and abbesses) functioning with the rights and privileges of bishops and even with secular jurisdiction.

Milburga functioned as a woman in a clerical office that exercised religious authority over a community that included men and was considered one of the most authoritative clerical offices at that time. Consider the description Jennifer Edwards uses to open her study of medieval female authority in Poitiers' Abbey of Sainte-Croix:

> Medieval abbesses were important and influential office holders, well-known public figures who offered spiritual guidance to the women under their care, protected their community's moral well-being, defended the abbey's property and economic interests, and performed the feudal duties they owed their lords and vassals. The female superior demanded not just the obedience of her own nuns, but of any seigneurial subordinates, or dependent communities— male or female. If head of a large or important community, the

abbess could rival bishops' power and claim the ears of kings and popes. These women's authority rested on the history of their communities, the strength of their advocates, and their own competence in defending their rights and privileges.[18]

The religious authority of an abbess like Milburga could rival that of a bishop—which means, I think, that she would have been more than a match for a pastor.

Was Milburga Ordained?

I don't remember his exact words, but I remember the gist of the question. It was a tweet asking for one woman in history who was ordained in the same way as a man. The tweeter qualified the request by insisting it not be a heretical tradition and that the ordination include the ability to officiate at the altar.

I started to respond, but then gave up.

It was a no-win situation. The question revealed how much the tweeter didn't understand ordination. It was going to take way more than 144 characters to answer, and I didn't have time for it.

I have time now.

Let's think about the tweeter's question. It presumes that a "real" (not heretical) ordination requires certain elements and enables the ordained to officiate at the altar. It also presumes that the definition of a "real" ordination has remained constant throughout Christian history.

Neither of these presumptions is accurate.

For the first thousand years of Western church history, ordination tied a particular function (think *pastoring*) to a particular office (bishop, priest, deacon, abbess, etc.) within a particular community (church, diocese, monastery, etc.).[19] While ordination could include administering the sacrament, it didn't have to. It could include consecration but didn't have to. It could include preaching and teaching but didn't have to. It could be connected to a clerical office but didn't have to be. As Macy reminds us, "The words *ordination* and *ordinare* were used to describe the ceremony and installation not only of bishops, priests, deacons, and subdeacons but also of porters, lectors, exorcists, acolytes, canons, abbots, abbesses, kings, queens, and empresses."[20]

The word *consecration* was also used interchangeably with ordination. Today, one may refer more to ceremonies involving sacred space (consecration) and one to ceremonies involving people (ordination). This distinction didn't exist in early medieval Christianity. Ordination, consecration, and even blessing recognized religious leadership functions.

When the text states that Milburga was consecrated by a bishop, it means she was ordained. Indeed, both abbots and abbesses were included on the lists of ordained clergy throughout the medieval era.

Let me put this into contemporary Baptist language.

For the first thousand years of Christianity, local clergy appointed men and women to fulfill specific functions within specific offices. This is one thing Al Mohler and I agree on: just as Baptists have no consistent theology of ordination and understand pastoral office and pastoral function as the same thing, the early medieval church had no consistent theology of ordination and understood clerical office and clerical function as the same thing.[21]

Milburga's *Life* records her as consecrated (ordained) to the monastic life when she became the abbess of Wimnicas, fulfilling the function of this office; this included exercising religious authority over both men and women. Her dying words seem to reflect this spiritual authority over a mixed-gender community, as she states how "like a mother" she piously cared for both her "sons and daughters."[22]

I know this might surprise you.

I know some of you might doubt me.

Some of you will find it hard to believe that there was a time in church history when women were ordained to ecclesiastical offices *and* fulfilled the function of pastors.

The historical truth is that they did. Until the rules changed.

Ordination Redefined

During the central Middle Ages, the concept of ordination shifted, moving away from ambiguity (with which Baptists and other more low church congregations are more comfortable) to more specificity (with which Catholics, Anglicans, Presbyterians, and other more high church congregations are more comfortable). Here is how Macy explains it in *The Hidden History of Medieval Women's Ordination* (if you haven't guessed, the title of this chapter is a tribute to his book).

First, in 1091 Pope Urban II linked ordination more narrowly to the orders of priest and deacon. Second, in the twelfth century Peter Lombard (author of *The Four Sentences*, a medieval systematic theology) linked ordination to sacred power. The ability to wield spiritual power (such as forgiveness of sins and celebration of the Eucharist) signified those who had received ordination. It marked them as set apart. Third, in the thirteenth century Lombard's definition was tweaked to limit ordination to offices that administered the sacrament at the altar.[23] This is the same century when, for the first time in Christian history, church leaders outlined the seven sacraments necessary for salvation that only ordained clergy could perform.

Can you see where this is going?

Ordination recognized Milburga's calling to serve the function and office of an abbess at a specific monastery. Three hundred years later, ordination imbued clergy with the sacred power to perform the sacraments regardless of which community they served. Instead of being ordained to a specific role, ordination now imbued a sacred *status* (remember this for the next chapter, as we will return to it). Only in this era did the Eucharist became tied to ordained status; that power to perform sacred acts signified a sacred calling to ministry.[24]

Conventional wisdom states that ordination was *always* associated with the sacramental power to celebrate Eucharist. But my students, both undergraduate and graduate, learn quickly that this idea wasn't crystallized (at least in the West) until 1215 at the Fourth Lateran Council. Macy describes the council as a "magisterial intervention to settle theological and pastoral discussions."[25] It uses the word *transubstantiation* to describe "the bread being changed by divine power into the body, and the wine into the blood. . . . And this sacrament no one can effect except the priest who has been duly ordained in accordance with the keys of the Church."[26]

There are fewer watershed moments in history than we often suppose, but I think that Fourth Lateran is one of them (at least for the Western church), because it was at Fourth Lateran that ordination and the sacrament at the altar became inextricably connected.

For those of you skimming to the good parts, you can start reading again because it is time to get to the point.

Remember the tweeter?

The ordination that he presumed (administering the sacraments) was not part of ordination in the early church; it was not part of ordination in the early medieval church; it was not part of ordination until the thirteenth century. As sacramental theology blossomed, ordination became more narrowly defined.

As the definition of ordination shifted, the rules for who could be ordained shifted too. I would give you three guesses about who the shifting boundaries of ordination impacted most, but I don't think you need more than one.

A Pastor in All but Name

I was proctoring the final exam in my summer history course when I realized that my tentative plans for the following day weren't going to work out. I had hoped to review a manuscript for one of my graduate students on the last day before I flew home to Texas, but I hadn't done enough research and now it was too late. Chagrined, I began making other plans—flipping through the English

Heritage site to see where I could use my membership one more time. Because of my previous visit to St. Martin's in Canterbury, early medieval women were on my mind when I saw the English Heritage listing for Wenlock Priory.

Two trains and one bus ride later, I stood beneath the soaring ruins of what had once been Milburga's monastery. As I walked through its tumbled walls, I thought about how Milburga's name has disappeared from history. I think it has done so for two (related) reasons.

First, the monastery that she once ruled was taken over by the Cluniacs after the Norman Conquest and flourished as a house for men until the Dissolution of Henry VIII in 1536. What people know about the monastery usually stems from this latter era (in fact, the ruins of the monastery reflect little of their early medieval origins).[27]

Second, another Benedictine monastery was founded at the politically strategic town of Shrewsbury, just a few miles down the road from Wenlock Priory. Under the leadership of Abbot Robert, Shrewsbury Abbey emerged as one of the most important monastic houses of that time and region.

Milburga, in other words, has been forgotten by history because historians have tended to focus on her male successors. The only reason we probably remember her name is because her late eleventh-century successors decided that a powerful saint would enhance the reputation of their abbey. They literally dug her up and proclaimed her story—not because her story was important in its own right (which it is), but because her story benefited a house of men. Her recently *rediscovered* relics brought them prestige and pilgrims.

Walking around the remnants of the lavatorium (used for communal washing up before meals), I could see two goose sculptures, woven from branches, standing in the yard. Their presence recalled one of the most well-known miracles associated with Milburga, involving the ability to control birds and prevent geese from destroying local crops.

As I stood on that quiet lawn, I realized that the eighth-century Milburga hadn't needed the miracle to bolster her authority. But the story lent her twelfth-century reputation credibility, enhancing the sanctity of the male monastic house (Wenlock Priory) that then occupied the site of her earlier Wimnicas community.

But Milburga herself never needed that reputation.

She never needed relics to put her monastic community on the map.

She never needed to be known as a miracle worker for her authority to be accepted.

Milburga had the support of her influential family. Her mother had ensured that she, along with her sister, received the education needed for monastic vocation. She also had the support of an influential clergyman—Theodore, archbishop of Canterbury—who consecrated Milburga into the monastic life. She had the support of her local community, both within and outside the walls of Wimnicas. To them, Milburga was the leader of their community, both spiritually and politically.

I love what Vivien Bellamy, a local historian who authored *A History of Much Wenlock*, writes—that Milburga, "like other royal nuns at this period, . . . was, in effect, the local ruler on behalf of the Mercian royal house." Bellamy describes Milburga as a "mitred abbess" who "ruled a double house of nuns and monks" and also managed "extensive landholdings" over her "thirty-year tenure."[28]

I'm a medieval historian who studies women and religion. I know that Milburga lived during a time when ordained women were more common and female leadership was not anomalous; a time when abbesses exercised pastoral and political authority over women and men, clergy and nonclergy. "Abbesses were exceptional women with extraordinary power," argues Jennifer Edwards. Yet, "there were many of them across Europe with access to similar resources and opportunities."[29] Women like Milburga were both extraordinary yet representative of broader patterns.

I know this.

Yet, as I stood in that spot, Milburga's ministry experience felt strange to me.

What would it have been like to grow up with the expectation (not just the possibility) that she could be an ecclesiastical leader as important as a bishop? That her ordination would be celebrated and overseen by one of the most important religious leaders in her world? That she naturally would have provided pastoral care to men as well as women? That her sex was not a barrier to a vocation in ministry leadership?

As I tried to imagine this, I thought about how Kathy Hoppe was ordained as a Southern Baptist woman in the early 1980s. She was a pastor's wife but felt called to be a chaplain. Her husband, a local pastor in North Dakota, supported her calling, but the broader SBC community did not—just as it did not support Sarah Wood Lee's wish to be called a minister. In a barrage of letters, pastors throughout the region fought against Hoppe's ordination, calling for her husband to be defunded as a church planter because his wife had been ordained. I have since learned from Hoppe that the furor over her ordination cost her growing family (she was pregnant with her first child at the time) their income from the Home Mission Board, despite that the SBC entity had appointed her husband with full knowledge of his wife's ordination.[30]

I also thought about Bertha Smith, a Southern Baptist woman who preached regularly in the pulpits of SBC leaders like Charles Stanley and Adrian Rogers. Daniel Akin, president of Southeastern Baptist Theological Seminary, described Smith as a "soul-winning missionary and woman of prayer." He's right: Smith served as a missionary in the Shandong Province in China and later in Taiwan. Her prayers influenced men like Stanley and Rogers to run for the presidency of the SBC. Isn't it ironic that one of the men responsible for the SBC's conservative resurgence, which pushed women out of its pulpits, was influenced to take leadership because of a woman who preached in SBC pulpits?[31]

Bertha Smith led a church in China, preaching, teaching, and pastoring men and women just as she pastored, preached, and taught men and women throughout the Baptist world when she was stateside.

Yet when Akin preached a sermon in honor of her at Southeastern, he described her ministry as sacrifice, prayer, and "personal witness." He emphasized that she, as a woman on the mission field, often did "the work which men do not go to do." He quoted her description of the church she led in China: "Miss Smith Baptist Mission," which she wrote on a sign and placed on a bamboo fence. People began to come, she wrote, and "in addition to the Sunday services, we had Bible classes Tuesday and Thursday evenings."[32] She was an evangelist and a prayer warrior, but Akin doesn't describe her as a preacher. He also doesn't mention that she spent more than twenty years at the end of her life preaching from pulpits in Baptist churches and teaching Baptist pastors.

Isn't it strange to think about Milburga from the context of Kathy Hoppe and Bertha Smith?

Milburga was an ecclesiastical leader in both office and function. She was recognized for what she did—ordained by the archbishop of Canterbury and given the same title of her male peers, abbess to their abbot. She is even depicted wearing the headdress (miter) of a bishop and carrying a crozier.

Bertha Smith was allowed to function like a pastor, but she was not given that title. She was appointed as a missionary, but I doubt anyone would recognize her as ordained.

Kathy Hoppe was ordained, but it was contested. It was okay for her to serve in ministry; she was expected to do that as a pastor's wife. But it was not okay for her to be ordained, nor to serve in a different ministry calling from that of her husband.

The problem isn't what these women were doing.

The problem is what we *call* the work these women were doing.

Milburga's world called her an abbess.

Bertha Smith's world called her a missionary.

Kathy Hoppe's world called her a minister's wife.

I can't help thinking about Elizabeth Marvel's words about women's ordination in the modern global church. "Ordination has less to do with what an individual can or cannot do in the church," she writes, "and more to do with the power or prestige assigned to their position while doing it."[33] I think she is right. History suggests that ordination has less to do with the work of ministry and more to do with how that work is recognized.

What do you think?

Is biblical authority really the reason behind the different ways we categorize women who do pastoral work? Or is something else going on—something that history shows us is connected to redefinitions of power, hierarchy, and authority working to privilege male clergy over female clergy and dependent ministry roles for women over independent ones?

4

The Rise of the Pastor's Wife

Once, at our former church in Waco, my husband suggested I have lunch with a friend. She was a graduate student and struggling in her program.

"Did you tell her I almost quit?" I asked him.

"Oh, yeah," my husband said. "That is why I thought you should talk with her."

Graduate school is one of the hardest things I have ever done. Although I am grateful for the excellent program I went through and for my superb adviser, I have no desire to return to those years.

I expected the never-ending research projects and papers, the complete lack of sleep for days on end, and even the drama among faculty and students.

What I didn't expect was how much I would fail.

Just to name a few of my early failures: I failed a classical Latin exam. The paper I hoped would be the genesis of my thesis came back with the words "This wasn't worth my time" scrawled across the front. I taught the 1381 English Peasants' Revolt completely wrong during a teaching observation. I never overcame the fear that gripped me when one professor spoke to me in Latin whenever we crossed paths (which was way too often for my stress level!). And, although my current students may not believe this, I almost never spoke up in seminar my first year. I was terrified of how much I didn't know. It really seemed that everyone else had not only read and memorized Foucault but also understood him so well that they could integrate his work into every conversation we had.

One day, when I was supposed to be brushing up on my German, I started thinking of alternate career paths. I had always wanted to write. Indeed, I became a history major because I liked writing and wanted to tell better stories. My goal was an alternative career path—one that would provide an income, be fun, and fit my life as a pastor's wife. At the time I still believed that one of the advantages of becoming a professor was having flexible hours; this is true to an extent, but I have learned that being a professor at a research university often involves way more than forty hours a week. The point is, I decided to try my hand at historical fiction. I had read a few Christian novels in high school and decided that I could do that. My angle, from the medieval perspective, would be different. In my naivete about the publishing industry, I didn't think it would take long to get published.

I started drafting a plot. The story is set in the aftermath of John Wycliffe's death in the late fourteenth century and centers on two young people who meet through their shared attraction to Wycliffe's teachings. They fall in love, of course, and secretly marry—but they don't live happily ever after. The woman becomes a devoted Lollard (as followers of Wycliffe came to be known), takes up street preaching, and helps to produce the Wycliffe Bible translation. The man follows in the footsteps of his uncle (who we later find out is his father) and becomes a priest. In a dramatic scene, the man declares the couple's marriage invalid and offers his wife a bag of coins as compensation for deserting the marriage. The next day he is consecrated a bishop. When the couple meet again, it is because the woman is arrested for heresy and taken to stand before the bishop who, of course, is her former husband.

Not only does he see her standing condemned before him, he sees that she is several months pregnant.

I titled the book, tentatively, *The Bishop's Wife*. The plot and characters are fictional but the historical events on which it is based—namely, what happened to the wives of clergy after the increased emphasis on celibacy in the wake of the eleventh- and twelfth-century reforms (often called the Gregorian reforms after Pope Gregory VII)—are true. What I didn't know at the time, as it was still early days in my graduate program, was that my role as a pastor's wife had been cemented by the medieval campaign for clerical celibacy.

It may seem strange that the seeds of what grew into the Protestant role of pastor's wife may have been planted in the thirteenth century. To be sure, the pastor's wife role is a Protestant development—nothing like it really existed before—and the peculiar version of the pastor's wife role in modern evangelicalism is a mid-twentieth-century creation. Yet when medieval church leaders began requiring celibacy for priests, they ended up writing women out of sacramental power, turning once respectable "wives and moms" into whores, and creating the building blocks that would one day be repurposed into an argumentative edifice that insists women's leadership always belongs under male authority.

Here is how it happened.

The Power of Medieval Nuns

Sometimes I wish *The Sound of Music* weren't so popular. Don't get me wrong, I love the movie, but it has contributed to misconceptions about medieval nuns. Despite stories of women like Milburga, most people today think medieval nuns were hidden inside monasteries with little outside contact. The cinematic version, released in 1965, drew international attention to Nonnberg Abbey in Salzburg, Austria. Founded in the eighth century, Nonnberg is still an active Benedictine house for women. If you are ever in Salzburg, you can attend services at the abbey church and still hear the nuns sing Gregorian chorales at 6:45 a.m. and again in the evening.[1]

In *The Sound of Music*, the nuns sang a different song. Remember "How Do You Solve a Problem Like Maria?" The problem with Maria (played by Julie Andrews) was that she didn't obey the monastery rules. Instead of staying within the walls, she was outside singing "The Hills Are Alive"; instead of praying quietly, she was waltzing and whistling in the stone corridors; instead of gentle submission, she was talking back to her female superiors and, later, her male employer. The problem with Maria is that she didn't act like the novice she was supposed to be.

Yet the reality is that earlier in history women monastics were free to leave the confines of the abbey. Claustration—the practice of nuns staying enclosed behind monastery walls—wasn't formally introduced until the thirteenth century. In 1298 Pope Boniface VIII delivered the decree *Periculoso* (papal decrees are named for the first word of the Latin decree; in this case, *Periculoso*, which means dangerous). It prohibited nuns from leaving the walls of the monastery for any reason; it also forbade people from entering the monastery. Historian Elizabeth Makowski notes that "the novel papal policy when enforced entailed radical changes in the discipline of female religious houses."[2]

Did you catch Makowski's qualification: "when enforced"?

Despite the gravity of the decree, evidence suggests that *Periculoso* was surprisingly ineffective. We know from the Nonnberg records, for example, that the nuns did not stay behind their walls, nor did the walls keep townspeople and visitors out. *Periculoso* was so difficult to enforce that in 1563 the Council of Trent reiterated it to reinforce it as the standard for female monastics. Still, we know from abbey records that enclosure wasn't strictly enforced at Nonnberg even in the seventeenth century.

Nine hundred years before the novice played by Julie Andrews sang in the hills outside Salzburg, another Benedictine nun left her cloister. Instead of just singing, though, Hildegard of Bingen went on a preaching tour through Europe. The tour was sanctioned by the pope himself. Janina Ramirez, author of *Femina: A New History of the Middle Ages, through the Women Written Out of It*, describes Hildegard as a "twelfth-century celebrity" whose intellectual and creative output can be compared only to that of "the polymath Leonardo da Vinci" more than three centuries later. Ramirez writes that Hildegard "broke the mold: she was part of a pan-European intellectual elite that included men and women, and was supported by those around her to rise to fame in a way that many men of her time could only have dreamt of."[3]

Many today do not consider Hildegard an exemplar of the medieval woman—they think she was an exception, not the rule. Those who reject the idea that women had pastoral authority in church history find her problematic and thus minimize her religious clout. Those who accept the validity of Hildegard's extraordinary life often categorize her as, well, extraordinary. Most women were not like her; therefore, she isn't a model for most women. Right?

Wrong.

First, describing women as extraordinary is often a subtle way of reinforcing patriarchy. If Deborah becoming a judge in the Hebrew Bible is understood as an exception due to extraordinary circumstances rather than something normative, then her appearance in that role doesn't threaten claims that the Bible supports male-only pastoral leadership. If Hildegard, a woman who preached to male clergy, including the highest ecclesiastical officials in her world, is just an exception, then her status as a preaching woman who exercised pastoral authority over men supposedly doesn't threaten claims that Christian history "speaks with one voice" on male-only pastoral leadership. Do you see how it works? Categorizing women who function as pastors as exceptional maintains the fiction that women are not pastors.

Second, Hildegard lived in a world ruled largely by men, but some women in some circumstances ruled too. Hildegard's coreligionists knew 1 Timothy 2, but unlike many modern Christians today, they did not interpret it as an impenetrable barrier to female leadership. Women (especially women from powerful families) who rejected marriage, dedicating their lives to the service of God in monastic communities, could achieve substantial authority both religious and political. "Elite women's exercise of power was commonplace in the Middle Ages," Jennifer Edwards writes.[4] Powerful men such as kings and popes supported the authority of women in religious leadership, and powerful women, like Hildegard of Bingen and Milburga of Wimnicas, flourished. John Van Engen describes the power of these women as surpassing that of queens. They weren't confined to their cloisters, nor were they barred from exercising spiritual authority over men. They were also, through their installation into clerical offices that had pastoral responsibility, ordained.[5]

Hildegard, in other words, may have been an extraordinary woman, but in her medieval context she wasn't exceptional. Women like her—who had dedicated their lives to the church and forsaken marriage and family—often became leaders. Put another way, being a female abbess who exercised pastoral authority independent of male clergy wasn't what made Hildegard extraordinary. There may have been more men than women in religious authority, but the women who wielded religious authority were not unusual.

Let's go back to *The Sound of Music*.

From the medieval perspective of women like Hildegard, the problem with Maria was of a different sort altogether. If you don't know the story of the movie, I apologize for the spoilers. Maria does not complete her monastic vows. She chooses instead to marry her employer and become stepmother to his seven children. From our modern perspective (especially the modern Protestant perspective), this is the climax of the movie. Love triumphs, and the possibility of a happy ending exists for everyone (except for the whole fleeing-from-Nazis thing).

From the medieval perspective, though, Maria chose the lesser part. She traded the bridegroom Christ for a mortal man; virginity for the marriage bed; being a spiritual mother for physical motherhood; and a life of ministry for a life of domestic toil. The medieval problem with Maria was that she got married.[6]

Both before and after Hildegard, a woman's path to religious authority was smoother when she forsook marriage (although virginity was not necessary if the woman was a widow or in a chaste clerical marriage). Not until after Hildegard did celibacy become required for men being ordained to the priesthood. Women like Hildegard continued to flourish, but by 1215 there had been a fundamental shift about who could be ordained as well as what ordination meant. Remember what I said in the previous chapter? Instead of ordination pertaining to a specific role, by this era, it imbued a sacred status.[7] A new clerical hierarchy would emerge out of this redefinition of ordination that would rank the male priest higher than any female office. Despite the religious authority of women like Hildegard, women's ministerial roles would henceforth be considered as less authoritative than the roles of men.

"The Manly Priest"[8]

To sum up about two hundred years of reforms: the redefinition of ordination centered the clerical hierarchy on the office of priest, tied it to the power necessary to transform the bread and wine at the altar into the body and blood of Christ, and gendered the identity of priests as masculine. By the tenth century, references within ordination ceremonies and liturgy consistently linked ordination with the priestly power to transform bread and wine into the body and blood. For example, one ceremony prayed that "through the offering of your people may they [the priests] transform the bread and wine into the body and blood of your Son by the undefiled blessing." The ceremony continued with the bishop consecrating the priest with holy oil and offering him the plate and chalice with the charge, "Receive the power to offer the sacrifice to God and to celebrate the Mass for the living and for the dead, in the name of the Lord."[9] Then, in 1215 the Fourth Lateran Council finalized the connection between the office of priest and the sacramental power to perform Eucharist, declaring, "Nobody can effect the sacrament except a priest who has been properly ordained according to the Church's keys, which Jesus Christ himself gave to the apostles and their successors."[10] With this one sentence, the Fourth Lateran Council effectively secured the office of priest as a sacred position.[11] A baptism could still be performed by anyone who performed it properly (include midwives baptizing babies at birth); but the words of consecration for Eucharist "worked" only if they were uttered by the sacred earthly proxy who stood in the gap between his parishioners and God.

This "explosive shift" to a "presbytero-centric hermeneutic" had far-reaching consequences.[12] To begin with, clerical orders leading to the priesthood and those advancing after priestly ordination were deemed the most important. "As the meaning of ordained ministry began to revolve around the Eucharistic celebration the understanding develops that one's ministry is 'ranked' according to one's liturgical role," explains William Ditewig. "So, by the twelfth century, the priest will be at the top because he is the one empowered to offer the sacrifice. . . . Other ministers, whose duties did not take them to the altar itself were simply not to be understood as 'ordained' in any sacramental sense."[13] To put it in Baptist terms, the ordained pastor was now the minister with the most spiritual authority. By the central Middle Ages, the office of priest was also gendered masculine.

With great sacramental power came great sacrifice. Up to this point, most clergy who did not take monastic vows married. Indeed, it could be hard to distinguish priests from their neighbors, as they lived, dressed, and behaved in similar ways—including training sons to follow in their fathers' career footsteps. The eleventh- and twelfth-century reformers (who were all monastics) rejected the all-too-common practice of "hereditary transmission of benefices" and passed laws against the ordination and inheritance of clerical sons, eventually declaring clerical offspring bastards.[14] To avoid legitimate heirs—who would then inherit church leadership and property—priests and those with priestly aspirations were required to give up their wives.[15]

It may not seem like much of a problem for the sons of clergy to assume the clerical position of their fathers. But think about it. Have you ever witnessed family dynasties taking over churches and other religious institutions? What about Jerry Falwell? At age twenty-two, he founded Thomas Road Baptist Church in Lynchburg, Virginia, and the national radio show, *Old-Time Gospel Hour*, that made him a celebrity. Ten years later he founded Lynchburg Christian Academy, followed a few years later by Liberty University. As his biography on the Liberty University website correctly states, he is best known for his political activism on behalf of evangelicalism.[16] When he died in 2007, his son Jonathan became lead pastor of Thomas Road, and his other son, Jerry, became president of Liberty. Jerry Falwell Jr. followed in his father's footsteps as a leading voice in evangelical politics—including supporting the rise of Donald Trump. He has become infamous, though, for his resignation from Liberty over a multimillion-dollar sex and extortion scandal, as well as several years of underreporting campus crime and alleged silencing of rape victims under his leadership at the university.[17]

Or what about Jack Hyles? Hyles was even younger than Jerry Falwell Sr. when he began preaching and became an influential Independent Baptist minister. He is best known for leading First Baptist Church of Hammond, Indiana, which became famous for hosting the largest Sunday school in the US. Hyles also founded the unaccredited Bible college Hyles-Anderson College and, like Falwell, created a family business out of his ministry. Hyles's son-in-law followed him as senior pastor of FBC Hammond, and his son, David, also became a pastor.[18] All three have since been involved in scandal, from alleged adultery to rape to financial mismanagement.[19]

Recognizing that sons can be ill-suited to religious vocation, I understand the desire of the medieval reformers to eliminate family inheritance patterns. But the concerns of the reformers were bigger than problem children—which is why their solution was so drastic. Hereditary inheritance of clerical positions also reduced the authority of the papacy (as inheritance rather than official appointment became the pattern for clerical succession) and alienated revenue from church property (as the land and income associated with clerical appointments became part of family inheritance). By allowing clergy to name successors and treat clerical appointments as family businesses, the medieval church lost both power and money, so legitimate heirs had to go.

The Problem of Female Bodies

Another factor concerning the reformers was sexual purity centered on long-standing disdain for the female body. They cited Old Testament teachings enjoining priests to "touch no unclean thing" and to practice ritual abstinence. Add to that beliefs influenced by Augustine of Hippo that "an active sexuality and ministry were conflicting values" and the growth of sacramental theology that centered the priestly role in Eucharist celebration. Thus, clerical celibacy developed in tandem with fears that sexually active priests wouldn't be able to transform the elements into the real body and blood of Jesus.[20]

I argue in *The Making of Biblical Womanhood* that the reform movement of the central Middle Ages strengthened the power of the church at the cost of women. As I wrote, "The reforms bolstering clerical status and ecclesiastical authority—and emphasizing the impurity of female bodies—distanced women from leadership in the medieval church."[21] Lynneth Miller Renberg states the problem even better: "If women's bodies were inherently sacrilegious, women could not ever attain the same access to holy matter, spaces, and perhaps even to a holy God as their male counterparts."[22] Female sexuality polluted the sacred. Not only did this exclude female bodies from performing sacraments, it also tainted married male bodies charged with performing sacraments. Janelle Werner catalogs the heightened concerns about female sexuality in the aftermath of the Gregorian reforms, including a thirteenth-century statute that "reminded priests that the same hands that touched 'the private parts of harlots' would also touch the body of Christ."[23] Some argued that clerics who remained sexually active should be banned from serving at the altar. The only solution for safeguarding sacramental power, argued reformers, was forsaking women for a celibate life.

With great sacramental power also came a financial perk that established medieval priests as householders, despite their single status.[24] The medieval papacy adapted a system that had been around since at least the ninth century to provide financially for new priests.[25] Ordained priests were to receive appointment to a benefice (also known as a living), which provided an endowed income in exchange for their fulfillment of religious duties.[26] "In a society in which many men faced limited economic prospects outside the Church," writes Hugh Thomas, "the prospect of an ecclesiastical income was undoubtedly an important practical incentive for many to enter the clergy."[27] Not all priests flourished financially, but enough did for accusations to swirl that some clerics became priests for economic gain.

Let's put the pieces together.

In her 2015 book, *The Manly Priest*, Jennifer Thibodeaux argues that the medieval clergy abstinence campaign created a new masculine identity. "The discourse promoted from the eleventh to the thirteenth centuries emphasized a different form of manliness, one that not only defined a code of sexual purity for the secular clergy but one that would also eventually encompass their bodily appearance and comportment"—elevating and separating the priesthood from the laity.[28] Masculinity continued to be defined by sexual conquest of the female body, but it was now also defined by conquest of sexual desire within the male body. The path to sacramental power for medieval men was rooted in a masculine identity that pitted male holiness against female sexuality.[29]

The Geese of Cross Bones Graveyard

The power offered by ordination came with the price tag of celibacy. Reality suggests that far too many priests didn't pay it. Thibodeaux reminds us that medieval masculine identity was built on struggle. The new masculine identity that emerged from the reforms wasn't any different, except the type of struggle changed; instead of struggling to dominate, it was struggling to resist. Priests could no longer openly marry or recognize their offspring as legitimate. But many couldn't stay away from women. Some continued about their business as married men within the community. Their wives were recategorized as concubines, but other than that, little changed. Some just took concubines in lieu of wives, even bringing them into their households under the guise of housekeepers. Some kept their households female-free and "visited" women in the village (including adulterous relationships), while others frequented brothels.

Would you believe me if I told you that some clergy participated in the business of brothels too?

Next time you are in London, take a walk across London Bridge. Not Tower Bridge—London Bridge. It isn't impressive, architecturally speaking. The structure isn't much older than I am, either, as it was built in 1973. The previous nineteenth-century London Bridge has the claim to fame as the largest antique ever sold, and the site of London Bridge marks one of the oldest parts of the city.

I usually take my students to London Bridge at least once when I am teaching in the city. We take the tube to Monument station and make our way to the church of St. Magnus the Martyr. On one particular tour, my students and I stay outside the church. We walk through the arch where the medieval London Bridge once stood and stop to touch an ancient pier remaining from the Roman bridge. We then walk up a staircase to the bridge. It takes us about fifteen minutes to get across (everyone stops for pictures), but once we reach the south side of the river, we walk down under the bridge to one of the most popular outdoor food markets in London, Borough Market. From the towers of cheese to the huge pans of simmering paella to the ever-present fish and chips, Borough Market never fails to dazzle.

About five hundred yards from the market, on the other side of a railway tunnel, lies our destination: a fenced community garden. I stop in front of the iron gates covered in ribbons, silk flowers, notes, and other memorabilia and point my students to a small circular sign: "Cross Bones Graveyard." A goose is engraved on the left with this description below: "In medieval times this was an unconsecrated graveyard for prostitutes or 'Winchester Geese.' By the eighteenth century it had become a paupers' burial ground, which closed in 1853. Here, local people have created a memorial shrine." At the bottom of the inscription are the words, "The Outcast Dead R.I.P." Today the site has attracted a mystical following that uses incense, symbols from various religions, and even magic.

Cross Bones Graveyard is an unmarked cemetery. John Stow wrote in his 1598 *Survey of London*, "I have heard of ancient men, of good credit, report that these single women were forbidden the rites of the church, so long as they continued that sinful life, and were excluded from Christian burial, if they were not reconciled before their death. And therefore, there was a plot of ground called the Single Woman's churchyard, appointed for them far from the parish church."[30] The Museum of London Archaeology has exhumed from the site 148 skeletons that they have identified as nineteenth-century paupers; some show possible evidence of syphilis, and female remains predominate.[31] Given that only 1 percent of the bodies buried have been excavated (and those mostly from the last fifty years that the cemetery was in use), it is possible that Cross Bones Graveyard marks an older burial site for women, perhaps the one mentioned by Stow.[32] It is more probable that Cross Bones Graveyard marks a nineteenth-century cemetery for paupers.[33]

Regardless, the commemoration of Cross Bones Graveyard has resurrected awareness about an ironic medieval reality. Underneath the ribbons, incantations, and constructed memory lies the historical reality of a medieval bishop who profited from the sex trade. Thirty-nine ordinances (which claim to date from the twelfth century) describe a legalized area for brothels licensed by the bishop of Winchester (hence the name Winchester Geese, as sex workers were later called) and proliferating in the Bankside area of Southwark—just outside the medieval city of London.[34] Indeed, the brothels (called "stews") were such a defining feature of Bankside that the area was sometimes called "Stewside." The landowner who regulated the sex trade was the bishop of Winchester. Eighteen licensed brothels operated under his jurisdiction and with his cooperation. By the fifteenth century, he directly owned two and profited indirectly from the others. Ruth Mazo Karras notes, "The fact that a churchman owned the most notorious brothels of the late Middle Ages is a sign not of the corruption of the medieval church but rather of the separation of the bishop's function as secular landlord from his religious persona."[35] You can still see the medieval remains of his luxurious London home right around the corner from the old Clink prison.

Regardless of legal distinctions between the bishop as religious authority and as secular lord, the fact remains that brothels proliferated in Southwark for at least three hundred years on land owned by the bishop of Winchester. For part of that time (if not the whole), the bishop licensed and profited from sex work literally in his backyard.

Once my students realize the implications of these facts, they are shocked. As they should be. During the very period when the medieval church was enforcing clerical celibacy and arguing that only men were worthy to perform the miracle of Christ's body, its leaders were also licensing a legal area of prostitution. Clergy profited from it and frequented it as clients. As for the women, they were deemed unworthy of Christian burial.

Let me put the story of the Winchester Geese into historical perspective.

As we've discussed, in the eleventh and twelfth centuries the medieval church began to redefine ordination as bestowing sacramental power. It began to differentiate clergy from secular men by requiring celibacy and providing a financial incentive for the ordained. A new masculine identity emerged, one built on resisting female sexuality. At the same time, the medieval church began to emphasize that only someone with a male body, which represented Christ, was worthy to perform the Eucharist. Clergy attempting to enforce clerical celibacy used terms like *whores*, *impure*, and *loose* to describe priests' sexual partners.

Yet, at the same time, the medieval church considered sex work a necessary evil. It was "like a sewer in a palace. Take away the sewer and you will fill the palace with pollution." Thomas Aquinas was thought (by medieval people) to have written these words in the thirteenth century. So when a bishop outside of London backdated an ordinance from the twelfth century to claim his fifteenth-century right to profit from the sexual exploitation of female bodies, no one balked.[36]

Who paid the price of the clerical celibacy campaign?

You tell me.

"From Priest's Whore to Pastor's Wife"[37]

By redefining wives as concubines and heightening fears about female sexuality, the reformers met many of their goals. The church gained control over the appointment of clergy and broke up family inheritance patterns. The church succeeded in distancing clergy from laity as only priests were imbued with sacramental power and priests could not formally marry.

But the church never really won the struggle for clerical celibacy, especially among lower clergy. Some priests, many of whom were good men who loved their wives and families, continued about their daily business as if they were legitimately married. Other priests maintained the fiction of celibacy. In some areas, the percentage of priests keeping concubines was as high as 40 percent.[38]

Do you see the problem? If clerical celibacy is required for sacramental authority, then the failure of priests to maintain celibacy jeopardized the sacraments. The only option was stricter enforcement of clerical celibacy, including the criminalization of concubinage. Unless, of course, clerical celibacy wasn't the solution. What if, in their zeal to distance the church from secular control, the eleventh- and twelfth-century reformers had allowed their own monastic lifestyle to influence their push to impose celibacy on nonmonastic priests? What if the solution to better priests wasn't celibacy at all, but rather allowing marriage? Admittedly, Protestant reformers were not the first to make this argument—there had always been Catholic proponents of clerical marriage. But it really isn't until Martin Luther that clerical marriage became a reality again in the West.

As Marjorie Plummer argues in her groundbreaking book *From Priest's Whore to Pastor's Wife*, "The rejection of the traditional practice of clerical celibacy formed one of the first and most definitive moves from an attempt to reform the church to one of the developments of a new church. . . . Ultimately the evangelical preachers rejected one of the most visible signs of clerical difference."[39] Seeing that the clerical celibacy campaign was ineffective, evangelical reformers advocated a different model. *Marriage* would become "a litmus test for confessional identity."[40] Instead of being a concubine, the sexual partner of a Protestant priest would now become the pastor's wife.

Except there were challenges.

The medieval celibacy campaign had been effective in some ways. It failed miserably in making priests celibate, but it succeeded admirably in convincing people that women in relationships with priests were whores. As the priest transitioned to an evangelical pastor, he lost his sacramental power and sacred identity. But as a husband and father he kept his masculine authority. His concubine (or ex-nun, as the case may be) did not fare as well. As the priest's concubine transitioned to the pastor's wife, she did not shed the negative ideas associated with a medieval priest's sexual partner. Instead of the "priest's whore," many still called her the "pastor's whore."[41] Her fight to be accepted as a wife would be an uphill, and sometimes dangerous, struggle. These women had more to lose marrying pastors than remaining concubines—as those who were imprisoned and executed soon learned.

But the pastor's wife made some gains too. She would gain the chance to "assume a significant spiritual function by assisting her husband in reforming the congregation and by serving as a female moral model to the community." She would gain the chance to confirm her husband's evangelical credentials (as "marriage was a necessary sign of evangelical belief for clergy") and fulfill her "clear Christian duty of service to Christ." And she would gain spiritual worth by becoming a wife and mother.[42]

It was at this moment, in the turmoil and fear and hope of early sixteenth-century Germany, that the pastor's wife was born. Today, Protestants continue to stress the importance of the pastor's wife for ordering the household and supporting her husband's ministry. As Plummer writes, "The priest's household, once exceptional in the community, would now look the same as those of the laity, but with the expectation of presenting the ideal model of Lutheran social piety."[43] Modern Protestantism owes much to these brave women who chose to become heretics and whores in the eyes of their communities as they simultaneously became grassroots symbols of hope for the spread of evangelicalism. Plummer shows that the first pastors' wives chose their role; it wasn't imposed on them by leaders. Unlike the bishop's wife in my never-written historical novel, the pastor's wife eventually gained the right to become a model of faith for her community and share a bed with the local clergyman.

I never wrote that book about the bishop's wife because I didn't quit my program. The next year was a turning point for me. Indeed, in my end-of-year assessment, my adviser wrote, "Beth blossomed this year." I figured out graduate school, and now, more than twenty years later, I'm a full professor at a research university.

But sometimes I wish I had written the book, because it is a story that needs to be told. It is a story about how the church in Western Europe created a new type of masculinity that elevated the priesthood by distancing women from both the clerical bed and the pastoral office. It is a story about how the pastoral role came to be redefined as inherently masculine. It is a story about families disrupted and women harmed in exchange for economic security and sacramental power.

It is also a story about the birth of a new role for women. It is strange to consider how the new role of pastor's wife emerged from the medieval campaign for clerical celibacy. It is strange to consider the Winchester Geese as part of the same storyline as Katharina von Bora—the ex-nun who married the ex-monk Martin Luther. I want you to consider, though, what these women do have in common—especially in contrast to the powerful medieval abbesses like Hildegard of Bingen. I want you to consider how the pastor's wife role, even while becoming a respectable position for women in the church, could never be more than a mediated role. Beneath the license of a bishop and the trappings of a marriage ceremony, both the priest's whore and the pastor's wife are defined by their dependent relationship to a man.

5

Two for the Price of One

During the five years my husband was a student at Southeastern Baptist Theological Seminary, we never lived on campus. Both of his jobs (the church where he worked as youth pastor for one hundred dollars a week and the Chili's where he waited tables for three dollars an hour plus tips) were about forty-five miles away from our home in Durham, while my university was about thirty minutes in the opposite direction. Once we got a second car, we compromised by living near the church. It was close to work for my husband and roughly equidistance from both of our programs, but it wasn't conducive to hosting seminary friends at our house.

I only did it once.

She was about my age and had two small children. Her husband worked as a music minister; he played piano beautifully and sang with a rich tenor voice. Unlike us, they lived in the graduate student housing on campus. They had one car, and he was gone most days. Like so many other wives of male seminary students, she did not work outside the home, which meant she was home most days in their tiny apartment with two kids under two. She was friendly, funny, and determined to support her husband as best she could in his ministry.

I invited her to our house one day. Her husband agreed to drop her off on his way to work and pick her up on his way back for an afternoon class at the seminary. She was all smiles as she carried the baby in through my apartment door, her toddler barreling in ahead of her.

The smiles stopped when the door closed behind her. I didn't notice at first, as I was watching the toddler make his way around the room. When she didn't respond to a comment I made, I looked up.

She was sobbing.

Bewildered, I took the baby from her arms. It was several minutes before I understood what the problem was.

I don't remember whether she was taking the seminary-offered course for pastors' wives taught by Dorothy Patterson, or whether she had attended any of the events on campus for seminary wives, or whether it was just the broader environment for seminary wives. Regardless, she had internalized the pressure placed on her to help her husband succeed—especially in matters of the home. A good pastor's wife was always ready to host; her home welcomed guests. A good pastor's wife kept her house clean and safe for her children, providing a nurturing environment. A good pastor's wife made sure her home was comfortable and orderly, full of good food, love, and even a "company box" that included ingredients ready to serve a quick meal for unexpected guests.

The pastor's wife, like her home, was always ready to serve.

The husband of this young pastor's wife attended Southeastern during the time that I knew her, the seminary where Dorothy Patterson reigned as "First Lady" between 1992 and 2003. It also overlapped with the time that Dorothy's husband, Paige Patterson, served as president of the Southern Baptist Convention (1998–2000). In her book *Handbook for Ministers' Wives*, Dorothy advises that the pastor's home "should welcome the family and others whom God may send through its doors. If a minister never knows whether he has clean clothes to wear or if he must wash his plate before dinner, he is defeated before he begins. Someone laughingly said that 'a sink full of dirty dishes at the parsonage may not be anyone's business, but the report will soon be everyone's gossip!'"[1] A few paragraphs later, Patterson outlines the "company box" to have on hand to make a "quick and easy meal or refreshment break appropriate for guests."

On the surface, this isn't bad advice. My pantry usually has ingredients for chocolate chip cookies, my famous brownies (just ask the undergraduate students I have lived with in the LEAD living and learning community for six years), and a strawberry-layered chocolate mousse I make on short notice for our small group. The problem is when the advice becomes a universal demand. Just listen to Patterson's words:

- "The home of the minister is in a peculiar way a public house."
- "The pastor's home does not need to be a showplace, but it should be furnished with taste and creativity."
- "The church should be able to point with pride to the parsonage regardless of its size, design, or location."
- "The pastor's wife, and every member of the family, should form a habit of keeping at least the entry and living room presentable and ready."
- "Especially should you learn to brew a good cup of coffee and, if I'm [Dorothy Patterson] coming, a wonderful cup of tea."[2]

Again, can you hear the expectation in those words—all the *shoulds*?

This young pastor's wife almost certainly did.

Whether or not she had read Patterson's book, I know she was struggling with shame because her home didn't meet these expectations. They didn't have extra money to spend on nice furniture and home decor, and she couldn't keep up with all the cooking and cleaning while caring for two small children, one of whom was still breastfeeding. Plus, I think her husband was more prone to messiness than neatness. The neatness of my home (due primarily to my husband, although the young pastor's wife didn't know that) and the niceness of my furniture (due to my grandmother, who was an antique dealer) had overwhelmed her.

She felt like a failure because her house was messy.

She felt so much like a failure that she burst into tears after walking for the first time into the home of another pastor's wife whom she barely knew.

I know that some of you reading this—those of you who have not lived the culture of an evangelical pastor's wife, especially in its Southern Baptist variety—may not understand her reaction.

But for the women who have, I expect you get it.

The pastor's wife classes at both Southeastern and Southwestern seminaries dedicated a whole lecture on how to pack your husband's suitcase properly. Indeed, Patterson wrote in her handbook that she had "learned to fold my husband's shirts professionally by sending one shirt to the laundry professionals and then carefully unfolding it and making notes on how it was folded. My demonstration on how to fold shirts and suits and how to pack a suitcase is a favorite in my class for ministers' wives."[3] Women in those classes were also told to practice getting in and out of a car as modestly as possible. They were told that the condition of their homes reflected the condition of their spiritual lives. That how they looked and how their kids acted reflected on their husband. That offering "Christian hospitality" is a "command from the Lord" that the pastor's wife is expected to extend not only to her family but to the whole church.[4]

I let the young pastor's wife cry for a while. After she drank some water and dried her eyes, I offered to come over and help organize her house, if she wanted. She finally smiled again.

While I cannot speak for all ministry wives' experiences, I can say that the two-for-one pressure this young woman felt is the pressure I felt too. After analyzing 150 books written for and by pastors' wives, I know we were not alone.

I can also say that, as a historian, I think I know where these expectations came from.

And they aren't from the Bible.

A "Universal Spare Part"

Let's talk about modern expectations for the pastor's wife role. The two-for-one model of pastoral ministry assumes that the labor and support of the wife is included in her husband's job. The ministry she does is expected to enhance and support the ministry of her husband. Like any other conservative Christian wife, she is expected to be a godly homemaker. But as a pastor's wife, the state of her home and ability to offer hospitality reflect on her husband's job performance.

This means that women like me, the wives of ministry students at Southern Baptist Convention seminaries, were taught that our marriage to a minister meant we were called to ministry. We were taught that the success of our husband's ministry depended, in part, on our success as ministry wives. We were taught to be content with our supportive role, one that's fulfilled without pay or a formal ministry title. We were to be ready for the wide-ranging duties expected of us that varied according to the current need of our husbands or churches—as Patterson puts it, each is to be a "universal spare part" able to "reverse gears and shift directions according to need."[5] We were taught that our ministry was to center our lives, from home to church, on our husbands:

> Make your husband a priority in your life. . . . Study your husband; learn all you can about his ministry; share at least some of his interests and pleasures. Be patient when you have to adapt the family schedule to the conditions of his ministry. When he has to work irregular hours, accept his inconvenient absence without resentment or recrimination. If he has to do his sermon preparation at

home, create an environment where that is possible. If you have a career or lifestyle that hinders his ministry, be willing to adapt or even give up your own pursuits to be his helper. Keep a happy countenance and joyful spirit.[6]

Patterson discouraged pastors' wives from working outside of the home unless necessary for finances. She discouraged pastors' wives from receiving compensation as paid church staff, as that would reduce flexibility. There is a difference between volunteering to fold bulletins for one afternoon and being required to work from 1 to 5 p.m. most days. The flexible pastor's wife should be available to host last-minute dinner parties, attend counseling sessions, and run errands for her husband.

Patterson isn't an outlier, either.

One of the final pastor's wife books I read while working on this book was written in 2010 by a blogger known as The Pastor's Wife. Her name is Lisa McKay, and her book *You Can Still Wear Cute Shoes: And Other Great Advice from an Unlikely Preacher's Wife* is entertaining and heartfelt. Her bouncy prose conveys her passion for ministry and dedication to supporting her husband's ministry. She also seems to have written this book at least in part as a reaction to Dorothy Patterson's *Handbook for Ministers' Wives*. Unlike other books, McKay says in a comment that seems directed at Patterson, this one is not going to tell pastors' wives how to make tea.

Her introduction gets straight to what she thinks of the two-for-one model. She tells a story of how a "well-meaning gentleman" gave her advice when her husband first entered ministry. "The best thing you can do for Luke is learn how to play the piano. He'll have a much easier time being called as a pastor of a church. Congregations love it when the pastor's wife can contribute. It's like they are getting two for one!"[7] McKay writes that after fifteen years of ministry experience, she has strong feelings about the "buy-one-get-one-free concept." She believes her job as pastor's wife is to support her husband's ministry, but she differentiates this from being at a congregation's beck and call. "It has taken years," she confesses, "but I thank God for helping me recognize that my most important role is as a helpmate to Luke and a loving mother to our children. In the midst of molding me into a godlier wife and mom, [God] has also placed the calling of minister's wife on my life, and thankfully nowhere in Scripture does it say I have to play the piano, wear polyester, or host the perfect party."[8] For McKay, her calling is to her husband, not the congregation, and this, in her mind, mitigates the two-for-one idea. The only script for a pastor's wife is obedience in exercising her calling in whatever way God has gifted.

I love McKay's optimism and admire her insistence on a more diverse model for the calling of pastors' wives. I also understand why McKay has the expectations she does for the pastor's wife role. Her husband's born-again experience saved their marriage when they were on the brink of divorce. A conservative Bible college admitted him despite his lack of a high school diploma, and he became a Southern Baptist pastor. I imagine that McKay found guides for her role mostly within this conservative evangelical community. She is teaching what she was taught.

Yet I am skeptical that diversity in how pastors' wives use their gifts resists the two-for-one model. I'm not sure that specific expectations to play the piano are different from more vague expectations to be visibly involved in church ministry. The most prominent idea throughout most of the books we analyzed in researching this book is consistent: the pastor's wife should help further the ministry of her husband through her presence, support, and activity in the church as well as her domestic management and hospitality within the home. Activity in the church could be playing the piano during church services, teaching, serving in nursery, or even just showing up at church events (preferably most of them). As one woman commented on McKay's blog, "As a layperson, I think it is obvious when a wife doesn't share her husband's passion for ministry. I don't believe a pastor's wife has to be everyone's friend or attend every church event. But I do think you can tell by her general demeanor if she is ministry-minded. And, rightly or wrongly, the vibe I get from her reflects on her husband."[9]

Isn't this still two-for-one?

Even Shevalle Kimber—who is ordained herself as well as the First Lady of First Calvary Baptist Church in New Haven, Connecticut, where she seems to carry more ministerial authority than her white counterparts—defines the pastor's wife role as "to support her husband and take care of her family solely. Additionally, she would publicly affirm her husband's decisions, helping him to navigate unpopular demands from church leadership, such as the deacons, trustees, and members, while singing in the choir, playing the piano, or occasionally teaching a Sunday School lesson."[10]

I've been a professor since 2008, and I can tell you no one cares whether my husband shares my passion for medieval history. How my colleagues perceive him doesn't come up in my performance reviews. When I am behind on preparing exams or writing my syllabus, I am not expected to ask my husband to help. I certainly don't ask him to fill in for my class when I can't attend.

Yet during the first two decades of my life as a pastor's wife, it was common for me to provide this type of assistance for my husband. I believed it was expected of me, and I felt pressure to do it. Once, after staying up past midnight the day before a youth trip helping assemble notebooks for forty or so participants, I told my husband I thought the administrative assistants should be doing this instead. He agreed but told me that they were only part-time and had other duties. They had helped print the material, and, well, we could do the rest. Don't get me wrong—I supported my husband's ministry and was active in teaching and leading alongside him. But, from my experience, labeling the contributions of a pastor's wife as "ministry" or "service" doesn't erase the reality that a pastor's job often includes the unpaid labor of his wife. I didn't mind helping my husband; what I minded was feeling like my help was an expectation for his job.

This is exactly the expectation that McKay underscores. She writes that a pastor cannot effectively do his job without his wife's visible and active help. She writes that a church "will not easily forgive . . . when you take a seat in the back and refuse to play a part—able or not. . . . The support the congregation perceives your husband receiving from you and your willingness to care for them even if you aren't able to do all that you'd like is a bridge between their hearts and your man's. . . . Your participation in his call is not only nice but necessary for him to effectively live out what God will do through him, whether you realize it now or not."[11]

Did you catch what she said? The pastor's wife's "participation in his call is not only nice but necessary for him to effectively live out what God will do through him." The pastor's wife shares the call of her husband. Her participation, her labor, is part of the deal. Certainly, it is okay for a pastor's wife to have her own ministry. But according to the manuals for pastors' wives that we surveyed, this ministry should meet two conditions: (1) it shouldn't interfere with "your first priority as his wife to affirm him in this role"; and (2) it should "broaden the scope of what he is able to do alongside you."[12] The pastor's wife is free to craft her role according to her own gifts and serve as she feels called—*if* her work, from home to church, enhances her husband's ministry.

Wife *and* Mom

My son was born on our seventh wedding anniversary.

My daughter was born the week of February 14, about five years later.

We find it amusing that our kids' birthdays overlap the two traditionally most romantic days for couples—a wedding anniversary and Valentine's Day. Instead of worrying about dates and gifts for each other, my husband and I have most often spent the first week of August and the middle of February hosting parties for our kids. I spent one anniversary icing an Eye of Sauron cake for my son while my husband led a *Lord of the Rings* version of capture the flag for twenty nine-year-old boys. We spent one Valentine's Day taking fifteen ten-year-old girls to a local performance of *Pinkalicious*.

It took more than thirteen years of marriage for us to become a family of four.

Since both my husband and I spent the first four years of our marriage in graduate school, this isn't that surprising, as many people earning advanced degrees delay having children. But let me assure you that family planning wasn't the only reason for the age gap between our kids.

My most difficult moment came when my son was around preschool age. It was clear by then that becoming pregnant was a struggle for us. I came to dread small talk at church because the conversations often drifted toward questions I didn't want to answer, such as: When were we going to have another baby? How often did I put my son in childcare during the week? Was I going to quit my job when I had a second child? Mostly, I feared the question about when we were going to have another baby. It was hard not to cry when people asked. I would find myself hiding with the friends I knew best, the ones in our small group, as they didn't ask these questions.

But sometimes I couldn't hide.

Take, for instance, the time I attended a homeschool graduation hosted at our church. I couldn't hide from the person who walked up to tell me how glad he was to see me with a child. It was great, he continued, for the pastor's wife to set an example for motherhood. Would we be expecting another baby soon?

I couldn't hide from the woman who came next, wondering whether I was going to take a break from teaching so I could stay home. My son was so cute. How could I stand leaving him to go to work? "I would never leave my children," she informed me.

I couldn't hide from the friend who suggested I talk to some of the homeschooling families, as now was the perfect time to get started. The other pastors' wives at our church homeschooled, and after all, the friend continued, my advanced degrees would make me a fantastic homeschool mom.

I was in tears by the time I got to my car.

As I fastened my son into his car seat, I found myself thinking about another pastor's wife from my teenage years. Her husband had served briefly at my childhood church as youth pastor. He wasn't a "good fit," people told me when they left. I had liked him and his wife. She was a full-time nurse, and they didn't have children. I was one of the first students to meet her when she and her husband were candidates. I am ashamed to admit I asked her when she was going to have a baby. Her husband answered for her, taking her hand. "God has promised us children," he said. She met his eyes and smiled briefly before looking away.

It wasn't until that moment, as I drove home from church with my three-year-old in the back seat and the tears fresh on my cheeks, that I understood the pain my childish curiosity must have caused that youth pastor's wife so many years before. If being a mother was the highest calling for an evangelical woman, and if being a pastor's wife was the highest ministry calling for an evangelical woman, what did it mean if the pastor's wife couldn't be a mom?

I understand the pain even better now.

Yvonne Garrett, for example, interviewed more than two hundred pastors' wives for her 1991 book, *The Stained Glass House: A Handbook for Ministers' Wives*. She asked the women a standard set of eighteen questions. While the questions did not presume the work status of the pastors' wives (asking whether or not they worked outside the home), they did presume children. Instead of prefacing the two questions related to raising children with "if" or "for those who have children," they simply ask, "How would (or did) you handle the situation if your teenage son or daughter decided not to attend services of the church?" and, "Do you think your child's behavior affects your husband's effectiveness as a minister?"[13] The questions presume that all those pastors' wives completing the questionnaire have children.

Likewise, McKay titled one of her chapters "How to Raise My PKs to Keep the Faith." She framed the chapter by quoting 1 Timothy 3:4: "He [the overseer or pastor] must be one who manages his own household well, keeping his children under control with all dignity" (NASB). She cites it to underscore there's a connection between the pastor's job and his household. She also writes, "It is imperative as we seek authenticity in ministry that we also consider how this applies to *raising our kids* in that same freedom."[14] Again, the language presumes McKay's readers are raising preacher's kids (PKs).

McKay isn't alone.

From Gayle Haggard to Gail McDonald, white pastors' wives writing instructional ministry books between 1980 and 2020 usually assume that motherhood is a part of their role—giving chapters titles like "Being a Devoted Mom," "The Taming of the PK," "How Rich Is the Child of a Minister!," "PKs Can Be OK," and even "The Insufferable Little Children." It goes without saying that Dorothy Patterson's *Handbook for Ministers' Wives* includes a chapter on child-rearing. In "Children of the Church—Orphans at Home," she states, "A minister's wife has no more important opportunity for service in the kingdom of Christ than nurturing her own children."[15]

This emphasis on home and family for pastors' wives explains why Kate Bowler dedicated an entire chapter in *The Preacher's Wife: The Precarious Power of Evangelical Women Celebrities* to "The Homemaker," showing how the idealized image of the godly wife helped launch evangelical stars like Jen Hatmaker and Joanna Gaines—women Bowler describes as "literally building Christian homes." In Bowler's sharp prose, "Mormon mommy bloggers' gorgeous photos of their children in matching chambray and bowties looked roughly the same as evangelical and pentecostal authors'

'About Me' section. The family was her primary advertisement, her expertise, and, often, the reason for her start in ministry, all disguised in three simple words: 'Wife and Mom.'"[16]

The primary job of the modern pastor's wife is being a wife and mom. Gayle Haggard is wife of Ted Haggard, formerly a prominent megachurch pastor and president of the National Association of Evangelicals. A mother of five, she wrote her book for pastors' wives in 2004 and confirmed, "As a pastor's wife, give yourself permission to place your responsibilities as mother over and above any responsibilities you have at your church. Being a great mom is a more important contribution to the body of Christ than anything else you do—other than loving your husband."[17] Two years later, Gayle learned that her husband had cheated on her with male partners and used illegal drugs. He lost his church, and his family lost their home and livelihood, but Ted did not lose his wife. Gayle told Oprah in 2010, "I'm a strong woman and I take care of myself, and these were my choices. I feel as though the betrayal had the potential to lead us toward greater health in our marriage, and that was the perspective I was willing to take because I do deeply love this man."[18] Whatever your thoughts about the Haggards, Gayle remained true to what she taught to other pastors' wives. She used her influence and public image to "strengthen and support her husband's ministry," even when her husband had failed her as well as his pastoral duties.[19]

Sic et Non: Yes and No

But has it always been this way? Has the pastor's wife role always been construed as a two-for-one model in which the unpaid labor of the wife as well as her homemaking skills are considered part of her husband's job?

I'm going to give you the answer my medieval history students know well, as it forms the basis of their regular *disputatio* writing assignment. The answer is both yes and no.

Let's start with the *no*.

My favorite pastor's wife story is recounted by Margaret Watt in her book *The History of the Parson's Wife*. Watt tells the story of a pastor and his wife on opposite sides of a religious controversy in late eighteenth- and early nineteenth-century Scotland. The wife was the daughter of a prominent member of the Burgher sect, which means her father supported public officials swearing allegiance to the Church of Scotland. The husband, however, was a dissenter who did not believe that public officials should be made to swear religious oaths. He voted to condemn her family at a synod in 1827. When she found out, she declared, "You have excommunicated my father and my uncle! You are my husband, but never more shall you be minister of mine." She remained married to him but stopped attending his church, instead riding every Sunday morning to a different congregation. As a fascinating note, her husband didn't oppose her decision. Watt writes that each Sunday, before he went to preach, he could be seen "helping her to mount his pony to ride into Jedburgh where she could find the doctrine and worship her injured feelings demanded."[20]

The pastor's wife role has not always been the two-for-one model, in which the wife's labor and identity, even as a mother, becomes completely subsumed under her husband's vocation.

Take, for example, the first pastors' wives in early sixteenth-century Germany. To be sure, marriage signified clerical allegiance to reform, and married ministry couples became a model of faith for their communities, but the pastor's wife was a new role. Marriage for clergy was just beginning to be accepted in this brave new world of the 1520s. For women, Marjorie Plummer reminds us, it came with considerable risk. "Becoming a priest's wife heralded a major shift in gender role and identity that was to have implications beyond any individual woman's life."[21] There was no script for the wives of these early Protestant reformers apart from general expectations for godly wives. It's important to remember that their husbands, formerly celibate clergy, probably had no idea what to expect from them either. David Whitford explains this well in *The Making of a Godly Man: Martin Luther and the Reformation of Masculine Identity*:

> All of the early reformers were educated and trained as priests and monks in a patriarchal and misogynist theological tradition that denigrated women, women's bodies, and human sexuality and who had lived for sometimes decades in exclusively male communities. Now, they were trying to figure out how to live and interact with an actual woman in a real family. For nearly all of them, this was an entirely new phenomenon. While some of the men who wrote tracts pleading for wives already had concubines that they married, none of the early prominent reformers, save Zwingli, did. Neither Luther, Bugenhagen, or even Karlstadt in Wittenberg knew their wives when they first began to embrace the idea of clerical marriage. Neither Martin Bucer nor Matthew Zell in Strasbourg had concubines, either. These men went directly from the cloister to the newly formed family home. These reformers were all theologians first, who then became husbands.[22]

As such, there would have been no "set qualifications" and a great deal of "latitude" for the first pastors' wives.[23] These women, and their husbands, were making it up as they went along.

Leonard Sweet nevertheless suggests these early pastors' wives were fulfilling the "companion" model of ministry, which sounds a lot like the two-for-one model, with a heavier emphasis on the home. They were "ministering angels who held up the sacred hands" of their husbands, writes Sweet.[24] I wonder what Katharina von Bora would have made of this description. While her husband, Martin Luther, described wives as submissive "nails in the house's wall," von Bora was not a submissive wife, nor did she focus on domesticity. She was a theologically engaged partner and businesswoman who kept food on the table and the bills paid. She had no problem telling Luther what she thought of him or his ideas, good and bad, and she didn't save her criticism for handwritten notes placed on his desk for him to read after he had recovered from a hard day of preaching. Von Bora wasn't trying to be a pastor's wife; von Bora was just figuring out her new life with Luther.[25]

Along with Katharina von Bora, Katharina Schütz Zell was among the earliest group of sixteenth-century pastors' wives, married to Strasbourg reformer Matthew Zell. She became a preacher herself. As the story goes, Matthew commissioned Katharina to be "Church Mother" on their wedding day, a task she took to most notably through writing and publishing biblical expositions in defense of her clerical marriage and to instruct her readers in the newly developing Protestant faith. From her earliest publication, "An Apologia for Master Mathew Zell," to her last, "An Open Letter to Sir Felix Armbruster," Zell embodied her role as Church Mother by transforming the printing press into her personal pulpit from which she delivered religious instruction and encouragement and defended the faith through her own biblical interpretations—as Katherine Goodwin Lindgren argues.[26] Zell's preaching and printing career changed after Matthew's death in 1548. At his graveside funeral, she gave an extemporaneous exhortation that was both eulogy and sermon. In it, she memorialized her husband's ministry and declared her intent to continue his legacy through her own pastoral work. "And so I say today, with and in the place of my dear husband, with Mary Magdalene, 'The Lord is truly risen and lives for us all!'"[27]

Ruth Tucker suggests Zell's ministry was an extension of her pastor's wife role: "Her role as a pastor's wife had become so much a part of her identity that it effectively continued long after her husband died."[28] But I rather think that Lindgren has a better measure of Zell, whose preaching at her husband's funeral is often perceived as the start of her independent ministry. Lindgren argues differently. "Likening herself to Mary Magdalene, the *apostal apostolorum* [apostle to the apostles], Katharina Schütz Zell placed herself in the tradition of female preaching that was a dynamic example of religious authority for medieval women," writes Lindgren. "However, this public claim to the medieval legacy of the preaching Magdalen and shared ministerial authority with her husband was not the start of her career as a lay preacher. Rather, it was the culmination of a preaching career that translated medieval patterns of performative female preaching in Strasbourg into the language of early modern reform through the rhetorical space of the printing press."[29]

This assessment of Zell is significant for two reasons. First, it disrupts the two-for-one concept of the pastor's wife role. It is true that Zell ministered alongside her husband and zealously supported his work. But she functioned more like a colleague than a "ministering angel" who labored behind the scenes. Her status as Church Mother granted her this opportunity to minister.[30] This opportunity placed her on similar footing with her husband as she shared in the very public work of caring for and preaching to their community. Second, it highlights medieval models of ministry that early modern women like Zell still had access to. Again, the role of pastor's wife was brand-new, while women serving in ministry as independent preachers and leaders was as old as the Bible. When Zell looked for ministry models, she did not look to her peers like von Bora; she looked to biblical women like Mary Magdalene, long considered an evangelistic preacher authorized by the apostle Peter.

I doubt that either Katharina von Bora or Katharina Schütz Zell would live up to Dorothy Patterson's standards for pastors' wives. Patterson even critiques Susanna Wesley, despite her raising John and Charles Wesley—the founders of the Methodist movement—and keeping her family together under difficult circumstances. "Susanna did not have the same commitment to her marriage" to Samuel Wesley as she did to her children, writes Patterson.[31] I find this an interesting statement considering Susanna bore nineteen children in twenty years. I also find it an interesting statement considering that Samuel left Susanna for more than a year because she didn't agree politically with him. His long absences contributed to the family's poverty. I wonder if Patterson's concern with

Susanna Wesley is that she assumed her husband's leadership, including his preaching duties, when he was gone. As Watt writes, Susanna had "remarkable success in attracting the congregation to listen to her teaching, or preaching, during one of these long absences of Mr. Wesley at Convocation. The people insisted on coming unbidden, to hear the religious instruction she gave to her own children, and coming in such numbers that her small room was crowded out, and the jealous curate accused her of holding a conventicle."[32] Susanna Wesley was a preacher, and Patterson accuses her of not being a devoted enough wife. Samuel Wesley's congregation, however, didn't seem to mind.

So, the answer to my question opening this section is no. The pastor's wife role has not always been construed as a two-for-one model in which the unpaid labor of the wife as well as her home-making skills are considered part of her husband's job.

At the same time, the answer is also yes. There are some obvious historical continuities in the pastor's wife role—namely the emphasis on wife, mom, and domesticity. But does this mean these continuities are ordained by God?

Hang onto your coffee (or tea, rather), because we are about to find out.

The Pastor's Wife Isn't from the Bible

We've established that the pastor's wife role emerged during the Reformation. As such, it isn't surprising that the role was heavily shaped by broader social trends that firmly ensconced women in domestic roles. As I argue in *The Making of Biblical Woman-hood*, the world of post-Reformation Europe strongly emphasized women's domesticity. The formation of the "Holy Household" during the Reformation era linked godliness to a patriarchal family structure; added to this were Enlightenment beliefs about the inferiority of women and the impact of the Industrial Revolution that disrupted and devalued women's labor.[33]

What I didn't talk about in *The Making of Biblical Woman-hood* is how the changing economic world of the fifteenth and sixteenth centuries created a new emphasis on domestic space. I find it interesting that the characteristics Sweet highlights to argue that von Bora's "greatest joy in life was to make Luther happy and useful" as an "industrious helpmeet in mothering and managing" were only recently gendered female in London.[34] Katherine French argues in *Household Goods and Good Households in Late Medieval London* that tasks like "cleaning, provisioning, and managing a household" that we gender female today may have been supervised by a housewife but were completed by male servants. French writes, "The economic crisis of the mid-fifteenth century drove women from better jobs in manufacturing into domestic service, thereby gendering urban housekeeping as female at both the supervisory and laboring levels."[35] As levels of consumption rose in the aftermath of the plague and work expectations for urban women (including elite women) shifted, household responsibilities shifted too. It wasn't until the sixteenth century, argues French, that "women both supervised and labored over housework in urban homes, and society identified and judged women by the quality of their housework."[36] It was also during this time, between the mid-fourteenth and mid-sixteenth centuries, that piety became more commonly associated with household items and "moralized the housekeeping tasks that were increasingly performed by women."[37] Take, for example, what Merry Wiesner-Hanks writes in *Gender in History: Global Perspectives* about why tea became a status symbol for women:

> Housekeeping itself became more elaborate, as international trade and then industrial production provided a steadily increasing amount of consumer goods to households in Europe and European households in the colonies. . . . This new consumer culture provided opportunities for men and women to socialize in new ways, with men gathering in coffeehouses and women in the homes of their friends or relatives around a teapot.[38]

What does this mean?

It means that the increasing emphasis on a woman's place in the home correlates with increasing consumerism for the home. It means learning to brew a good cup of tea became important to European households as a marker of economic success. Biblical stories about Martha of Bethany, the sister of Mary, who oversaw the arrangement of a dinner for Jesus, and even Sarah, who bore the promised child Isaac and called her husband "lord," threw a biblical aura over the work of these housewives. But the historical reality is that the afternoon tea Dorothy Patterson planned for the 2006 SBC Ministers' Wives' Luncheon—themed "Filling Your Home with God's Beauty" and including an interior designer as the speaker and advertisements for Premier Designs jewelry—was much more a product of early modern capitalism than of the Bible verse quoted in the program: "By wisdom a house is built . . . ; through knowledge its rooms are filled with rare and beautiful treasures" (Prov. 24:3–4 NIV).[39] It also means that the modern conservative movement that glorifies housework, childcare, and family management was born of the growing international trade and consumption of domestic goods in early modern Europe.

To be sure, when modern pastors' wives began looking for models to sacralize their callings, they found them in the Holy Household of the Reformation era, which emphasized male authority and female submission.[40] They found them in the Catholic households of early modern Europe that treated women's caregiving as acts of Christian devotion.[41] They found them in "the mistress of the New England parsonage" who "defined her role totally in relation to her husband's home life."[42] They found them in the busy wives of nineteenth-century ministers who spiritually trained their children, visited the sick, and cared for the poor. They found them in the bustling housewife polishing her spoons and reading devotional books, the purchase of which marked her family as successfully middle class.

But these historical models were less influenced by the Bible than by the secular world around them. Indeed, we may have early capitalism to thank for the two-for-one ministry model. Wiesner-Hanks explains how "urban investors often hired whole households, but paid wages only to the male head of household." She uses the example of mining, in which men were paid per basket but women and children provided the labor required for breaking the ore apart and washing it. Both their payment and labor were subsumed into the "work" of the male household head. This type of wage structure evaluated women's labor on the basis of their husbands rather than "the quality of their work"—and it rings a bell in the ears of the evangelical pastor's wife.[43]

The Case of Delilah Morrell

Just a few days before my husband was fired in September 2016, we went to a wedding deep in the heart of Texas. Wide open fields dotted with cattle and the occasional John Deere tractor were broken by scattered farmhouses. The roads were narrow and dusty; population signs for the small towns counted inhabitants by the hundreds; and notices posted at the reception (held in one of the nearby small towns) warned guests to keep all alcoholic beverages *inside* the church fellowship hall instead of the other way around.

The ceremony took place at Little River Baptist Church.[44] With its bright white beaded wood and tall Gothic windows, the 1873 building still looks today much as it did at the turn of the twentieth century. In a truly communal effort, the church was built by dedicated congregants working with the local Masonic lodge. In 1906 the building was expanded to accommodate the largest congregation in Milam County.

A tombstone for Delilah Morrell, 1804–1883, stands tall in the cemetery surrounding the church.[45] A few other tombstones date from 1866, some perhaps earlier. Morrell's stone marks more than a memorial to her life. It also testifies to a fascinating event from the early history of Little River Baptist Church: the divorce of a pastor's wife.

Delilah Harlan, a widow, married Z. N. Morrell, a widower, on October 27, 1845. Delilah then helped her husband found Little River Baptist Church in 1849. Morrell became the first pastor of the new church, and Delilah became the first pastor's wife. In 1857 she gifted several acres to the church, including the site for the first church building on which the church today still stands. When she died, Delilah Morrell's grave was marked prominently in the cemetery of the church to which she had dedicated more than thirty years of her life.[46]

Delilah's dedication to her pastor husband, however, proved less enduring.

For some, Z. N. Morrell is a legend. A preacher known as "Wildcat," Morrell planted churches in Mississippi, Texas, and Honduras; fought as a frontier soldier (including against the Mexican army); raised funds for a Baptist university close to my heart (Baylor University); rode as a circuit preacher; and even wrote a full account of his work as a Baptist missionary.[47] Possibly enamored with Z. N.'s impressive reputation and probably confident in his husband quality, Delilah Harlan married this preacher.

Shortly after, in 1845, Morrell accepted an appointment as a state missionary by the Domestic Mission Board of the Southern Baptist Convention. His job included church planting (hence the founding of Little River Baptist Church), organizing Baptist associations (including the first Texas convention of Baptists in 1848), and regularly making the long and arduous three-hundred-mile round trip (circuit) on horseback between Cameron and Corsicana, preaching and policing Baptist beliefs. Morrell preferred the peripatetic, unpredictable, and risky lifestyle of a circuit preacher to that of a settled pastor.

In other words, he was rarely at home with his wife.

When Morrell did return home, it was usually because he was sick and needed Delilah to nurse him back to health. After fifteen years of this, of never knowing when (or if) her husband would come home, Delilah called it quits. She asked Little River Baptist Church to allow the marriage to be terminated. As she wrote to the disciplinary committee, she considered herself "parted" from her husband. Modern members of the church still whisper that Delilah's extreme distress over Morrell's long absences convinced the church to help her despite the nonscriptural basis of her request. In 1860, they allowed Delilah to divorce their church founder and first pastor. Morrell was exonerated of wrongdoing (i.e., he could still preach), but he ended his membership with Little River shortly after.

This is remarkable, in no small part because Baptists in 1860 were at the cusp of a crackdown on divorce laws. As historian Rufus B. Spain writes, "Baptists considered marriage an institution of divine origin, initiated by God in the Garden of Eden and validated by Christ at the marriage feast in Cana. The increasing divorce rate in the late nineteenth century was therefore of grave concern to Baptists. To combat this trend, they stressed the absolute necessity of strict compliance with God's marriage laws."[48] Some Baptists in nineteenth-century Texas practiced "churching" (exclusion from membership and access to ordinances) against immoral members: drunkards, criminals, and those who got divorced. Indeed, churching was enforced at the First Baptist Church of Dallas in 1877 when a woman was excluded after divorcing her husband for "lunacy" and then remarrying. A meeting of the San Antonio Baptist Association in 1898 affirmed an equally rigid position on divorce, stating that "ministers and members of Baptist churches . . . forbid divorce for any other cause than adultery or fornication, and do not authorize remarriage of the divorced."[49] Contemporary Baptist attitudes toward divorce seem clear: it wasn't allowed, except for sexual sin.

Yet Delilah Morrell was granted a divorce by the fourth Baptist church established in Texas for reasons other than these biblical exceptions.

Can you imagine?

Can you guess what happened next?

Delilah Morrell stayed in Little River Baptist Church. She remained an influential member, not only as a divorced woman but as a divorced pastor's wife. She was influential enough when she died to be buried prominently in the churchyard. Her family remains connected to the church today. Her ex-husband, on the other hand, is no longer associated with Little River Baptist, despite the fact that he founded the church alongside Delilah; he was buried at a different church a hundred miles away.

Delilah's story is remarkable because neither Delilah nor her husband fit typical expectations for a pastoral couple. Even without the divorce, Delilah, as a woman who seems to have contributed little to her spouse's peripatetic ministry, does not fit modern expectations for a pastor's wife.

But in nineteenth-century Texas, her Baptist church did not seem to mind.

Two Roads Diverging

The two-for-one approach to pastors' wives is rooted in changes in the early modern world that placed wives under the authority of their husbands. Indeed, the pastor's wife developed along with the spreading branches of Protestantism. Her story intertwines with the emergence of capitalism, Enlightenment ideas about gender, and the nineteenth-century emphasis on women's work as domestic and subordinate to the work of men.

But her life, through the early twentieth century, was less circumscribed than we have imagined. To be sure, there were pastors' wives who fit Dorothy Patterson's ideal of holding the ladder for a husband to climb. There were also women like Delilah Morrell who did not. In many ways, marrying a pastor before the early twentieth century was not much different from marrying any other Protestant man. The pastor's wife may have received more attention within the community and been upheld as a model, yet what was expected of her—even the two-for-one business model—paralleled what was expected of other wives.

But something significant had changed.

Marriage had become an expectation for good Protestant women, which meant that even women called to ministry were also expected to be wives. Is it any wonder that women's path to ministry began to blur with their path to marriage? Is it any wonder that women's calling to ministry began to blur with their roles as wives and mothers? Is it any wonder that, as a wage structure developed that subsumed women's work under that of a male household head, this affected the pastor's family too?

The medieval Milburga disappeared into a distant, Catholic past. With her disappeared the once-familiar emphasis on women's independent ministry. Mary Magdalene, who had once been revered as a preaching apostle to the apostles, disappeared under the flowing hair of a reformed prostitute. She prayed and asked for forgiveness, but she no longer preached.

Women continued to serve in ministries separate from their husbands and fathers, and women like Delilah Morrell did not become subsumed under the identity of their pastor husbands. But as the correlation increased between being a wife and being a godly woman, so did the correlation between being a woman in ministry and being the wife of a minister.

6

The Best Pastor's Wife

A friend once told me about a jarring event in her life. She, like me, had continued to a PhD program in history. She had also married a pastor. We had commiserated before about weird things people said to us or situations we had encountered from our double lives as academics and pastors' wives.

But what happened to her never happened to me—at least not overtly.

Her husband had applied for a pastoral role at a new church. He had made it far in the candidate process, and it looked like he might be invited to the church in view of a call. Before the church committee recommended him, however, they wanted to talk with his wife. She was mother to a toddler, expecting another baby, soon to graduate with her PhD, and working full-time. She asked them about expectations for pastors' wives. There wasn't much else she could fit into her life. The question surprised the committee, leading them to ask more probing questions. They learned that her husband had relocated for her PhD program instead of for his current pastoral position. They learned that although she supported her husband, she herself did not feel called to ministry.

Shortly after, they informed her husband that the other candidate had been selected. "You were the top candidate," they told him. "Until we talked to your wife."

When she told me the story, I shared her bemused outrage.

But neither of us was surprised.

We had been pastors' wives long enough to know the underlying assumptions. We both were historians who specialized in women's and gender studies, which meant we knew that our experiences as pastors' wives were shaped by the patriarchal forces of history. We both might laugh at Ryan Gosling as the marginalized Ken in *Barbie* singing "I'm Just Ken"—"Doesn't seem to matter what I do I'm always number two. No one knows how hard I tried, oh-oh."[1] But we also knew the hard reality of patriarchy lurking behind his words.

Patriarchy is a fancy word for a social system that centers some men and privileges their power. Sociologist Allan Johnson explains it as such in his book *The Gender Knot*: "A society is patriarchal to the degree that it is male dominated, male identified, and male centered." By this definition, patriarchy means that "core cultural ideas about what is considered good, desirable, preferable, or normal are associated with how we think about men and masculinity."[2] Women are valued in patriarchal societies for how they relate to and support men. They are typically not valued apart from their connection to men.

Doesn't that sound like the pastor's wife role?

Could it be that church hiring committees value pastors' wives for how they relate to and support their husbands rather than who they are as whole persons in and of themselves? Could this be why church hiring committees feel justified in expecting pastors' wives to be called to ministry and to work as unpaid laborers? Could it be why they feel justified in expecting wives to be part of a two-for-one ministry package?

Instead of valuing my friend for who she was as a full, complex person, the church hiring committee saw her through the lens of her husband. They measured her by the way she would support her husband's ministry and, by extension, the ministry of the church, and they found her lacking.

I don't think my friend (or her husband) regrets not getting that church job.

But I worry about the broader church today and the consequences of a ministry model that reduces the value of a pastor's wife to the ministry calling of her husband. I know there was a time not that long ago when evangelical women, even in the SBC, were encouraged to serve in a variety of roles, both as pastors' wives and as single women, both as helpmeets to their husbands and as teachers and preachers in their own right. I know there was a time when even the literature aimed at pastors' wives encouraged them to follow their calling and not disappear behind their husband.

And I know there was a time when it changed.

Don't get me wrong. There was never a golden age for women in ministry. Even in the 1970s and '80s, when more women were enrolling in seminary and on track for ordination, they still were paid less than men (if they were paid at all) and faced more challenges in finding employment. The barriers for women in ministry paralleled broader challenges faced by all women. But it is important to understand that there is a history behind the absorption of a woman married to a pastor into the calling of her husband, and it is a history connected to the battle over women's ordination.

Let me show you what I mean, although it will take the next chapter too.

Let's use the SBC as a case study.

The Irony of Willie Dawson

Every October, my parents took our family to the State Fair of Texas. Big Tex, a twenty-foot-tall cowboy animatronic in Levi's, would greet us as we walked into the Dallas fairgrounds. My little sister was disconcerted by his giant square jaw and big eyes that moved with jerky twitches as he waved and made speeches. I imagine, when he caught fire a few years ago, the sight of his oversized features garishly lit by orange flames and blackened by smoke probably scarred more than one child who witnessed it.[3] But we all loved the food trucks. My brother would try almost every type of fried thing, including the fried Twinkies and even fried butter once, while my dad would buy us as many tamales as we wanted from our favorite vendor. Cool gadgets and toys filled the science and technology center, and one year my little sister and I talked my dad into buying monkey puppets that allowed us to annoy our older sister.

My mom would take us to the Women's Building. Beautiful quilts, embroidered panels, amateur photography (my dad really liked this aisle), handmade toys, and rows and rows of preserves (or "weird jellies," as my sister called them) filled the cases around the walls, each one bearing a prize ribbon for the skills showcased that year. My mom, a practiced needleworker, would tell us about the intricacy of the lacework and the finely embroidered panels as she pointed out her favorite pieces. I never became competent with the needle (my husband tailors better than I do, thanks to his college job at a tuxedo shop), but my mother taught me to love the beauty of the craft. To this day, one of my favorite shops in London is Liberty, which, from its faux-Tudor building on Great Marlborough Street, has specialized in designer fabrics since 1924. When I walk on the third floor through the stacks of fabric, I can almost see my mother and my grandmother walking ahead of me, touching the fine lawn with their expert hands.

As a child, I saw the Women's Building as one more familiar part of the State Fair experience. I didn't know that the history of the Women's Building at the fairgrounds—created to showcase women's decorative and homemaking skills as well as their philanthropic pursuits—began a century before I was born. I also didn't know that, almost a quarter century before I was born, a similar yet distinctly different public prize arose that would also showcase

114

women's work. Rather than at a State Fair, this one would emerge within the Southern Baptist Convention to honor the pastor's wife.

The organizers of the third annual Southern Baptist Pastors' Wives' Conference, held in May 1958 at River Oaks Baptist Church in Houston, dreamed up the Distinguished Service Award (later renamed the Mrs. J. M. Dawson Award and renamed again as the Willie Turner Dawson Award, which is how I will reference it) to recognize the outstanding ministry contributions made by pastors' wives.[4] The women who won, especially in the early years, were wives and mothers engaged in traditional ministry work, such as teaching Sunday school and providing pastoral care. They were also visible leaders at local, state, and even national levels. Many were theology and Bible teachers for college and seminary students and speakers at large events whose audiences included men and women.

Let me stop and tell you about the first time I saw the name of this service award. From August 2018 to May 2024, I lived as a faculty-in-residence in Dawson Residence Hall on the campus of Baylor University. Nearly every day during that time, I walked past "Willie" (as the students call her). She presides from an ornate frame hanging above the piano in the residence hall lobby, watching over our boisterous karaoke nights and coffeehouse performances. You can imagine how it surprised me to see a picture of that same portrait staring not from the wall of my home but from a folder in the Southern Baptist Historical Library and Archives.[5]

Described as "a regal woman with a commanding stage presence" and as a "powerful and convincing" orator, Willie Turner Dawson was the pastor's wife of First Baptist Church in Waco for thirty-one years (1915–46). She was a Bible teacher, a preacher, and a leader in her own right who had been baptized into the faith by George W. Truett (the namesake of Truett seminary on the Baylor campus, which trains women alongside men for pastoral ministry).[6] She helped popularize the Lottie Moon Christmas Offering for international missions, fundraised for the Women's

Memorial Dormitory on Baylor's campus, delivered international addresses to the Baptist World Alliance in 1947 and the Baptist World Congress in 1950, served regularly on state and national SBC committees, and became the first woman to be nominated for election as vice president to the Southern Baptist Convention.[7]

Dawson also served on the committee delivering the Women's Missionary Union (WMU) report to the 1933 national convention. The report makes it clear that the leadership of women was "a positive force for good" for not only the mission of the church but also the SBC. "Since Christ came into the world woman has been in the ascendancy," it proclaimed. "For during his few years on earth the Master forgave woman, praised her, safeguarded her, comforted her, and set her free. Some of his most ardent friends were women. Notable among these were Mary and Martha of Bethany. Women hastened to the empty tomb and sped away with the resurrection message." Just as women played a prominent role in the "rise and spread of early Christianity," the report emphasized the prominent role played by the WMU in the success of the SBC. At the height of the nationwide depression, it noted, the WMU single-handedly contributed half of the yearly funds for the national SBC Cooperative Program, 60 percent of the budget for the Foreign Mission Board, and more than 70 percent of the budget for the Home Mission Board. Women like Willie Dawson literally "kept alive the fire of evangelism" in the SBC.[8]

The SBC Pastors' Wives' Conference was created in a world that recognized women's religious authority even while honoring them as wives and mothers, an SBC world that still lived under the powerful shadow of the WMU. When two Georgia women proposed that SBC pastors' wives would benefit from a national organization, not everyone saw a need for it. The executive director of the Tennessee Baptist Convention, Chas. W. Pope, wrote in 1949 that, "since our ladies are organized in the Women's Missionary Union, I have not, personally, seen a need for an organization of pastors' wives."[9] Nevertheless, they persisted (if I may use that phrase), just as their WMU forebears had, and launched the SBC Pastors' Wives' Conference in 1956 to meet alongside the national convention. They raised money, elected officers, wrote a constitution, organized childcare and transportation for attendees, and designed programming. As Loulie Latimer Owens wrote, the organizers hoped "that the wives conference, adapting itself constantly to the changing times, will continue to provide inspiration and fellowship, and that it will always help to interpret the high significance of the unique role of the individual minister's wife."[10] The significant work that these women did, and the significant role they played in affirming one another, is remarkable.

How they perceived their role is also remarkable. Certainly, these women emphasized caring for their families and supporting their local churches. Yet, when the awards committee began evaluating nominations for the 1965 Mrs. J. M. Dawson Distinguished Service Award (later named the Willie Turner Dawson Award), they listed the basic requirements in order of importance. The award committee did not want to reward "Mama" for shining "before the WMU Executive Board" while neglecting delinquent children and hungry husband, but neither did they emphasize the home as first priority. It was listed as last priority, just after local church activity. The top three requirements to qualify for the pastor's wife award were versatility of interests, a.k.a. well-roundedness, followed by uniqueness of the contribution, which the committee described as "something beyond the usual minister's-wife-routine." The most important characteristic was breadth of influence. "The award was for 'the most outstanding contribution to the denomination.' She must do something that would reach beyond a single state, or a few states." Rather than celebrating a woman who focused primarily on being a domestic helpmate, the SBC pastor's wife award—as it was designed in 1959—emphasized women who went beyond quotidian duties and made significant contributions at the state and national levels.[11]

This attitude persisted throughout much of the conference history. Well into the late 1990s, conference organizers emphasized that the Dawson Award should recognize a woman who made a "distinguished" contribution "in her own right," instead of only recognizing the wives of notable men.[12] In the same spirit, Alice Marshall (president of the Ministers' Wives Conference, 1994–95) explained in a June 26, 1995, letter her reason for not publicly recognizing Bobbye Rankin, wife of then SBC International Mission Board president Jerry Rankin, at the conference: "I believe in recognizing women for their accomplishments and not because of their husband's achievements."[13]

Ministers' wives may have married into the job, but—throughout much of the SBC Ministers' Wives Conference history—they were expected to earn their own recognition.

Who Is the Best Pastor's Wife?

Not everyone agreed that the independent merit of a pastor's wife was more important than their dependent role of supportive wife. Let's look more closely at the 1959 Distinguished Service Award.

That year had a record number of nominations. Award Chair Marian Grant was astonished by both the volume and content of the nomination letters she received: around three hundred letters nominating at least 160 ministers' wives across more than twenty states.[14] Ultimately, the award went to Mrs. M. Jackson White of First Baptist Church of Clarendon in Arlington, Virginia. Twenty-five women received honorable mentions, and eleven (including Mrs. White) were finalists. One newspaper article from May 1959 recounted that "among her [Mrs. White's] numerous activities was teaching courses on the Old Testament and on the life and teachings of Jesus at the University of Richmond extension department," as well as frequently speaking, leading marriage conferences, and serving on the executive board of the Virginia Women's Missionary Union. In short, Mrs. White fit the requirements for the award: she went beyond normal wifely duties at home and even at church to become a college educator and public speaker within her home state.

Before a winner was named, Grant wrote to the president of the SBC Pastors' Wives about the nominations. "These people LOVE their pastors' wives!" she told them. "And for good reason. I've been inspired and made ashamed too, to see what some are doing." She suggested she could write something, maybe a book, using the nomination letters, to showcase the women's wonderful work.[15] A book never materialized, as far as I can tell, but Grant did write an article for her local newspaper. Quoting from some of the letters, she wrote, "Pastors' wives are versatile, that's for sure, doing anything from 'filling the pulpit in the absence of her husband' to 'preparing food and bringing it to the workers and assisting with the actual work on the pastorium—sanding, painting, cleaning windows, even helping a little on putting down the hardwood floors.' Teaching study courses, Sunday School classes, Training Union, and young people's groups is taken in stride as well as being able to 'prepare a program with 15 minutes' notice.'" She continued to list many of the other qualities that nominees had displayed, from musical talent to homemaking, from faithful denominational service at state and national levels to local community work.

Grant concluded the article with this assessment: "Southern Baptists love their preachers' wives, but they do not want 'a dictator nor a church mouse.'"[16] They want pastors' wives active in ministry but only those who do not overstep their authority. One of the letters, nominating Ruth Harrell Bobo in 1959, illustrates these expectations:

> Her greatest single qualification is consecration. Whatever task she does, she does for the glory of God. Ruth is a qualified elementary school teacher, but she accepts teaching only when there is a great need for her services. She prefers to spend her time serving in the

church. She is a graduate of Mercer and the Carver School. She serves tirelessly in every activity. She advises all the other teachers and counselors in the church. If the problem comes to her, she says, "Let's pray about it." She teaches Mission studies for country churches. She visits the sick and the shut-ins. She earnestly tries to enlist everybody, and she is such an inspiration to us that she usually succeeds. Ruth Bobo has done more to raise the spiritual level of our church than any other person. She has done it not by preaching (but she could if she were needed) but by her daily life of dedicated consecrated service. She is the most selfless person I ever knew.[17]

In Wooten's words, Ruth Bobo had done more for their congregation than anyone else, even her husband. Yet she did not do it by preaching (although she had the education and the ability to do so). She did it as a sacrificial wife who only took on paid work when she was needed and when it would help others.

Many award recipients and nominees continued to distinguish themselves through denominational work at the state and national levels. Bobo, however, distinguished herself by supporting the work of her husband. James O. Duncan, a leader in the District of Columbia Baptist Convention, wrote in 1959 to the awards chair regarding a finalist. He commented that the award guidelines privilege women who serve the denomination more broadly at the state and national levels. "We who are pastors, however, I feel, would rather have a wife who is a constant companion by our side helping us with our local work or local program in our own church—counseling, giving advice, ministering to the women . . . than to have one who becomes a leader in the denomination."[18] Women like Willie Dawson are to be commended; but according to Duncan, the best pastors' wives are those who support their husbands' ministry.

Forty-seven years after Duncan expressed his preference for a pastor's wife who stays by her man, Dorothy Patterson became president of the SBC Ministers' Wives conference. She nominated

Carol Ann Draper for the Willie Turner Dawson Award in 2006 because of her "commitment to the priorities and boundaries of Scripture" as she served alongside her husband, James (Jimmy) Draper. At the time of his wife's award, Draper had just retired as president of Lifeway, the publishing arm of the SBC, and was considered a "pastor to pastors." Patterson applauded Draper's wife for the public platform she developed that focused on teaching and encouraging women, as well as her role as homemaker and caregiver. "Carol Ann," wrote Patterson, is "worthy of the award for helping her husband in ministry."[19] Perhaps Carol Ann would have agreed with this assessment by Patterson, as she described herself as earning a "PHT (Put Hubby Through!)" on her résumé.[20] Jimmy Draper's wife won the award named in honor of Willie Dawson, but for different reasons than the namesake of the award did.

The same characteristics remained qualifications for the best pastor's wife award throughout its history, but now they were in reverse order. The most important quality for a pastor's wife was not to earn national recognition in her own right but rather to support the ministry of her husband. Patterson was careful to emphasize that even when Draper served in the denominational arena, as required for the award, she did so as a wife alongside her husband, not merely of her own accord.[21]

The best pastor's wife in 1963 preached internationally and exercised both state and national denominational leadership.

The best pastor's wife in 2006 held the ladder for her husband to climb.

What Pastors' Wives Taught Each Other

When Willie Dawson served alongside her husband at First Baptist Church Waco, only one or two books for ministry wives were published every decade or so.[22] By the time she was nominated for the Distinguished Service Award in 1963, the number of books meant for pastors' wives was growing. At that time, they were split between different denominations, with evangelicals publishing a number of these books but not the majority. By the late 1970s and '80s, this began to change. It is significant, I think, that the uptick in pastor's wife material correlates with increased interest in the pastor's wife role—exemplified by Barbara O'Chester's wildly successful retreats for pastors' wives during the 1970s. Indeed, O'Chester later won the Willie Turner Dawson Award for her "dynamic retreat ministry."[23] Elizabeth Flowers writes that O'Chester deeply influenced how SBC ministry leaders understood womanhood and that by the 1990s, her retreat ministry "boasted 20,000 women per year at her church alone."[24] Given such increased visibility in the pastor's wife role, it isn't surprising that Christian publishers targeted this growing consumer market.

Of the 150 books we examined for this study, one-quarter were published between 1950 and 1989. The message of these books reflects a diversity of pastors' wives—from women like Willie Dawson to women like Ruth Bobo. Resist the pastor's wife mold (i.e., you don't have to play the piano if you don't want to), they urged, and find how God uniquely gifted you. Take, for example, Denise Turner's 1982 *Home Sweet Fishbowl: Confessions of a Minister's Wife*. She writes, "I used to be one of those ministers' wives whose identity is bound up in her husband's call. I proofread all of my spouse's sermons, tagged along to his seminars, and poured his coffee at his board meetings. The fact that I had no time left over for myself was irrelevant. There was no self. There was only the minister and his shadow." Then she learned to find and use her own talents, her own gifts, explaining that "whenever I'm not using any of the abilities that God has given me, I just don't feel very good about myself."[25] Turner's words show that she once thought the role of pastor's wife was "bound up in her husband's call." Her words also show that she found this mold (serving in the shadow of the pastor) obscured her own gifting. So she pushed against it and urged other pastors' wives to follow suit.

Some of these earlier books made it clear that the authors weren't against the idea of "ministers' husbands," but simply chose to focus on ministers' wives, because they comprised the majority of ministry relationships.[26] *The Minister's Mate—Two for the Price of One?* explains, "We make no apology for having ministers' wives as the primary target for this resource. This is not to say that we believe males are the only suitable ministers, and therefore females are only suited as mates to the minister. It is to say that the current reality is that the vast majority of ministerial couples in our Convention are aligned in this more traditional way."[27] Published in 1986, *The Minister's Mate* is an SBC publication from the SBC Sunday School Board. In 1986, then, this recognition of men as potential ministry spouses indicates the SBC's awareness, even approval, of female pastors.

In short, similar themes appear within books from the 1950s to the 1980s, themes such as resisting stereotypes, finding one's unique spiritual gifts, prioritizing family time, and raising pastors' kids (PKs). To be sure, there are discussions about pastors' wives as hostesses, the importance of maintaining the appearance of one's home and body, and whether the role was a "calling." There are also discussions about the submission of wives and the headship of husbands—but they are less frequent and less rigid. In the case of Martha Nelson's 1977 *This Call We Share*, it is a short conversation that leans more egalitarian. As she writes, "We read Paul's admonitions to wives, interpreting them within the framework of our particular marriage and the times and culture in which we lived. If we promised to obey our husbands (we'd have agreed to almost anything in that romantic glow), our obedience was probably closest to the word's Latin derivative which means 'to listen to.' It worked for most of us. With our husbands we struggled toward oneness, giving a little, taking a little, misunderstanding sometimes—at our best, yielding to one another out of love."[28] An emphasis on female submission and male headship has long been part of the pastor's wife story, but it was a less visible, less consistent, and less critical part before the last decade of the twentieth century.

Diane Langberg's 1988 *Counsel for Pastors' Wives* helps us see the emerging shift in pastor's wife books. "Scripture is very clear that our first loyalty is, without question, to God himself," she writes. "Our relationship to him and our obedience to his Word are to be above any other priority in our lives. When anyone or anything would lead us to disobey him, we must obey God and not man—even if that man is one's husband."[29] Almost fifteen years later, Patterson's 2002 *A Handbook for Ministers' Wives* modifies Langberg's advice. "In matters of conscience in which you have a word from God, you will obey the Lord rather than any man; but in the inevitable choices of life, you will learn to give and take, to cooperate with each other, and ultimately to defer to your husband as the divinely appointed head of your household, for better or worse."[30] Women should submit to God rather than man—unless that man happens to be their divinely appointed husband.

In the 1990s, the number of books written for pastors' wives began to increase significantly (more than two-thirds of the books we examined were published after 1989). We also find in the 1990s an increase in clearly articulated expectations of male headship and female submission (what I have categorized as submission language).[31] By the early 2000s, it is fair to say that books published for the evangelical pastor's wife role largely support complementarian teachings. This finding fits with Melody Maxwell's description of evangelical women's ministries, which were growing rapidly in the 1980s and '90s. "Instead of urging women to consider issues of gender equality that had previously been significant to a number of evangelicals, most women's ministries propagated conservative views about gender." The pastor's wife epitomized biblical womanhood, so it is no surprise that the increasingly conservative trend in pastor's wife literature matches an increasingly conservative trend among evangelical women more broadly.[32]

Beverly Hyles, wife of Jack Hyles, provides an example. She weaves male headship and female submission throughout her entire 1990 book *Life as Viewed from the Goldfish Bowl*.[33] "Are you pleasing your husband?" she asks her reader. "'Do you know what He [sic] wants? Do you periodically stop and ask him if there is something he would like to have changed or if you have become perhaps something other than he wants?' You should know what pleases him, and you should do everything you can to do what pleases him." This includes, she continues, making him your "top priority," "accepting him unconditionally," and always being ready to "satisfy your husband's physical needs. I mean all the time."[34]

Much work still needs to be done on the genre of pastor's wife literature, and I plan to continue the work I have started. But this preliminary study suggests a measurable shift in perceptions about the pastor's wife role. While authors writing between 1923 and 2024 mostly agree that a pastor's wife should support her husband, it isn't until the late twentieth century that more began to expect submission too. (In the final chapter, we will consider another measurable difference within the pastor's wife genre— that of Black authors.)

Why the increase in submission language from the 1990s onward?

Let me give you three reasons (and they are interconnected).

First, in 1989 a statement (previously written in 1987) was published in *Christianity Today* that, in some ways, expanded on the SBC 1984 declaration that only men could be pastors because of the sin of Eve. It is known as the Danvers Statement and formally summarizes complementarian theology. The Bible, from Genesis to Paul, specifies God-ordained gender differences that reserve leadership within church and family to men. It prescribes that husbands are called to leadership and wives are called to submit. Four of the six SBC seminaries adopted the Danvers Statement as a confessional document, and three SBC seminary presidents still serve on the council for the Council on Biblical Manhood and Womanhood, the self-defined "flagship organization for complementarianism" that is housed at Southern Baptist Theological Seminary.

Second, in 1991 Crossway Books published the first edition of John Piper and Wayne Grudem's *Recovering Biblical Manhood and Womanhood: A Response to Evangelical Feminism.* Seth Dowland describes this volume as clarifying complementarianism. "By enlisting a lineup of leading evangelical intellectuals to write sustained defenses of male headship, *Recovering Biblical Manhood and Womanhood* reinforced the conclusions of the Danvers Statement, which the book reprinted in an appendix."[35] Essay after essay reinforces the crux of complementarian theology, that God called men to lead and women to submit. Let's remember that *Christianity Today* named *Recovering Biblical Manhood and Womanhood* as book of the year for 1992.[36]

Third, the SBC made two revisions to the Baptist Faith and Message, the denomination's confessional document. It added the "submission statement" in 1998, declaring that a wife should submit graciously to the servant leadership of her husband, followed by the 2000 declaration that only men could serve in the office of pastor. "While both men and women are gifted for service in the church, the office of pastor is limited to men as qualified by Scripture."[37]

In sum, between 1987 and 2000, the largest evangelical denomination (which controlled several seminaries, religious institutions, and a publishing company), another influential evangelical publisher, and a small, interconnected group of male leaders who together exerted a disproportionate amount of influence over evangelical culture made decisive and public demonstrations affirming the "biblical" teaching of male headship and female submission. Neither Piper nor Grudem, two of the most influential of these evangelical leaders, are Southern Baptists, but through their shared participation in the Evangelical Theological Society as well as the Council on Biblical Manhood and Womanhood (which they both helped found), they colluded well. "Functioning as theological think tanks, CBMW and SBC seminaries provided resources for denominations, organizations, and local churches, helping to build a network of evangelicals committed to advancing a patriarchal version of Christianity," explains Kristin Du Mez.[38] Indeed, two chapters from Du Mez's *Jesus and John Wayne*, "Tender Warriors" and "Holy Balls," confirm Elizabeth Flowers's argument that Southern Baptists both "reflect and illumine"[39] evangelicalism—influencing even as they are influenced.

From this perspective, it makes sense that at the same historical moment when submission language crafted by the SBC and CBMW began to flood the evangelical world—rewriting the Baptist Faith and Message and taking over the glossy pages of *Christianity Today*—such language began filling books for pastors' wives too.

Lorna Dobson's 1995 book *I'm More Than the Pastor's Wife* is another notable example of the rise of submission language. One of her chapters is titled "Mutual Submissions: Partnering in Godliness." While Dobson is not SBC, her language echoes the 1984 SBC resolution. As a reminder, the 1984 SBC resolution states that women are to be excluded from pastoral leadership "to preserve a submission God requires because the man was first in creation and the woman was first in the Edenic fall."[40] In a similar vein, Dobson emphasizes the "Edenic fall" in her explanation of a submissive role for wives: "Since Adam and Eve acted with a spirit of independence as well as disobedience, human relationships have been fractured by a need that can be met only through the restoring grace of God and sacrifice of Christ on the cross. Harmony in marriage is achieved by mutual consent, with the husband mirroring Christ's example of servanthood, being the primary initiator of love, sensitivity, provision, and spiritual concern for the family. The wife responds to his initiative by submitting to Christ and to her husband."[41] Dobson's words are almost certainly informed by the rapid emergence of complementarian teachings between 1984 and 2000. Dobson does make an insightful point when she argues that being a minister's wife is important not only for pastors' wives' ministry but because they "are observed and therefore are role models for others."[42]

The impact of pastor's wife books like Hyles's and Dobson's has been twofold: reinforcing the importance of submission for pastors' wives and, in turn, reinforcing the importance of submission for all the women who look up to their pastors' wives.

The Power of the Pastor's Wife Example

Do you remember when Starbucks introduced quotes on their cups? I do.

It was around 2005, and in my role as youth pastor's wife, I had started a coffee hour for teenage girls. We'd hang out for an hour or two at a coffee shop, play games, and sometimes have a short devotional.

Today, Waco has more coffee shops than I can keep up with. In 2005, I could count them on one hand. At first, we rotated among them, but the girls increasingly just wanted to go to Starbucks. So we did—until my husband came home after the pastor spoke with him.

Apparently, a parent had complained to the pastor. Starbucks, according to the parent, promoted anti-Christian values with the quotes from famous Americans that it featured on coffee cups. I didn't know it at the time, but this accusation against Starbucks was started by Concerned Women for America, who claimed the Starbucks quotes were part of a liberal agenda.

Honestly, I'd never read the quotes on the cups. Mine were usually covered by a cardboard sleeve. I'm not sure the girls paid much attention either. We were too busy playing Apples to Apples and laughing.

But it didn't matter.

It was suggested to me that, as a model for these young girls, I should do better and not introduce them to Starbucks's anti-Christian values.

128

I was angry, in part because they hadn't talked to me about it first. I expressed my anger to my husband. He agreed with me, but we knew the smart thing to do was acquiesce even if we thought the complaint was nonsense. So, at least for a while, the Starbucks gatherings stopped.

It is ironic to me now when I realize that, regardless of where I took the high school girls to get coffee, as the youth pastor's wife I was serving as a model of biblical womanhood, whether I wanted to or not. Just by being a pastor's wife serving in an unofficial ministry role, I was modeling that concept to these girls. My husband was paid for the ministry he did; as his wife, I was expected to serve in ministry as an unpaid volunteer.

Benjamin Knoll and Cammie Jo Bolin, as research for their book *She Preached the Word: Women's Ordination in Modern America*, conducted a national survey on "Gender and Religious Representation," which they describe as "a series of national representative public opinion surveys" that gathered data "from hundreds of American congregants from all major religious traditions." They also conducted several face-to-face interviews with congregants from across denominations.[43] One of the questions they asked was how the gender of their church leaders mattered. While respondents stated that personality and experience mattered more than gender, they also stated that female clergy served as positive role models for the younger generation.

Knoll and Bolin found that another sort of female role model existed within congregations. They write, "Other individuals from traditions that do not ordain women, or that do ordain women but who currently have a man serving as the primary religious leader, mentioned the 'first lady' (the pastor's wife) or other women who teach Sunday school or lead studies of religious texts as serving as role models for women within the church."[44] Knoll and Bolin found that these women not only served as role models but compensated for a lack of female clergy. Respondents explained how the pastor's wife and other women serving in volunteer and less authoritative roles showed that women were not limited within their churches. As one respondent explained, "There are so many other avenues in our church to lead. Whether it's in women's ministry or whether it's in a Bible study. . . . It's not like some churches where the women are silent and they don't do anything. I mean we have so many opportunities within our congregation for women to step up and lead. . . . To my knowledge, no one has had an issue with not being able to preach or lead an adult ministry."[45]

Or, as another explained, "Women can do a host of things. It's just that the office of the pastor is reserved for men." Knoll and Bolin summarize this response well: "Because women see that they have 'plenty of opportunities to serve,' even in religious traditions in which they cannot be the primary religious leader, they may not think that their congregation's policy on female ordination 'hinders [them] from teaching or being effective in the ministry or having a voice.' By looking to the ways in which they can be involved, women within congregations that do not ordain women can still feel that '[they're] all important people' and not underprivileged."[46]

I sat back in my chair the first time I read that. It hit hard.

On the one hand, I'm so glad my role as pastor's wife has empowered women to see that they have a pathway to meaningful and important ministry. "Just being married to a pastor puts you in a position of leadership and gives you influence over many people's lives," explain Lori Wilhite and Brandi Wilson in their 2013 book *Leading and Loving It: Encouragement for Pastors' Wives and Women in Leadership*. "You have an impact on the lives of your church family and ministry."[47] On the other hand, I'm troubled that my role as pastor's wife within a congregation that opposed women's pastoral leadership helped to perpetuate a theology that limits women too.

By providing women an alternative to professional clergy, the role of pastor's wife empowers women to find many important ministry opportunities.

By providing women an alternative to professional clergy, the role of pastor's wife can undermine the professional ministry of women too.

From this perspective, it's worth noting that as the role of evangelical pastor's wife grew in visibility and significance during the last decades of the twentieth century and into the early twenty-first century, it corresponded to the decreasing visibility of women serving in professional ministry. Kate Bowler, for example, found that women in ministry are invisible on the websites for staff of SBC churches. "The fact that Southern Baptist Convention congregations do not have a female pastor is not surprising," she writes. "What was surprising, though, was how much they obscure their entire staff other than the male ordained clergy. SBC congregations were especially difficult to determine if they had women on staff, much less the titles held by these women."[48]

Except, on reflection, I no longer find it that surprising.

Gendered representation matters.

For more than thirty years, the SBC has been rendering their most visible and acceptable women in ministry, their pastors' wives, as unofficial and unpaid volunteers who are designated by God to support the professional ministry of men. Should we be surprised that this is how they treat their female staff too?

Before we move on to the next chapter, consider your own experience with pastors' wives. Perhaps what you have seen is different from what I have described with the SBC. Perhaps it has included women married to ministers who have maintained their own identity (either staying home with children or working outside the home) or shared ministry more equally with their husbands, even becoming co-pastors. The pastor's wife books written by Jill Briscoe and Kay Warren reflect this more egalitarian impulse. While writing this book, I met Leanne Friesen (currently the executive minister for Canadian Baptists of Ontario and Quebec) who shares a vocation in ministry with her husband Dallas. They even served on staff together at a church before her election to the executive minister role—but in their case she was the senior pastor and her husband was the associate. If your experience is more like this, then I am grateful.

But if this is your experience, it suggests to me that the pastors' wives you know were not formed by the steadily increasing number of pastor's wife books published in the evangelical (and evangelical-adjacent) world that emphasized women's submission.

It suggests to me that the pastors' wives you know weren't formed by the SBC seminaries, either.[49]

The pastors' wives you know weren't influenced by Patterson's reign as the "matriarch of complementarianism" who "worked with leading evangelicals outside the Southern Baptist context" as well as within the SBC world to "construct a more nuanced understanding of biblical womanhood called 'complementarianism.'"[50]

Who is the best pastor's wife?

By the year 2000, in the evangelical world that influenced and was influenced by the SBC, it isn't Willie Dawson.

It is the pastor's wife desired by James Duncan in 1959 (remember him, the pastor who weighed in on the Distinguished Service Award): a "companion" who supports and submits to her husband.

7

The (SBC) Road Less Traveled

It was spring 2021.

I picked up an advance reader copy of *The Making of Biblical Womanhood* and walked down a hall of the Graduate School at Baylor University.

"Dean Lyon," I said, knocking on the open door. "I don't know what is going to happen, but I think you should know what I have written." Larry Lyon, professor of sociology, dean of the Graduate School, and vice provost at Baylor University, was my supervisor at the time. He took the book from me and later read it, then preordered copies for everyone in the graduate school. Then he sent me a YouTube link.

"Beth, you've got to watch this *Designing Women* episode," he said. I laughed, relieved by his response. I remembered *Designing Women* from my teenage years. Set in Atlanta in the late 1980s, the storyline revolves around four white women and a Black man who run an interior design business. I didn't remember this particular episode,[1] so I watched it.

Lyon was right. It is an incredible episode. In one scene, one of the protagonists, Charlene, tells her Southern Baptist pastor that she can no longer attend a church that rejects women in ministry. Just listen to this dialogue.

> CHARLENE. I've been up all night, and I just can't figure out how I can belong to a church that doesn't think I am fit to preach God's word.
>
> REV. NUNN. You want to be a minister?
>
> CHARLENE. Well, I've never told anyone this before, but as a matter of fact I did. When I was about six or seven, I got my first Bible. It had my name embossed in gold across the front. My parents gave it to me the night I was baptized. I'll never forget it came with this beautiful cardboard bookmark that had Jesus with a pink halo painted on it. . . . I couldn't take my eyes off of it. I thought, "Boy, that's for me." I was gonna travel the world preaching and teaching—maybe even become a saint.
>
> REV. NUNN. What happened?
>
> CHARLENE. I don't know. I guess I figured I couldn't make saint. Anyway, my point is, I had that dream because no one told me I couldn't. But what about all those other little girls out there, hundreds of them, just waiting to become ministers and spend their lives preaching God's word—except for the fact that you and a bunch of other people got together and decided that God doesn't want that? That just doesn't make any sense, Reverend Nunn. I mean, for what possible reason would God not want that?
>
> REV. NUNN. That's not for us to say, Charlene. I don't think we should question his wisdom.
>
> CHARLENE. I'm not. I'm questioning yours.

My jaw dropped the first time I heard Charlene's words. Baptists today may have forgotten our long history of women in ministry, but in the 1980s it was still a memory that Charlene knew.

Leon McBeth estimated in his *Women in Baptist Life* that more than 1,600 women were enrolled in SBC seminaries in 1977, and many of them intended to seek ordination after graduation.[2] By 1982 there were so many SBC women in ministry that the Women's Missionary Union (WMU) sponsored a Women in Ministry Dinner alongside the annual SBC meeting. This proved popular enough for a similar gathering in 1983, attracting thirty-three Baptist women ministers, and by the 1984 SBC annual meeting, more than 250 women and men attended a gathering for women in ministry. When Charlene told her pastor that she dreamed of being a minister because no one told her she couldn't, she was speaking historical truth.

My favorite line from the episode, though, is spoken by another character, Bernice. "Just remember," she says to Reverend Nunn, "after Christ was crucified on the cross, and all his men had gone home, it was women who stayed until the bitter end. And it was women who first heralded the news of his resurrection. So just put that in your pulpit and smoke it."

Who knew that a 1980s sitcom would encapsulate, in less than thirty minutes, so much of the SBC debate about women in ministry? While it is true that many Southern Baptists would not have declared Charlene unfit for pastoral leadership in the 1980s, by the year 2000 most would have. The transition to moving women out of ministry in the SBC was just that—a transition.

It was a transition that intersected with increasing emphasis on the role of the pastor's wife.

Who Is a Minister?

I have gone to just one conference for pastors' wives.

It was one of my favorite women's conferences that I attended. It was nice to be around other women who knew what it was like to be a pastor's wife within evangelicalism. One woman shocked me when, after learning I was a professor as well as a pastor's wife, she patted my knee and said, "Don't let them get you down, honey. You be who God called you." I can't tell you how often I have thought of her words since writing *The Making of Biblical Womanhood*. If she reads this book, I want her to know I am grateful.

I remember some of the sessions I attended too. One of the speakers performed an interpretative dialogue in the character of a New Testament woman. It was so powerful that, after she finished, a crowd of women came forward to ask questions. One wanted to know how she was able to leave her children for speaking engagements. The speaker explained she told her children it was the ministry that God had called her to and thanked them for letting her go speak. Another wanted to know how the speaker wrote her material and, as a follow up, whether she could have a copy of the dialogue for use in her church. The speaker explained that the dialogue was her intellectual property but that she would be happy to perform it at the woman's church in a professional capacity. That answer caught the questioner by surprise; she hadn't realized the speaker's ministry was a paid job. Even though the speaker did ministry, she had not been perceived as a professional minister.

Historically speaking, the perception is common. The question has never been whether women are *fulfilling the function of ministry* in the church—they always have been. The question has always been whether their function of ministry is recognized as *paid, professional ministry*.

What if I told you that the SBC conversation about who qualified as a paid, professional minister (i.e., who can be ordained) became a concern at the same time that—claims of biblical inerrancy notwithstanding—external cultural changes challenged both male power and local church autonomy to define a minister?

Let me tell you what happened.

Let's start with the 1973 annual meeting of the Southern Baptist Convention, where a pastor's wife stood on the floor of the convention and publicly challenged women's ability to serve in independent leadership roles (such as pastor). Jessie Tillison Sappington, the wife of Richard Sappington, pastor of Cloverleaf Baptist Church in Houston, Texas, proposed a resolution titled "On the Place of Women in Christian Service."[3] Because "there is a great attack by the members of most women's liberation movements upon scriptural precepts of the woman's place in society," the resolution declared, and because "the theme of the Convention is 'Share the Word Now' and this Word we share is explicitly clear on this subject," it should be resolved that God's "order of authority" is "man the head of the woman." When the Committee on Resolutions tried to soften her language, clarifying that the SBC appreciated women's "leadership," Sappington refused. Her resolution was not binding on local churches. What it did was provide a warning to SBC women that their place in Christian service was under the authority of men.[4]

I can't say for sure why Sappington chose 1973 to introduce a denominational resolution that challenged women's independent pastoral leadership. I do know that she couched it in terms of biblical inerrancy (an "attack . . . upon scriptural precepts of the woman's place in society"); she couched it in terms of opposition between "women's liberation" and the Word of God; and she couched it in terms of God's "order of authority"—that men are called to lead and women are called to follow.[5]

The timing of her proposal seems significant.

Her resolution came one year after a Baptist church in New York became SBC, thereby transforming its female pastor, Druecillar Fordham, into the denomination's first ordained Black woman pastor. By 1973, not only were growing numbers of white women receiving ordination, but an ordained Black woman served as a senior pastor at an SBC church.[6]

Sappington's resolution—coming as it did from a respected pastor's wife—passed by an easy majority. While she did not speak specifically against female pastors, another pastor's wife did. Joyce Rogers, the wife of Adrian Rogers (pastor of Bellevue Baptist

Church in Memphis, Tennessee, and later president of the Southern Baptist Convention in 1979), argued that women's leadership
is only appropriate "among women and children."[7] I agree with
Elizabeth Flowers that, even though Sappington's resolution did
not directly address female ordination, it was a portent of things
to come. Another pastor's wife named Dorothy Patterson would
not only carry Sappington's torch to the SBC finish line, but—as
the queen of complementarianism—she also would help make
SBC's endorsement of female submission and rejection of female
pastors mainstream evangelical.

Flowers's book *Into the Pulpit* provides an in-depth analysis of
the SBC gender wars and their connection to broader American
culture. In her chapter focused on the 1970s, Flowers shows how
SBC concerns about female autonomy and independent leadership
roles coincided with increasing agency for women. As students
in my freshman history class learn, it was only in the 1960s and
'70s that women in the US gained legal protections against wage
discrimination, credit discrimination, sexual harassment, and
gender discrimination within the workplace. They also gained
legal access to birth control and abortion. My students are most
shocked to learn that women still have not gained "equality of
rights under the law." Without the Equal Rights Amendment, the
rights affirmed by the US Constitution are still not guaranteed
equally to women. The import of this has been especially poignant
to students in my Votes for Women history class, as they watch in
real time conservative courts (at local, state, and national levels)
threaten access to no-fault divorce and even a doctor's discretion
to perform life-saving procedures for pregnant women.[8]

Flowers connects the dots among the SBC (and more broadly
evangelical) rejection of female pastors, their rejection of equal
rights for women, and the growing leadership of pastors' wives
in promoting traditional womanhood. Joyce Rogers, for example,
drew inspiration from the biblical womanhood retreats hosted
by Barbara O'Chester during the 1970s. These began as retreats

for pastors' wives but "became so popular that she opened the doors to all women." Flowers describes how these weekend retreats taught women about "wifely submission, child-rearing, and the act of marriage (or sex)." A friend of O'Chester, Rogers published an influential pamphlet in 1974 which articulated "biblical justification for submission." Along with arguing that submission "freed women," she proclaimed that biblical leadership roles for women came only by submitting to male authority. "Any responsibility that demanded she serve as a king rather than a queen violated God's word," summarizes Flowers.[9]

If we were in my classroom, I would pause for a minute.

Then I would make sure my students understood not only the connection Flowers makes between the rise of the notion of biblical womanhood and the subsequent decline of women's independent pastoral leadership but also the role played by pastors' wives in this shift. Because of the pastor's wife role, the SBC could argue for its support of women in ministry.

Of course, women are free to lead in the SBC. They are free to lead however God has called them, right? Because God—at least in the SBC—only calls women to ministry roles that are subordinate to male authority.

For the SBC, the pastor's wife became more than a helpmeet to her pastor husband; she also became a helpmeet for the SBC's rejection of female pastors.

Let me add one more possible piece to this puzzle. I confess I am not quite sure how it fits, but I think it does—at the very least because it helps contextualize the SBC's focus on ordination during the latter decades of the twentieth century.

You see, it was also in the 1960s and '70s that the SBC began to redefine who could be ordained. At first, it expanded who could be ordained. In May 1959, the Southern Baptist Convention adopted a resolution declaring that missionaries serving under the Foreign Mission Board of the SBC "are in the same category as ordained ministers as far as Christian purpose, commitment, and vocation are concerned." Indeed, it continued, "we declare the fact . . . that those whom our denominational terminology has termed 'commissioned missionaries' are 'commissioned ministers.'"[10]

Just let that sink in for a minute.

With one resolution, the SBC turned every missionary serving under the authority of the Foreign Mission Board into a minister of the gospel.

Why did it do this? At least part of the reason—as a file on the IRS and the parsonage exemption in the Southern Baptist Historical Library and Archives files for the SBC Executive Committee make clear—was to help more SBC ministers have access to a tax exemption. The IRS was making it increasingly clear that only those officially ordained to the office of ministry and fulfilling professional ministry functions (performing sacraments, conducting worship services, and overseeing or teaching in religious institutions) could receive what has become known as the parsonage exemption. This exemption allows "ministers of the gospel" to set aside a portion of their salaries as a tax-exempt housing allowance. From ministers of education to chaplains to missionaries to even seminary professors, the SBC began to ordain positions that were once only commissioned into "ministers of the gospel"[11]— primarily, it seems, for the goal of receiving this tax exemption.

In its zeal to help their "ministers of the gospel" financially, I think the SBC failed to consider the impact of more expansive language used for ordination.

It had the potential, for example, to compound problems for the IRS. By the early 1980s, so many people qualified as "ministers of the gospel" that the IRS began cracking down on those claiming exemption. The Treasury Department even recommended doing away with the exemption in 1984. Too many people claimed to qualify, and it was too difficult to discern who really did. Moreover, the expanded definition of "minister of the gospel" deprived the government of a lot of revenue. The Treasury Department only relented from eliminating the tax break after more than 150 clergy wrote arguing that the exemption was necessary to make up for low clerical salaries.[12]

It also created problems for those advocating against female ordination. The SBC didn't have a problem with women doing the ministry work of missionaries, chaplains, and church planters. The SBC auxiliary Women's Missionary Union trained women exactly for these types of roles. "Girls in action, Girls in action, Mission study and mission action. Praying, giving money so, the world may know of Jesus' love." I remember singing those lyrics in my WMU training for preteen girls at my childhood SBC church. Go and do, our leaders taught us, because God called women too. The problem was that the more expansive definition of ordination increased accessibility for women who often served in nonpastoral roles. The outrage Sarah Lee and Kathy Hoppe experienced regarding their ordination in the early 1980s is a prime example of how this unexpected side effect caught the SBC off guard. They had intended the expanded definition of "ministers of the gospel" to help ministers of education and seminary professors obtain the tax exemption. Yet it allowed the wives of church planters to be ordained too.

Again, the SBC did not have a problem with Sarah Lee and Kathy Hoppe sharing in the ministry of their husbands. What the SBC had a problem with was these women receiving ordination for ministry roles. I find it rather interesting that, just as the IRS was curbing eligibility for the tax exemption by demanding higher thresholds for who qualified as a minister, the SBC shifted to a more conservative view on women in ministry that refused to ordain women, thereby excluding women from the tax exemption. In 1974, for example, Tom Reynolds made a motion to amend the SBC Constitution under "Missionary Qualifications" to restrict women from roles that functioned as pastors (such as chaplain).[13] The motion failed in 1974, but by the 1980s the SBC North American Mission Board (previously the Home Mission Board) was defunding church plants led by women pastors and by the early 2000s no longer endorsing ordained women chaplains.[14]

Of course, the tax exemption wasn't the only factor at play for the SBC as it argued against women's ordination. But it was a factor.

Ordination became the golden ticket for the parsonage exemption even as ordination became increasingly difficult for SBC women to achieve. Women could—and did—function as ministers if they were okay with facing more challenges than their male counterparts, including not receiving the authority, title, or tax benefits men received for the same work. SBC churches welcomed women to do the work of ministry—as long as those women were content not being recognized officially as ministers. Elgee Bentley wrote in 1989, "Ordination has become Southern Baptists' weapon of choice." Refusing to ordain women allowed the SBC to reserve its "most desirable jobs," which qualified for the most benefits, for men.[15]

Who is a minister?

For the SBC, anyone who performs the function of ministry and is recognized by their church as fulfilling this function is eligible for ordination.

Unless the person performing the function of ministry is a woman.

As Susan Lockwood's SBC pastor father told her when she started seminary in the early 1980s, "Don't get ordained. You can do all kinds of ministries and I want you to do that. But don't get ordained because that will just create such a storm around you and might keep you from having certain opportunities. So just don't get ordained, okay?"[16]

Do the work of a minister, the SBC told women—just don't be ordained as one.

A Pastor's Wife and Her Pastor Daughter

In November 2022, I was in the Texas Collection archives at Baylor, researching an academic article. My focus was Bill Estep, a historian who taught at Southwestern Seminary for more than fifty years.

I got sidetracked by a pastor's wife whose story encapsulates the growing tension between the role of pastor's wife and that of female pastor.

The pastor's wife's name was Peggy Bartley. She and her husband, Jim, were career missionaries in Uruguay, sent by the Southern Baptist International Mission Board and serving from 1952 to 1993. Jim was a seminary student and pastor when he met Peggy in 1951; he already felt called to be a missionary in South America and was very serious about this call. He had ended a previous engagement because the young woman "had no sense of calling to foreign missions." Three months after meeting Peggy in 1951, "the sweetest girl I had ever known," he asked her to marry him. "I never knew anyone could be so happy as I became," Jim wrote.[17] They married in January 1952 and by January 1953 were living in Uruguay. They served for forty-one years as SBC missionaries in Uruguay until retiring in 1993.

Peggy began writing her own progress reports back to the SBC Foreign Board (now known as the International Mission Board or IMB) in 1954. As a ministry couple, Jim and Peggy received twice the pay as a single missionary. He was responsible for the ministry work; she was responsible for providing the domestic support that would help her husband succeed.[18]

Peggy's annual reports to the SBC Foreign Mission Board are what caught my attention. She identified fully with the "home and family" designation for her role, describing herself as a "missionary homemaker" and her work outside of the home as flexible and supportive.[19] When she taught for the Baptist Theological Institute in Montevideo, Uruguay, she stressed she wanted to "be able to teach in a satisfactory way whatever I might be called upon to teach." Also, when her husband later became institute director, she expressed her uncertainty about how his new role would impact her. "I trust that if any added responsibilities are mine because of my husband's change from professor to director that they will be made clear and that I will accomplish them to the best of my ability," she wrote.[20]

Yet, regardless of her full-time responsibilities at home with four young children and a husband who traveled frequently, she did a remarkable amount of ministry work. Listen to just some of what she did between July 1954 and July 1955:

> In addition to making the usual pastoral visits with my husband I have served as counselor of the Y.W.A.'s [Young Women in Action], director of the Sunbeams [a Christian education program for children ages four to nine] until the last of June at which time a young woman was found to replace me, treasurer of the W.M.U. [Women's Missionary Union, which was in charge of the Sunbeam program mentioned above], and until January superintendent of the nursery department in Sunday School. In January I gave up my work in the nursery department to become teacher of the class of young women from 17–24 years of age. I was privileged to speak at two of the trimestral meetings of our Women's Federation. In connection with my part on one of these programs I translated from the English to Spanish a stewardship study book for the Sunbeams. In regard to my language study—for the majority of this past year I have studied with a private teacher having at some times two classes a week and at other times only one class.[21]

At this time, she was the mother of a toddler and around seven months pregnant with her second child. She also continued in her "usual duties" of household chores, cooking, cleaning, and caring for her young daughter. One year later, in her third annual report, she expressed the hope that in the future, when her kids were older, she would be able to "give a larger percentage of my time directly to the work."[22] By July 1961 she was expecting her fourth child. She had been teaching summer Bible studies, serving as a nursery teacher, teaching teenage girls, serving as president of the associational WMU, serving as treasurer for the national WMU, serving as secretary for an ad hoc group of pastors and missionaries who gathered monthly, serving as leader for a monthly missions study, and working as a counselor to GAs (Girls in Action). But she decided to resign the last in anticipation of her fourth child. As she said, "I have seen the necessity of limiting my church activities" on account of her parenting responsibilities.[23]

But I'm not sure she did limit her ministry work.

Not really.

By 1966 Peggy had completed her master of religious education degree from Southwestern Baptist Theological Seminary (using their furlough from December 1964 through June 1966 to finish coursework). Also, in addition to the rest of her activities, she was teaching at the Baptist Theological Institute. The amount of ministry work Peggy accomplished and time she invested in supporting the ministry of her husband seems astonishing, especially considering expectations that she would be the primary caregiver in charge of household responsibilities. The SBC mission board defined her duties as domestic. Yet, by her own hand, Peggy felt like she wasn't doing enough as a missionary. "My two major weaknesses as a missionary are difficult to admit because they are such basic points," she once confessed. "My devotional life isn't all that it should be and one of my goals is to change this. My other weakness is in personal witnessing."[24]

As the children finished high school and, one by one, returned to the US for college, Peggy struggled with their absences. The miles separating Peggy from her children weighed on her until she eventually sought mental health treatment. In 1982 she wrote that "the doctor said I had the classic symptoms of depression." She took a three-month medical leave, received counseling, and proclaimed "God's grace" had brought her through. "I still find being separated from all the children difficult and many times I lack the motivation in the work that I would like to have, but I trust and pray that in due season He will honor me with the blessing of happiness and fulfillment in the work once again," she told the SBC mission board in her annual report.[25]

One child brought her great joy by choosing a ministry vocation. By 1969 Peggy reported that Nancy, the oldest child, was demonstrating "spiritual depth" and "evangelistic zeal." Peggy expressed hope that perhaps her investments in the home front as a missionary would finally bear fruit. They had. Jim Bartley reported on July 6, 1982, that "Nancy has become our only child in the pastorate. She is pastoring a Spanish-speaking church in Chicago."[26]

Peggy and Nancy Bartley provide a fascinating example of ministry options available for women even in the early 1980s. When I started reading the Bartley papers, I did not know about Peggy's ministry as a pastor's wife or her daughter's ministry, which included service as a pastor. Nancy's parents had commented on her faith trajectory in many of their letters, including how she felt called by God into ministry. Of course, despite her SBC missionary upbringing and her own husband's SBC seminary training, Nancy's congregation in Chicago (which she saw as a mission opportunity) was mainline Protestant instead of evangelical.[27]

Nancy's SBC parents were not upset about her vocational choice. They express no condemnation of their daughter's ministry calling nor her pastoring outside of the SBC. Jim Bartley doesn't even seem concerned about reporting to his SBC employers that his daughter had become a pastor. Jim and Peggy express only pride and joy.

Isn't that interesting?

Did Peggy and Nancy know about the economic forces that had been shaping their ministry roles for the past few decades? I suspect Peggy did not know that her role as a pastor's wife might be disadvantaging the paycheck of her daughter. A 2017 article in the *Sociology of Religion* journal suggests that the inability of female clergy to "offer the informal benefit of a 'clergy spouse'" might be one reason that women in ministry are paid less than men. Listen to what it argues:

> A "pastor's wife" was expected to play a role in the life of the congregation, often in an unpaid capacity. Some of their tasks included menial work such as making coffee as well as substantive labor such as being active participants in worship services and assisting with children and youth. This role marked an important and informal benefit to the congregations when hiring a male clergy person. In contrast, husbands of female clergy are not held to the same expectation. In many cases, "the pastor's husband" does not attend their wives' services or volunteer to be a more active participant in congregational life. This lack of a "pastor's husband" may be affecting pay of the women clergy, as they may be receiving less pay because congregations assume they will not be able to offer this informal benefit.[28]

It seems plausible that, given the two-for-one deal with married male clergy, congregations might also privilege male candidates—who brought a pastor's wife—over female candidates whose husbands would be less engaged for pastoral positions. Nancy became the pastor of a Spanish-speaking congregation. Growing up bilingual in South America would have been a clear asset for her, perhaps offsetting any concerns about her sex that the church might have had. But—despite the fact that Nancy did the same type of work as her father, even taking on a first church at about the same age—evidence suggests that she would have earned less, perhaps significantly less, than he did.

Peggy, on the mission field far away from Baptist politics and furloughing mostly in the company of Southwestern Baptist Theological Seminary before it was taken over by the conservative faction, may not have known how pastors' wives like Joyce Rogers and Dorothy Patterson were actively working against women becoming pastors. I do suspect Peggy would have learned that a pastor's income came to benefit from an IRS tax break since Jim would have met the qualifications for "minister of the gospel." She might not have known, though, that her daughter would be less likely to receive this tax break. She might not have known "how the parsonage exemption intersects with sex discrimination concerns."[29] Despite her pastoral office, Nancy would need to prove ordination to claim the tax exemption. Evidence shows that women face more challenges than men in obtaining ordination for the same ministry work.

In short, by the time Nancy Bartley Gatlin became a pastor in 1982, women in ministry faced more economic challenges than men, in addition to the "usual" challenges regarding denominational support. They were discovering that the existence of trained pastors' wives who came two-for-one alongside their ministry husbands had the potential to limit not only the salaries of female pastors but also their opportunities to be hired.

Pastors' wives, in contrast, were becoming more visible throughout the evangelical world. By 1992, for example, the SBC had launched the Women's Enrichment Ministry program for the broader denomination and all six SBC seminaries had established women's programs. While not focused exclusively on ministry wives, both the denominational and seminary programs taught the concept of biblical womanhood (a theology of Christian womanhood that emphasized female submission and male headship) and developed programming specifically for ministry wives.[30]

By 1997 Al and Mary Mohler had established the Seminary Wives Institute (SWI) at Southern Baptist Theological Seminary to prepare "God-called ministers' wives" for service alongside their husbands. The 2023 Essentials courses were team-taught by faculty wives at Southern and required for all institute students. The assigned readings for these courses were *The Pastor's Wife* by Gloria Furman (2015) and Christine Hoover's *How to Thrive as a Pastor's Wife* (2022).[31] The courses focus on "your calling as a Christian and a ministry wife," "your influence on children," and "mentoring, time management, listening and discerning skills, hospitality, starting well/finishing well in various settings and more." The Leadership Skills for Women course (also required) examines "what leadership looks like for women in the home, the church, and in the community." Tom Schreiner and T. J. Betts also offered a Bible survey course (also required) that was described as "life-changing" by "two SBTS scholars who have taught grateful student wives in SWI for decades."[32]

Both Peggy and Nancy Bartley were women in ministry, but only one of them served in a ministry position that the SBC would recognize as a legitimate role for women.

The Road Less Traveled

My daughter's favorite Taylor Swift album is *1989*. For months now, she has been irritated with me because, instead of calling the album *1989*, I call it *1984*. I'm thankful my daughter doesn't have to belong to a church where the events of 1984 limit her. I'm thankful she doesn't know why I can't get that year out of my head.

It's the year Mrs. Minette Drumwright received the Willie Turner Dawson Award for Distinguished Minister's Wife from the SBC Pastors' Wives' Conference. Her husband, a pastor, professor at Southwestern Baptist Theological Seminary in Fort Worth, Texas, and former executive secretary-treasurer of the Arkansas Baptist State Convention, had died three years prior. Drumwright at the time worked for the Foreign Mission Board of the SBC and authored the *Women in the Church* college-level curriculum series for a seminary extension course created in 1977 specifically to better educate SBC ministers-in-training on the reality of women's work within the church, including women serving as pastors and leaders. One section was titled "Should Women Be Ordained? A Controversial Issue." It outlined examples of women in the Bible serving in ministry roles (such as deacon) as well as women serving in ministry in the SBC, including as pastors' wives. Indeed, it treats ministers' wives "like women in other roles" in church ministry.[33]

As one of the lessons states, "It is not too late for the church to be redemptive as it confronts the issue anew. Our best hope for a community of truly liberated human beings is the body of Christ . . . Jesus had the idea first: Because of him, women can be free! In the meantime, where is the church? Where are you?"[34]

At the same Kansas City meeting in 1984, the Southern Baptist Convention adopted a resolution on the role of women in SBC life that directly contradicted the curriculum created by Drumwright, now recognized as the SBC outstanding pastor's wife of the year. The resolution stated that SBC churches should stop ordaining women because "the Bible excludes women from pastoral leadership because the man was first in creation and the woman was first in the Edenic fall."[35] This resolution, its authors stated, was necessary to "preserve a submission that God requires" because man was created first and woman sinned first. Never mind the fact that, as a local newspaper remarked, a survey from around that time showed 80 percent of SBC female clergy had advanced graduate degrees, "far surpassing the average educational level of male Southern Baptist pastors."[36]

Ironically, many Baptists have argued that ordination is irrelevant. Because of the priesthood of all believers, everyone is a minister. "Baptists do not hold to the ecclesiastical tradition which leads some to consider ordination the channel through which the ordained receive special ministerial grace or powers not afforded to others," reminded H. H. Hobbs in the 1958 *Encyclopedia of Southern Baptists*. "The silence of the New Testament as to the form and meaning of the rite of ordination tends to indicate that it was nothing more than a setting apart or approval of the ordained for the work of ministry." Moreover, because of the Baptist emphasis on the autonomy of local churches, it is the prerogative of each congregation to decide whom it will ordain.[37]

It is true that this 1984 resolution was not binding on local churches.

It is true that SBC women continued to seek and receive ordination by local congregations.

It is also true that the 1984 resolution marks the tide turning against the ordination of SBC women. The denomination's pastoral women had joined together as "Women in Ministry," but it was only an unofficial group. "We don't have an official voice in the convention. Right now, there is no way to speak through an official channel, and there is no one to speak for us. We have no voice. We are not represented in any group in the convention. We're not fundamentalists, and we're really not part of the moderate group. We're not on any boards, and we're the last people who would be put on them," stated Susan Lockwood, pastor of Cornell Baptist Church in Chicago and cochair for the Women in Ministry resolutions committee.[38] SBC women had been preaching as pastors for many years, but their voices were becoming more difficult to hear.

By 1986 the Home Mission Board was defunding church plants pastored by women. Marv Knox reported in the *Baptist Press* on October 29, 1986: "The board voted October 8 not to give future financial support to any woman who is pastor of a local church." Female SBC pastors responded that they were "deeply grieved" and that the vote was "an obvious affront to Christian women and men who understand pastoral leadership as a gift given by the Holy Spirit not according to gender" as well as "an even greater affront to the autonomy of the local church and to the Good News of the gospel, which declares that there is neither male nor female in Christ."[39]

By 1989 the SBC Foreign Mission Board refused to appoint the husband-wife missionary team of Greg and Katrina Pennington because both were ordained. In an open letter to the Home Mission Board that year, pastor Nancy Hastings Sehested wrote, "You can continue your relentless efforts to contain the Spirit of God, squelch it, silence it and damage it, but it will not die in us. . . . I pray that we will have the courage to follow our Lord into a kingdom where enemies are loved, where sons and daughters prophesy, even behind pulpits, and where God's Spirit is poured out on all flesh."[40]

By 1998 Dorothy Patterson helped write an amendment to the Baptist Faith and Message that declared wives should submit graciously to their husbands. By 2000 the SBC had declared the pastoral office to be reserved for men.

Elizabeth Flowers concludes her study of the Southern Baptist gender wars by reminding us that Baptist battles impacted Christian attitudes and practices far beyond the SBC. "The struggle of Southern Baptist women and the Southern Baptist struggle over women also constitute a 'story within a story,' which is postwar American religion and culture."[41] The SBC may have only been "one of many evangelical denominations and subcultures" that began fighting over women in the 1970s, but it was also the biggest and loudest.[42] Two roads had always diverged for Southern Baptist women in ministry—one that led to independent ministry as a pastor, missionary, professor, preacher, or leader; and the other that led to dependent ministry through marriage to a minister. Through most of SBC history, these two paths ran side by side, even supporting each other. One had always been less traveled, but both had always been options. But after 1984, the road to independent ministry for SBC women became increasingly difficult to traverse. After the formation of the Council on Biblical Manhood and Womanhood and the publication of the Danvers Statement in *Christianity Today*, women throughout the conservative evangelical world shared the same challenges as SBC women.

The ministry of pastors' wives would help fill the gap, but there would be a catch.

In the words of Kate Bowler, the pastor's wife was the "safest" ministry position because it embodied conservative gender theology.[43] The pastor's wife was literally defined by her relationship to and dependence on a man. Just as Dorothy Patterson's trademark hats covered her hair, serving as an outward symbol of submission to male authority, the model of the pastor's wife covered the absence of female pastors, serving as a visible symbol that women could still be active and visible in ministry even in churches that wouldn't ordain them.

8

The Cost of Dorothy's Hats

I stood in the atrium of our recently built $2 million church build-
ing. It was in the early days after my husband was fired. My sleeve-
less shirt was gauzy blue. I remember because the tears I fought
to suppress came anyway, sliding down my face to stain my shirt.
The shirt hung loose on me; for the first (and only) time in my
life, I had lost my appetite. The stress of what was happening to
us, my disbelief that the people who knew us so well would let
this happen to us, had overwhelmed my body. I stopped eating; I
stopped sleeping; I stopped laughing. That Sunday morning, I followed one of the elders out of the worship service on a whim—a
last-ditch effort to plead for my husband's job.

Sympathy showed in his face as we stood in the morning light
that flooded through the tall windows and pooled on the polished
concrete floor. He was my friend, but in that moment it wasn't my
friend listening to my story. It was a male church elder, authorized
by a particular interpretation of 1 Timothy 2–3. I watched when he
walked away to stand by another elder. I could tell he was conveying
my words. Only a few feet separated us, but I wasn't invited to join
them. Their posture, backs turned away and heads bent, signaled
a closed space almost as clearly as if they had shut an office door.

This didn't surprise me.

As a pastor's wife in a conservative evangelical church, I had served like a leader for fourteen years. I had been interviewed like a leader before my husband was offered the job, I had conformed to leadership expectations, and I was perceived as a leader by the church congregation.

But I wasn't one.

I reflected pastoral authority but carried none of my own. I was a glorified volunteer who invested several hours a week in ministry work yet was not included in any official leadership role. At best, my efforts that morning would be received as that of a suffering wife, perhaps helping to soften the blow of the sudden job loss on our family. They wouldn't be received as that of a leader with wisdom about the implications this decision had for the community. I had played a significant role for fourteen years teaching and guiding a subset of the congregation, yet my voice was excluded from a conversation about the fate of that ministry.

The worst part wasn't the realization that my last-ditch effort would fail (which it did).

The worst part wasn't my growing concern with a theology and ecclesiology that concentrated church governance in a very small group of men.

The worst part wasn't understanding, perhaps for the first time in my experience as a pastor's wife, how contingent my role was—that all the influence I had wielded, authority in ministry I had carried, had come only as an extension of my husband's job.

I didn't understand the worst part until later, after I had time to reflect, and even then, I didn't fully know the worst of it.

I do now.

The worst part is knowing, historically, how I had come to be in that atrium; knowing how women like me had become ministry leaders without ministerial authority; knowing how the disappearance of women's independent leadership and the rise of a dependent ministry role tied to marriage had little to do with the Bible; knowing how removing women from leadership positions equal to those of men and tying their authority to subordinate positions increased women's vulnerability.

You see, during a research trip to the Southern Baptist Historical Library and Archives in Nashville—exactly one week before the 2023 annual Southern Baptist convention in New Orleans—I began to uncover a story hauntingly familiar to the sex abuse crisis plaguing the SBC. A story connecting the dots between a gender theology that rejects women's independent pastoral authority and a culture that privileges male clergy over clergy abuse victims. A story that shows the precarity of the pastor's wife role.

It took me eight months to piece together the story, with the assistance of the SBC archives in Nashville, the Canadian Baptists of Ontario and Quebec at their main office in Toronto, and the archives in the neighboring town of Hamilton, as well as conversations with former church members at Dufferin Street Baptist Church in Toronto.

The story I uncovered reinforced for me how lucky I am in my personal experience as a pastor's wife.

I may have been powerless in that atrium seven years ago, but I have never been powerless in my marriage. I am married to a kind and generous man who loves Jesus, has integrity, and believes fully in the dignity and equality of women. He majored in social work and became a pastor because he felt called to help people—not because he wanted to build a social media platform and preach before thousands of people. Neither money nor power motivate him. He isn't perfect, but he is a man after God's own heart; he loves me and our children deeply.

I am lucky.

Not all pastors' wives are.

Unearthing the Cost

It was Friday, June 2, 2023.

My daughter sat at the end of the table in the Southern Baptist Historical Library and Archives. She had been waiting for her cousins to return home from vacation that evening. We had plans to cook them enchiladas for dinner. She was ready to leave. It was toward the end of the day, exactly 3:12 p.m. (courtesy of the time stamp from my iPad), so I promised her this would be the last box of documents I would go through.

For those of you who aren't in the Baptist world, the timing of our trip means we were in the SBC archives on the eve of the 2023 Southern Baptist Convention in New Orleans. If that still doesn't mean anything to you, let me remind you what happened there.

Rick Warren, the retired pastor of Saddleback Church in Lake Forest, California, and Linda Barnes Popham, the pastor for thirty-three years of Fern Creek Baptist Church in Louisville, Kentucky, failed to convince the SBC to allow their churches to remain in fellowship with the convention. The issue was women's ordination, and the twelve thousand delegates in attendance voted overwhelmingly to uphold their decision to reject churches with female pastors.

Ironically, it was because Warren raised the issue of ordaining SBC women at the national level that Popham became a known figure, and her church, along with Warren's, was targeted by the SBC Executive Committee.[1]

What is even more ironic (and I mean actual irony, not as sung by Alanis Morissette) is that the SBC's quick response to Warren as well as its landslide vote to oust churches with female pastors came even as the SBC remained woefully slow and ill-prepared to address sexual abuse within its body. Southern Baptist women who are sexual abuse survivors have had to wait years not only for a response by the SBC but for their voices to even be heard. Christa Brown, for example, began asking the SBC in 2004 to investigate the pastor who allegedly abused her as a teenager. It wasn't until 2019, after the *Houston Chronicle* published its far-reaching investigation, "Abuse of Faith," that the SBC finally began to pay attention to her allegations.[2] Just think about what it means that nearly twelve thousand messengers voted in a landslide against female pastors, but only about fifty of those same messengers gathered for a breakout session to discuss sexual abuse toward adults. Even one of the speakers on the floor of the convention commented that the SBC is quick on the draw to shun female pastors but slow to respond to victims of sexual abuse perpetrated within SBC churches and often by SBC pastors.

As I concluded in an op-ed for MSNBC, "At a time when they should be listening to the voices of women and lamenting the sex abuse scandal still rocking the denomination, the Southern Baptist world has chosen to strengthen the voices and the power of men. I can't begin to imagine the cost."[3]

This wasn't entirely true, though. I could imagine at least some of the cost.

I could do so because I had found it in the archives.

The box was from the James T. Draper Jr. Papers, in collection AR 607, box 2.[4] Draper served as president of the SBC between 1982 and 1984, which means he was president during the 1983 uproar over the ordination of two women, Sarah Wood Lee and Kathy Hoppe (whose stories we heard in chapters 1 and 3). Their story is why I had asked to see the Draper files, and the first document I took a picture of concerned Lee and Hoppe. It was a letter from Tom Edwards, pastor of First Baptist Church in Shelby, Montana. He was writing on December 27, 1983, to thank William Tanner, the president of the SBC Home Mission Board (HMB), for responding to him about the two women's ordination. He was also writing to take issue with part of Tanner's response.

> Dr. Tanner, let me assure you, we hold to the doctrine of the "Priesthood of the Believer," too. We question, however, if the Holy Spirit would move a believing individual to knowingly violate the very Scripture He authored. The criteria, Brother Tanner, is not ours—it is the Bible's. The question is this: Does any agency of the SBC have the right to give implicit support to one side of an issue which is currently hotly debated? The appointment of those who approve of the ordination of women does imply (and only imply) HMB [Home Mission Board] approval.[5]

To be sure, Tanner had assured Edwards that they had been "unaware" of Lee's plan to be ordained and stated that the state leadership could have stopped the appointment of Hoppe if they had so chosen.[6] But Tanner had also resisted Edwards's claim that the ordination of women violated Scripture. "I think you will find that there is also a doctrine called the Priesthood of the Believer allowing the Holy Spirit to speak to each of us regarding His Word. What you and your church have spoken says that Home Mission Board does not have the right to support anyone whose theology is questionable by your criteria," Tanner wrote.[7] Both Tanner and Edwards might personally believe that the ordination of women was wrong, but that doesn't mean other faithful Baptists could read the same Scripture and think differently. Tanner was emphasizing to Edwards that the criteria of his church wasn't (and shouldn't be) the standard for the Home Mission Board, which represented all the churches of the SBC. Edwards, in contrast, was pushing an idea that would soon be typical in the SBC and eventually be clearly expressed at the 2023 SBC convention: women's ordination—more precisely, the rejection of women's ordination—was a core gospel issue.

I finished reading Tanner's response and turned to the next letter in the file. I fully expected a continuation of the saga about ordaining Lee and Hoppe. But the next letter was different. It was written on March 1, 1983, by James (Jimmy) Draper, then president of the SBC. Draper wrote in response to an accusation of clergy abuse made against a male pastor currently employed by the SBC. In brief, a man named H. P. Wu alleged that Mario Acacia, "a Special Minister to Embassy Personnel" in Washington, DC, working for the Language Missions Division of the Home Mission Board, sexually abused one of his congregants (who I later learned was a woman on church staff who had asked for counseling). This is what Draper wrote in his response to Wu:

> I certainly appreciate your taking time to write to me. None of us could ever condone the kind of acts which you have described

in your letter. I assure you that ever[y] attempt will be made to investigate and to take the proper action. I am sending your letter to Dr. Bill Tanner at the Home Mission Board. He is president of the Home Mission Board and a very close personal friend. I will urge him to take every step necessary to rectify the situation.

May God bless you is my prayer.

In His love, James T. Draper, Jr.[8]

What I found next on that sunny June day in Nashville was the beginning of an eight-month-long journey that would end on a cold January day in Toronto. And what I found in Toronto was far more than I expected. In addition to the full story of clergy abuse alleged by H. P. Wu, I found a pastor's wife named Maria Acacia.[9]

Without downplaying the severity of what happened to the victim, the story of Maria helped me more fully understand the impact of Christian patriarchy on women trapped in the homes of abusers. The life of Maria is a striking example of all the ways conservative evangelical gender theology fails women.[10] Her life as a pastor's wife began before the hard conservative turn taken by her Baptist world. But the moment she might have finally been seen and helped by SBC leaders was the moment the SBC made that hard turn.

It is striking to me that Jimmy Draper played a central role in both the hard turn of the SBC against women in ministry as well as the circumstances involving Maria's husband. The year after Jimmy Draper closed the correspondence about Maria's husband, he closed the door on Susan Lockwood—an ordained SBC pastor who wanted to speak on the convention floor against the 1984 SBC resolution that condemned women's ordination "to preserve a submission God requires because the man was first in creation and the woman was first in the Edenic fall."[11] Lockwood's microphone was literally turned off, and when she sought Draper out, asking him as the SBC president to give her a chance to speak, he said no. "Well, I've decided that I'm not going to let you speak," he told her. "I feel we followed things correctly in our procedure and I'm not going to let you speak."[12]

At two different moments during his presidency, Jimmy Draper had the chance to see the reality of the path the SBC was choosing; the reality of the cost for women.

But Draper didn't see it.

He didn't see the consequences of a theology that rendered women's spiritual calling only through the role of helpmeet to men.

He didn't see how rendering women as subordinate, in both marriage and ministry, rendered women's voices, contributions, and value as less than those of men.

He didn't see how removing women from leadership roles equal to those of men removed women's ability to advocate effectively and be heard when speaking against male predators.

He didn't see how limiting women's religious authority to dependent roles increased the vulnerability of all women.

He didn't see the victim of Acacia's clergy abuse.

Neither did he see a pastor's wife named Maria.

Maria

It was Tuesday evening, April 18, 1961.

I imagine that Maria Acacia sat in the pew of College Street Baptist Church in Toronto, Ontario, Canada, her short dark hair waving around her face as it did in her profile picture for the SBC Home Mission Board file. Her choir voice might have joined the congregation gathered that evening to celebrate her husband's induction service. I imagine her hands would have held the hymnal for her two young children, encouraging them to sing the familiar words with her. Or her hands may have cradled her youngest, still a baby. I don't know whether Maria would have stood up as the Reverend Kenneth Allaby called her husband forward. Her body, only a few months postpartum, was already nurturing a fourth baby. She may have chosen to stay seated and let her feet rest. She would have heard, standing or sitting, the ceremony start for the induction of her husband as a Baptist minister in Canada. Reverend Allaby spoke:

> Dear Christian friends, we are assembled here in the name of Jesus Christ and at the invitation of the Home Mission Board and the Toronto Association to induct our brother, Rev. Mario Acacia, into the ministry of Christ in this city.[13]

Only a few days earlier, on April 4, 1961, the Acacia family had arrived in Toronto at the behest of Canadian Baptists of Ontario and Quebec (CBOQ) Home Mission Board. The aftermath of World War II had triggered large-scale immigration, and many immigrants had made new homes in Toronto. Dufferin Street Baptist Church, in the West End, had begun supporting a ministry for Italian immigrants in its neighborhood. Church records indicate that the Acacia family was called for this mission. "Rev. and Mrs. Mario Acacia were brought from Switzerland by the Home Mission Board and we were happy to receive them into fellowship with us. Office space and telephone are provided at Dufferin Street and services in Italian at Ossington Avenue. Classes in English, held Monday evenings, provide opportunity for Members to teach and Witness to these New Canadians." They hadn't come directly from Switzerland. Their time in Switzerland had ended in August 1960, and they had been at a church in Rome for the previous few months. But they did come across the Atlantic, recommended by the SBC and the Baptist World Alliance, to take up this pastoral missionary post in Toronto.[14]

I wonder what Maria would have thought about the transatlantic move.

She had given birth to their third child in Lugano, Switzerland, where her husband had served at Lugano Baptist Church from March 1955 to August 1960. They then moved to Centocelle

Baptist Church in Rome, where they were from September 1960 to February 1961. Rome was Maria's childhood home and where her family still lived. Would she have wanted to leave again? Mario had previously served at Ronciglione Baptist Church in Ronciglione, Italy, from September 1953 to February 1955. Maria would have lived in four different countries with her husband (the US, Italy, Switzerland, and now Canada) since their marriage in 1951.

Maria had the courage, the adventurous spirit, for the peripatetic turn her life as a Baptist pastor's wife had taken. Born in 1924, she had become fluent in enough languages (English, French, and some German in addition to Italian) by the early 1940s that she translated for the Allies at their headquarters in Rome during the Second World War. Somehow, during that chaotic time she received a scholarship to Northwest Bible Institute in Seattle, Washington. It was an Assemblies of God school, and since Maria had been raised in a charismatic tradition in Rome, it was a good fit. It became Northwest Bible College during her studies, and today is Northwest University. She graduated with an honors degree and went to Louisville, Kentucky, to continue her education.[15]

It was in Louisville that she married Mario. They had known each other in Rome, where they both grew up in evangelical homes, although Mario was Baptist. Mario had taken an educational route similar to Maria's—he was offered a scholarship by New Orleans Baptist Theological Seminary but transferred to East Texas Baptist University to earn a BA. He entered a master of divinity program at Southern Seminary. I am uncertain how Maria reconnected with Mario in the US, but a brief newspaper article from April 15, 1961, states that "Mr. Acacia studied for the Baptist ministry in the United States where he met his Italian wife who was taking similar training."[16] By 1951 Mario and Maria were married. Two years later, on June 7, 1953, Mario was ordained as a Southern Baptist pastor at Broadway Baptist Church in Louisville, Kentucky.[17]

I wonder what Maria would have felt about the words used to induct her husband into his new ministry in Toronto:

It is the duty of the minister devoutly and reverently to order the Service of God's House, and, as much as lieth in him, to lead a quiet and peaceful life in all godliness and honesty, remembering that this is good and acceptable in the sight of God, our Savior, who will have all men to be saved and to come unto the knowledge of the truth.[18]

I can't help but think that she hoped this mission, this church, would be the one at which they stayed. At least for a while. That her husband would live the charge that he had been given—to preach the gospel always and care for his family and the congregants of his mission with the love of God. I wonder how she felt to be, once again, a pastor's wife.

Would she have been excited?

Would she have been hopeful? Thankful for this chance, in a new city, a new country, to start fresh?

Would she have been worried?

At the end of the ceremony, the presiding minister declared that "in the name of the Lord Jesus Christ, the Head of the Church, and by the authority of the Home Mission Board, and the Toronto Association of Baptist Churches, I commend you to this ministry. May the Lord preserve your going out and your coming in from this time forth, and even for evermore."[19] Perhaps Maria joined her voice with the congregation one more time, singing "Hark the Voice of Jesus," before her husband—as the newly installed pastor of the Italian Mission for Dufferin Street Baptist Church—gave the benediction.

The congregation would have bowed their heads, listening to Mario pray. I imagine Maria prayed her own prayer. I imagine she would have asked God for the strength to face what came next. She would have prayed for her children, born and unborn. I imagine how tightly her arms would have cradled her baby daughter.

I don't know what Maria prayed for that day, but if I had been in her shoes, I would have prayed for this time to be different.

A Tale of Two Pastors' Wives, Part One

In 1951, the same year Maria married Mario in Louisville, Kentucky, another young woman married an SBC minister in West Palm Beach, Florida. We have already met her as she is quite well known in SBC circles. Her name was Joyce, and her husband's name was Adrian. Adrian Rogers.

In many ways, the two women's lives ran on parallel tracks. They both married young to men they had known in childhood. Both of their husbands expressed a calling to full-time ministry. The SBC ordained both of their husbands to the gospel ministry, and both women became pastors' wives (although Maria was more precisely a missionary pastor's wife). Both supported the ministry of their husbands as they also managed homemaking responsibilities, childcare, and some part-time work. Maria worked as an assistant at the school near their home in Toronto and was an adjunct oil painting instructor at a nearby community college. Joyce mostly confined her work to ministry. They both had five children during the first twelve years of their marriage (although Joyce lost one child to sudden infant death syndrome, and Maria later had a sixth child in 1967).

It is possible both women felt personally called to vocational ministry. I did not find Maria's own words stating this, but from what I learned about her when I visited the main office of the CBOQ and from her choices in educational institutions and her major in theology, it seems likely she was pursuing vocational ministry.

Joyce articulated a ministry call. She tells how, during a service at a Christian retreat center, she stood by Adrian when he declared God calling him to ministry. He was sixteen and she was fifteen. The pastor told Joyce that she should have gone forward to join Adrian at the altar. "You know that a preacher's wife must be called too," he said to her. After that conversation, Joyce filled out a card declaring a call to full-time Christian service. "Deep in my heart I knew that one day I would be Mrs. Adrian Rogers, pastor's wife," she said.[20] Three years later, at age eighteen, she married Adrian and became the pastor's wife she believed God had called her to be.

In other ways, however, the lives of these two women were different.

Joyce's husband became pastor of one of the most prestigious churches in the SBC, Bellevue Baptist Church in Memphis, Tennessee. The church grew from nine thousand to twenty-nine thousand members within a few years. Before Bellevue, Adrian had served as pastor of four churches in Mississippi and Florida between 1954 and 1972. He served at Bellevue from 1972 until his retirement in 2004.

By contrast, the longest term that Mario Acacia served as pastor was eleven years as the senior pastor of Dufferin Street Baptist Church (1967–78), and during that time membership declined. In 1967, when Mario assumed the pastorate, Dufferin had a membership of 122; by 1972 that membership had decreased to ninety-two.[21] Joyce's ministry as a pastor's wife focused exclusively on SBC churches in Florida, Mississippi, and Tennessee; each time she left a church with her husband, it was their choice. Maria Acacia's ministry as a pastor's wife was more scattered and had less security as her husband moved from place to place. Great distances, including the vastness of the Atlantic Ocean, stretched between Maria's moves, whereas Joyce served in only three Southern states.

The churches where Joyce served as pastor's wife grew bigger and more financially stable during her husband's tenures. She faced trials, including the death of her infant son and a time during which she was told by a Christian counselor that she was a "very bitter woman" (because she felt left out of helping her husband's ministry at the church), but she never doubted the love of her husband nor regretted her life as a pastor's wife. "I lived for fifty-four years with a man who loved, lived, believed, and preached God's Word," she wrote in 2013. In her own words, she served "at five wonderful churches," "traveled all over the world," "met four presidents of the United States," and watched her husband retire with accolades from a church he had pastored for more than three decades.[22]

When Mario had to leave his position, again, in 1978—leaving his family, again, with uncertainty about the future—Adrian was on his way to becoming the president of the Southern Baptist Convention. Joyce expressed great joy and confidence in Adrian. She explained how, at first, he did not believe God was calling him to the presidency. But after receiving assurance from his wife as well as from Bertha Smith (the preaching missionary who pastored churches in China for the SBC whom we met in chapter 3), he agreed—after an extended prayer time in a hotel room alongside Jerry Vines and Paige Patterson—to run for president of the SBC at the 1979 convention. Patterson and Paul Pressler intentionally courted Adrian for the election; they hoped he would help the conservative faction take control of the SBC and keep it for at least ten years.[23] "What they needed was a good candidate, so they recruited Adrian Rogers to be the candidate they would run in 1979 to try and win," historian Barry Hankins noted. "He was a winsome personality with a great preaching voice. He was staunchly conservative in his theology, in favor of conservatives having a sort of test for leadership in the convention, but he was not in any way a hard-edged personality type."[24]

Rogers was a beloved preacher and pastor, in other words, who had gained the trust of thousands of Southern Baptists. The day after he had prayed with Vines and Patterson, 51 percent of the fifteen thousand delegates at the Houston convention elected him the next president of the SBC. His election marked a turning point, as the conservative faction rose to prominence. Joyce writes how she wrote a song of celebration that she sang to him. "I'm so proud, I'm so proud, I'm so proud of my husband! I'm so proud, I'm so proud of God's man!"[25]

Maria, in contrast, divorced her pastor husband in 1997 after more than forty-five years of marriage. She was seventy-three years old at the time.

Saint Fabiola

Dufferin Street Baptist Church stands on a once bustling street corner in West Toronto. The front doors, now blocked by stacked boxes, would have opened wide for Maria as she welcomed the diverse neighborhood into the church her husband led—first as pastor for the CBOQ Italian mission (housed at Dufferin) and later as the senior pastor of Dufferin. Those who remember Maria describe her as "gifted and talented," "warm," "beautiful," and "caring." She had a way of seeing people, knowing when they needed encouragement, caring how they were doing.[26]

Maria had taught herself English during the war. Besides Italian, English, French, and German, she also had some knowledge of Greek and Russian. Maria's proficiency in languages would have served her missionary life with Mario well. During the first two years of his CBOQ appointment as a missionary pastor, he traveled throughout Canada—to Vancouver, Calgary, Edmonton, Winnipeg—visiting with new Canadian families from all over the world. The February 1964 *Baptist Advance* described Mario as having "given leadership among Baptist churches in the program of reaching other new Canadians and establishing them in Baptist churches."[27] Maria probably stayed in Toronto instead of traveling with him, but the Dufferin Street neighborhood would have provided ample opportunity for her linguistic prowess.

Along with learning languages, Maria had learned to paint as a young girl in Rome. Her vibrant flowers swirled through the Vacation Bible School she helped run in the summers and the Jordan River flowed more clearly behind the baptistery mural after she repainted it. One image must have drawn her, as she painted it throughout her life—giving it away to a family member or friend before painting it anew and giving it away again. The image is one of the most reproduced paintings in the modern era, copied by so many amateur and professional artists that an entire art show has been dedicated to these portraits and keeping the memory of the lost original alive. The image is of a young female saint, a fourth-century Roman martyr, profiled with a red robe draping her head. Her name is Fabiola. It is possible that Maria, like so many other artists who have reproduced her portrait, found comfort and joy in painting this woman. Perhaps it reminded Maria of her childhood in Rome, a little piece of her Italian heritage.

It is also possible, given what I am about to tell you, that Maria had another reason for painting Saint Fabiola.

The Acacias served at Dufferin between 1961 and 1978; Mario served as the primary pastor for eleven of those years. The congregation hovered around one hundred. The Acacia family grew during that time, from five to eight. Maria would have been busy caring for her family as her husband not only served as pastor but also taught as an adjunct at the University of Toronto, working on a doctorate in Italian studies. During those years, Maria fit the pastor's wife image of a "universal spare part"[28] to a tee. She sang in choir, organized the annual VBS, played piano, and provided pastoral care in place of her husband—visiting congregants in hospitals and nursing homes. She also oversaw the Christmas pageants—writing the scripts, sewing costumes, and painting scenery. Maria themed one memorable pageant "Jesus Is the Light of the World," dressing the children of Dufferin's diverse congregation in costumes representing their global heritage. Her ministry reached almost every part of the church, her hands were in everything, as one former congregant told me, and she was both loved and appreciated.

Until December 1977.

The 1977 annual report for Dufferin Baptist Church still exists in the CBOQ archives. I found it strange to read, knowing what had happened that year.

The pastor's report, signed "Keep up the good work in Christ's name" by Mario Acacia, focuses on the words of Jesus in Luke 19:10–13: "The Son of man is come to seek and to save that which was lost. . . . And he called his ten servants . . . and said unto them, Occupy till I come" (KJV). Mario spoke in broad generalizations, commenting that some members had kept busy and lots of good things had taken place, including "a good number of baptisms." He also remarked on problems that existed in the church but were solved "in a brotherly fashion." He commended the congregation—ninety-one active members—and claimed the year closed in "victory and praise."

Maria also appeared in the report, writing about a new program on Sunday mornings. "The 'Mission Bands' of Dufferin Street Baptist Church had resumed activities for children under 8 or 9 years of age during the morning service," she wrote, explaining that the program would introduce children to missions and missionaries. "Trusting in God's guidance," she concluded before signing the report. She was slated to serve as assistant organist for 1978, as well as on the teller committee, the flower committee, and supervising the mission bands.[29]

But by January 1978 her husband no longer pastored at Dufferin Street.

I wonder whether Maria already knew what happened when she submitted the mission bands report. Did she know that her time at Dufferin was about to end? I wonder what she felt when she learned her husband had been engaging in a long-term sexual relationship with a much younger married congregant who had two young children. I wonder whether she was home when the younger woman's angry husband confronted her husband, demanding that he confess. I wonder whether she knew that the young woman, a recent immigrant who was having trouble adjusting to her new home, had come to Mario as her pastor, requesting counseling. Instead, the young woman's husband charged that "he slept with her." I wonder whether she knew that Mario had insisted the "affair"—which we have come to rightly understand as clergy sexual abuse—was instigated by his young congregant, despite the power differential between them of not only age but also employment.[30] The young woman served on his church staff.

Did Maria have to listen to a description of the young woman's "very soft skin" and admission that the woman resisted "some but not over much"? Did Maria know that the official documents in the CBOQ office asked whether it was "rape" or "adultery" next to a description of the "emotional relationship."[31]

I can't help but wonder what she thought when Mario was allowed to keep his license and resign from the pastoral position. Maria was told, the documents state, and was "fully aware of the situation." She was reconciled to her husband, the male authors of the documents assure.[32]

But was she?

Did she know she could ask for help? I wonder if anyone spoke to her directly, without her husband in the room. Did they ask the children how things were at home? Did they tell Maria that, if she didn't want to stay in the same house with her husband as she was processing what he had done to her and their family, they would provide a safe place for her? Did they connect her with a counselor?

Maybe they did.

Or maybe they didn't. As was common at the time, the representative from the CBOQ as well as the deacon from Dufferin and the husband of the victim accepted Mario's confession and repentance as enough.

Nothing in the documents suggests further help was offered to Maria. Nothing in the documents suggests how she would have felt knowing the cost her husband's infidelity would have on her family or on her both personally and professionally. No evidence remains to tell us what Maria really thought.

Except, perhaps, Saint Fabiola.

Throughout her forty-five years of marriage, as they had moved from church to church, Maria had painted the same portrait of Saint Fabiola over and over, giving it away again and again.

Do you know who Fabiola was?

She was a fourth-century Roman woman who scandalized her community by divorcing her abusive and adulterous husband.

170

Saint Jerome preserves her story. He writes, "So terrible then were the faults imputed to her former husband that not even a prostitute or a common slave could have put up with them. If I were to recount them, I should undo the heroism of the wife who chose to bear the blame of a separation rather than to blacken the character and expose the stains of him who was one body with her." Today Fabiola is remembered as the patron saint of difficult marriages, divorced persons, and survivors of unfaithful and abusive spouses.[33]

Fabiola was also remembered by Maria Acacia, who chose to paint the saint's image throughout her life as a pastor's wife.

Did Maria know that Fabiola was the patron saint for abused spouses? Did she know that Jerome called Fabiola "heroic" for not exposing the deeds of her abusive spouse?

I can't say for sure.

But I suspect that she did.

A Tale of Two Pastors' Wives, Part Two

The greatest difference between Maria Acacia and Joyce Rogers stemmed from their greatest similarity: they were pastors' wives in a culture that privileged male authority and increasingly emphasized female submission.

But the way they experienced that culture was different.

On the one hand, the patriarchal milieu in which both Maria and Joyce grew up was rooted in the war-torn Western world. Maria and Mario grew up in Italy during the decades between World War I and World War II—a time in which the government sought to increase the birth rate by institutionalizing family values and honoring mothers who raised more than five children. Merry Wiesner-Hanks describes how the totalitarian government of Italy (along with the governments of Germany and Japan) "mounted propaganda campaigns setting out their view of the ideal family, which was one in which fathers ruled and wives and children obeyed."[34] Ideas about women's "natural" role, Wiesner-Hanks continues, fueled government policies "promoting maternity and limiting women's employment."[35]

Joyce and Adrian Rogers grew up in a similar patriarchal culture in Florida. They too experienced an increased emphasis on "traditional family values" in which the father worked outside the home and the mother stayed home with the children. Wiesner-Hanks summarizes that in both "dictatorships and democracies," working women were "denounced as taking jobs away from men" and "vigorous propaganda campaigns" defined work as inherently masculine and the home as inherently feminine. The influence and power women had wielded in their churches as missionaries, taking on pastoral roles in Asia and Africa even while denied ordination at home, "evaporated" in the aftermath of World War II.[36] The suffrage movement may have earned women the right to vote by 1920, but the brave new postwar world of the 1950s in which both Maria and Joyce married insisted that the right place for women was in the home.

At the same time, the increasing SBC emphasis on female submission and male headship was representative of broader evangelical trends. It was also representative of white Southern culture. "More than 80 percent of SBC members are white, and more than 80 percent live in the South," writes Elesha Coffman.[37] Joyce's husband climbed to power within the SBC, which upheld these patriarchal (and racist) structures as biblical. Coffman summarizes how Rogers, and the conservative faction that helped elect him, interpreted women's advancement during the 1960s and '70s as an attack against Christian values. Legal and economic parity between women and men in the US seemed possible, from the rise of federal legislation like the Equal Pay Act (which prohibited sex-based wage discrimination), Title IX (which mitigated sex discrimination within schools and protected against sexual harassment and assault), and the Equal Credit Opportunity Act (which mitigated sex discrimination regarding mortgages, loans, and credit), to court cases protecting women's access to contraception and, in some cases, abortion, to the passage of the Equal Rights Amendment by Congress.[38]

Adrian Rogers did not applaud these gains for women. Coffman quotes the fear Rogers expressed in 1980:

> WHAT IS HAPPENING TO AMERICA IS NOT "JUST HAPPENING." It is the result of a well orchestrated plan with Satan waving the flag. FEMINIST THINKERS ARE OUT TO SUBVERT YOUR WOMEN AND TO BRING IN THEIR HEATHEN HEAVEN to do this through a HUMANIST/FEMINIST/SOCIALIST [*sic*]. There is a move to deny God, debase man, destroy the family, the world. Their plan is to free your children from the [*sic*] of their puritanical parents. . . . IN A WORLD GONE MAD I THANK GOD FOR SOME CONCERNED WOMEN WHO ARE SAYING "BACK TO THE BIBLE." STAND UP AND BE COUNTED BEFORE THE TIME RUNS OUT FOR AMERICA.[39]

Joyce's husband emphasized male headship and female submission, which played a key role in the conservative takeover of the SBC. Joyce proved a strong support in this endeavor. The conference she helped launch in 1980, for which her husband's words above were written, attracted more than four thousand concerned women. It emphasized "submission and domesticity as God's design for women" and included such keynote speakers as Elisabeth Elliot and Beverly LaHaye.[40]

Two years after Adrian Rogers stepped down from his first term as SBC president, Jimmy Draper would step into the role, presiding from 1982 to 1984. A 2016 *Baptist News Global* article linked both Rogers and Draper with Bill Gothard, the fundamentalist Christian founder of the Institute in Basic Life Principles, whose teachings fueled purity culture, patriarchal authority, and the homeschooling movement among conservative families. As the article reports, "In 1998 Gothard joined Southern Baptist leaders Adrian Rogers, Charles Stanley, Jimmy Draper, and Ed Young in a letter to pastors comparing the views of presidential candidates." The language of both the Danvers Statement and the Baptist Faith and Message 2000 echoes Gothard's "cornerstone belief" about the husband having an "umbrella of authority" over his wife. But even before the Danvers Statement, SBC moderates like Roy Honeycutt and Andrew Lester worried about "Gothard-style hierarchalism" that was floating around SBC leadership.[41]

It is true that Rogers served only one year as SBC president, but men like Draper carried on his legacy, including supporting the success of the 1984 resolution that foreshadowed the complementarian takeover of the SBC. Appealing to the "delegated order of authority" in Scripture, the resolution stated that women are excluded from "pastoral leadership to preserve a submission God requires because the man was first in creation and the woman was first in the Edenic fall."[42] When Wayne Dehoney of Louisville, Kentucky, opposed the resolution on constitutional grounds, Draper refused to sustain his objection, arguing that the resolution was not binding on local churches and therefore not in violation of the constitution. When Susan Lockwood, an ordained SBC pastor from Chicago, tried to speak against the resolution, her microphone was turned off. When she appealed to Draper, he refused to allow her to speak.[43] The resolution passed.

Joyce Rogers's husband helped launch the sharp conservative turn taken by the SBC that reinforced Christian patriarchy. To be sure, Joyce praised her husband as a kind and godly man. He loved his family, he loved his congregation, and he treated the people in his life well. Adrian Rogers inspired men like Draper who, during his presidency, oversaw the 1984 resolution and the fight to remove ordained SBC women from ministry roles.

While Joyce was singing the praises of her husband's election to the SBC presidency, Maria Acacia was packing up her belongings to become an SBC missionary wife. I don't think Draper ever knew her name, but he would prove to be a powerful force in the direction of her life.

"Forgive and Forget"

On February 20, 1983, a Mr. H. P. Wu, a former member of Dufferin Baptist Church, wrote a letter to then SBC president Jimmy Draper. He was writing because of a "Watergate case of serious moral turpitude within your SBC." The letter alleged that

> Mario Acacia, a Special Minister to Embassy Personnel in the D.C., [address and phone number omitted], who committed sexual acts repeatedly for a considerable length of time with a person for whom he was rendering his service, resulting in substantial injury to her and the family, has remained active in the sacred post continuously. Subsequently, his self-proclaimed repentance includes minimizing and distorting the facts, intimidating and blaming the victims.[44]

Wu further alleged that Oscar Romo, the Director of the Language Missions Division for the SBC Home Mission Board—which had oversight of Acacia—shirked responsibility to raise concerns or investigate the allegations, citing the autonomy of local churches and saying, "It is up to the local SBC anyway." As such, Wu was writing to ask Draper to revoke Acacia's ordination.

Draper at first responded with concern, reaching out to Bill Tanner, president of the Home Mission Board. Tanner acknowledged that his office had heard from Wu for several years. Tanner, in turn, reached out to Romo.[45]

Romo responded to Draper in March 1983. He affirmed that Mario Acacia was a well-known SBC figure, educated in SBC undergraduate and graduate institutions. He also confirmed that the Home Mission Board had been made aware of the allegations about Acacia at the time of his appointment to Washington, DC:

> After having become acquainted with him, our division asked the Department of Missionary Personnel to process him for work with Internationals. Missionary Personnel recommended that Language Missions appoint him to serve in the metro DC area

among diplomats. Dr. Acacia was appointed and arrangements were made for his immigration to the United States and the moving of household goods. The moving van had departed Toronto when a Mr. Wu called and made various accusations.[46]

The Home Mission Board confronted Mario, who "acknowledged that problems had existed and that these problems had been discussed with the Convention officer assigned the responsibility of issuing credentials to pastors related to the Convention." Romo stated that the "appropriate office in the Ontario-Quebec Convention was contacted concerning the situation. . . . It was acknowledged that such a problem had existed several years before."

And then they did nothing.

As Romo explained:

> It is my understanding that the credentials committee of the Ontario-Quebec Convention met with Mr. Wu, Dr. Acacia and church leaders. After reviewing the situation, the consensus of the group was to permit his certification as a minister to be continued. Also, I understand that after prayer and dialogue it was agreed by the group to forgive and forget and to place the entire matter in the hands of God. Thus, the situation was closed, as agreed by the group which included Mr. Wu.
>
> In the past Mr. Wu has called; and when asked to indicate the identity of the "victim," he has refused to provide the information either verbally or in writing. Often when he has called and I was out of the office, Mr. Wu has shared the details of the situation with whomever answers the phone. It seems that he has an obsession that continues to affect his life and perhaps his family.
>
> Several years have elapsed since the problem occurred. Dr. Acacia has been related to us for some five years. To the best of my knowledge, history has not repeated itself. Dr. Acacia has been advised that if the same problem occurred again it would be necessary for a reevaluation of relationships.

A review of Mr. Wu's extensive correspondence with numerous persons seems to indicate that the only acceptable response to him is for Dr. Acacia to be dismissed from any position in any type of religious work.[47]

I wonder about the evidence on which Romo based his surmise that "history has not repeated itself." Did he talk with the Acacia family? Did he interview the people Acacia worked with, especially the women who traveled with him and worked closely with him? Did he go to the Acacia house and inquire about Maria? Did he ask about their children, or at least the only one who remained in their household? Did he even know Maria's name?

I worry, too, about how Wu was dismissed again and again. Romo suggested Wu was obsessed and unreasonable in his expectations. I searched for the "extensive correspondence" from Wu that Romo admitted once existed. I have not yet found it.

Draper was satisfied with Romo's response. I wasn't. So, in January 2023, I went to Toronto.

With the full cooperation of the CBOQ executive minister and board, I found Mario's confession and the full allegation made by H. P. Wu (in which I learned the identity of Acacia's victim). It was quite a moment when we found the drawer containing records of deceased ministers and saw two envelopes marked "confidential" in Mario Acacia's file. Following CBOQ protocol, the envelopes were opened and read by the executive minister, who then gave permission to me. The phrase used more than once by CBOQ executive board members was their desire "to be a part of bringing the truth to light." The first envelope was sealed on February 9, 1978, and contained Acacia's confession. It related what we define as clergy sexual abuse—a sexual relationship between the pastor and a woman on his staff who had come to him for pastoral counseling. The second envelope contained notes from a conversation between a guidance counselor and the husband of the victim confirming the details of Acacia's confession. We also found former members of Dufferin Street Baptist Church who were there when this scandal happened, who knew the family, and who were willing to speak with me.

What I learned was more than I thought possible.

I learned that a pastor's wife named Maria had spent her life serving the church. She had served faithfully even while living with an abusive spouse who was not faithful to her and who abused another woman in his congregation.

I learned that at each moment when Maria's husband might have been exposed and she might have had a chance for a better life, nothing happened. Her husband would find a new job and Maria would start over. In her dependent role, she had few choices.

I learned that after the SBC hired Mario, Maria was hospitalized twice for serious accidents that occurred in her home. I learned that her body often bore evidence of domestic abuse. I learned that, after she received third degree burns from her neck to her waist, she gained the courage to divorce her pastor husband.[48]

She received most of the furniture from the divorce proceedings. But she refused to take the bed.

From what I can tell from the documents, Romo did not know about Maria's plight as the wife of a pastor who abused his power—who should have lost his pastoral title long before. Draper didn't know it either.

They didn't know because I don't think they asked.

Here is how Draper concluded the correspondence about Mario Acacia:

Dear Oscar: I appreciate your very kind and detailed reply regarding the accusations of Mr. H. P. Wu. You have certainly adequately responded and I believe we need to leave the matter in the hands of God. We must be a redemptive community. Certainly there are many problems relating to each of us and we all stand under the grace of God. I think you have handled it wisely and I have no further suggestions to make. God bless you dear friend. In His love, James T. Draper, Jr.[49]

The letter was dated March 16, 1983. A little over a month after receiving Wu's letter, Draper closed the investigation.

As far as I can tell, no one ever asked Maria.

In Remembrance of Maria

I found this correspondence on the eve of the SBC 2023 convention, just before the SBC voted in a landslide decision to disfellowship churches with female pastors. What does this story of a pastor's wife abused by her husband have to do with the rejection of women's ordination? Think about it. Both reflect what happens when male power is privileged at the cost of women. Both reflect women's precarious status in the SBC as dependent on male authority. Both reflect how SBC women lack the agency to follow their callings or to protect themselves from violence—especially violence perpetrated by male pastoral authority.

On the eve of the 2023 SBC annual meeting, I learned that—at the same time Adrian Rogers, Jimmy Draper, and Paige Patterson were laying the groundwork to permanently exclude SBC women from leadership roles equal to those of men—a woman who was under the pastoral care of a Baptist pastor, who was an employee on his staff, was subjected to repeated sexual acts that caused severe damage to her and her family. When the pastor was confronted with the allegations, he admitted to having "problems." The CBOQ representative and deacon from Dufferin Street Baptist Church who learned what Acacia had done, who heard his confession, met and prayed together, deciding to "forgive and forget." He was allowed to remain in ministry. I learned that the Home Mission Board knew about the accusation and confession when it moved this pastor as an SBC missionary to Washington, DC.

I learned that the year before the SBC's 1984 resolution declaring women unfit for leadership because of the sin of Eve, the presiding SBC president—Draper—had declared, "We must be a redemptive community" because "there are many problems relating to each of us" and so closed the inquiry on this pastor. I learned that, while Draper was willing to forgive a male pastor who had confessed to serious abuse of his pastoral authority that harmed a woman under his pastoral care, he was not willing to give an ordained SBC female pastor the microphone to speak against the 1984 resolution.

Mario Acacia continued serving in a position of SBC pastoral authority until he retired several years later.

No one ever knew what he had done.

No one ever knew that the highest leaders in the SBC Home Mission Board and Executive Office had learned about the accusations against him and dismissed them.

No one ever knew that long before the *Houston Chronicle* broke the news about the sex abuse crisis in the heart of the SBC, long before Paige Patterson lost his job over his mishandling of Megan Lively's rape (Lively had been counseled by Patterson in 2003 to not report her rape to the police), long before Christa Brown begged SBC leaders to listen to her story, the SBC president chose—based on third-party information—to dismiss a serious allegation against a male pastor; chose to allow the pastor to remain in a position of spiritual authority; and (from the evidence available) chose not to check on the pastor's family or coworkers.[50]

Don't you find it interesting that at the same moment the SBC was building its male-only leadership model, it was protecting a male pastor who had confessed to clergy sexual abuse?

For more than five decades, conservative evangelical theology has been teaching an increasingly restrictive gender hierarchy that privileges male power and authority while subordinating and marginalizing women. The sex abuse scandals that are currently plaguing the SBC are not anomalous; rather, they are the product of a systemic culture teaching that women are worth less than men. Such a culture teaches men it is okay to "forgive and forget" when a man admits to causing harm to a woman and her family; it allows such a man to remain in ministry until his voluntary retirement.

Proponents of this theology and culture have gone so far as to tie their patriarchy explicitly to the gospel of Jesus, claiming they are upholding biblical authority. To be a Christ follower, they argue, is to privilege male power. They have been so busy decrying the evils of women preaching the gospel, launching a revolution that would enshrine masculine authority into the Godhead itself, that they haven't considered the impact of their theology on women less fortunate than Joyce Rogers.

But it is okay, right?

It is okay because, as Mario Acacia and Jimmy Draper both said, they all had problems. The SBC thought it was more important to vilify women preaching the gospel than to protect the sexual victims of male pastors.

It is best to be a redemptive community.

To forgive one another.

To forget about a victim of clergy sexual abuse.

To forget about a pastor's wife named Maria.

9

Together for the Gospel

My daughter has converted me to *Doctor Who*. The BBC television series about a traveling time lord who guarded the galaxy long before Marvel's Star-Lord was born has become a staple in our household. Our favorite doctor and companion pair are David Tennant (the tenth doctor) and Catherine Tate (Donna Noble), but my favorite episode is one with the eleventh doctor (played by Matt Smith) and his first companion, Amy Pond (Karen Gillan). The storyline revolves around the painter Vincent van Gogh. Amy and the doctor help him defeat an alien monster that has been terrorizing his village, but the subplot focuses on his mental illness. Van Gogh died from suicide when he was thirty-seven after two years of incredible artistic output (many of his most famous paintings were made during this time). His work was not well received during his life, and he died a pauper.

Smith's doctor gives Van Gogh the gift of time traveling to a modern art gallery featuring his paintings. The astonished joy on Van Gogh's face as he stands amid the circular room filled with people admiring his work, seeing for the first time the impact of his art, never fails to bring me to tears.

Pond hopes this positive experience will help Van Gogh overcome his mental illness. When she learns that it doesn't, that Van Gogh still dies by suicide, she despairs. It is at this moment that the eleventh doctor tells Amy something profound. "The way I see it, every life is a pile of good things and bad things," he says. "The good things don't always soften the bad things, but vice-versa, the bad things don't necessarily spoil the good things and make them unimportant. And we definitely added to his pile of good things."[1]

Like the eleventh doctor, I can't change history.

No matter what I say to conclude this book, I can't undo the impact of decisions made by SBC leaders like Jimmy Draper and Adrian Rogers on women. I can't stop the theological and cultural crosscurrents in evangelicalism that helped the SBC and similar-minded institutions like the Council on Biblical Manhood and Womanhood mutually strengthen their ideas about women. I can't undo what happened to Maria Acacia any more than I can undo what happened to me.

Van Gogh died by suicide.

John Piper and Wayne Grudem published *Recovering Biblical Manhood and Womanhood*.

The SBC declared the role of a submissive wife to be a woman's highest calling, and Dorothy Patterson taught pastors' wives how to pack their husbands' suitcases as part of a seminary curriculum.

I can't undo what pastors' wives like Joyce Rogers and Dorothy Patterson have done to help lead the SBC charge to reject women called to pastoral ministry.

I can't soften how some pastors treated Kathy Hoppe and Sarah Wood Lee; I can't mute the male SBC pastor who called Susan Lockwood a "handmaiden of Satan."[2]

I can't remove the bad that was done to women by the SBC or the broader world of US evangelicalism any more than the eleventh doctor could save Van Gogh.

What I can do, though, is add to the good.

I can offer you some hope.

The SBC Can Be Different

Located on the wall of a brick pavilion right between the two oldest buildings on the Baylor University campus is an engraved stone tablet memorializing one of Baylor's earliest female professors. It wasn't until a student, Anna Redhair Wells, prompted me that I finally noticed her.

"Dr. Barr," Anna said, "I think you will like Dorothy Scarborough."

She handed me a note, taken from her afternoon archival research. I taped it on my computer so that I wouldn't lose it. This is what it said: "Emily Dorothy Scarborough prof. at Baylor from 1905–1915 taught a college men's Sunday School class at FBC Waco." The note stayed on my monitor for quite a long time. So long that the name stuck in my head too. Then, one day, as I walked through that brick pavilion, I looked up and saw her. Dorothy Scarborough. Baylor graduate, faculty member at both Baylor and Columbia, folklorist, and novelist. Right where she had always been, immortalized in one of the busiest pedestrian thoroughfares on the campus where I had taught for over twenty years.

There is so much I could tell you about Dorothy Scarborough.[3] I could tell you how she was Texas born and bred, living for several years in West Texas not far from where my father grew up. I could tell you how she was one of the early women graduates from Baylor, how she relentlessly pursued a PhD in literature—spending summers in graduate school at the University of Chicago and one year in residence at Oxford University, and finally earning her PhD from Columbia University in 1917. I could tell you about her skills as a teacher and researcher. Columbia immediately hired her as faculty after she completed her doctorate, and her dissertation was so "widely acclaimed by her peers" that it became "a basic reference in the field."[4] Baylor later recognized the scholarship of Scarborough, awarding her an honorary doctorate in 1923 after the publication of her first novel. I could even tell you how bad her handwriting was as I read through letter after letter, manuscript after manuscript, of her papers in the Texas Collection archives on campus (although I was secretly pleased to see a fellow scholar with handwriting almost as bad as mine).

But what I want to tell you about is just one ordinary part of her life that gives me hope for women in ministry.

It is what Anna Wells wrote on that sticky note so long ago: Dorothy Scarborough, a single woman in the early twentieth century, taught a "popular and influential" Sunday school class for college men at an SBC church in Waco, Texas.

Those of you who have read *The Making of Biblical Womanhood* can understand why that fact stuck with me. The triggering event that led to the firing of my husband as a youth pastor at a large evangelical church in Waco—the story I tell in *The Making of Biblical Womanhood*—was his attempt to gain permission for a woman to coteach high school students. Yet, one century earlier, an SBC church in Waco recognized a woman teaching its college men's class as one of their most "popular and influential" teachers.[5]

Scarborough wasn't a pastor's wife; she wasn't an ordained pastor either. She was a single woman serving in an independent ministry role exercising spiritual authority over men in a prominent SBC church.

This means there was a time in Southern Baptist history when women were not always defined by their relationship to male relatives, when women could serve in ministry and lead men without causing controversy, and when women's ability to teach and preach the Word of God was less challenging than it has become today.

Scarborough is a far cry from Milburga, the medieval abbess of Wimnicas. But like Milburga, she resists the mold of what the evangelical world has tried to teach us about women in church history. She also shows us how different the SBC once was.

Did you know that one year before the 1984 resolution condemning women for the "Edenic fall" and discouraging women from pursuing "pastoral functions and leadership roles entailing ordination," the SBC passed a resolution that did the opposite?[6]

It is hard to reconcile the 1984 convention with the 1983 expression of gratitude for women's ministry, affirming "those women who labor for the Lord and the churches in places of special service to which God has called them."[7]

It is hard to reconcile the 1984 convention that proclaimed God requires female submission because of the sin of Eve with the 1983 encouragement for SBC institutions and churches to pay women fairly and guard against gender discrimination in the workplace.

But both are the SBC.[8]

What I find most interesting about the 1983 resolution are the back-to-back statements first affirming "women who serve the Lord as homemakers" in their "special calling" and then affirming women who work outside the home. Instead of declaring that God calls women primarily to dependent ministry roles as homemakers and pastors' wives or declaring that God calls women primarily to independent ministry roles as pastors and missionaries, the SBC made room for both.[9]

Can you imagine?

Can you imagine if, when SBC women expressed a call to ministry, they weren't told it was probably a call to marry a minister?

Can you imagine if women like Joyce Rogers, who loved her role as a pastor's wife, hadn't insisted that all women called to ministry do what she felt called to do?

Can you imagine if pastors' wives like Rogers and Dorothy Patterson had followed the lead of the 1983 resolution—encouraging women who worked outside the home as much as they encouraged homemakers?

Can you imagine if the Home Mission Board had listened to Sarah Lee when she told them she wanted to be a minister instead of a minister's wife? If, instead of forcing her into the "church and family" category, they had encouraged her to follow the calling God gave her?

Can you imagine if, when H. P. Wu contacted the Home Mission Board about Mario Acacia, the SBC entity had responded like the Canadian Baptists did when I first reached out to them, saying "let light shine in the darkness" and pursuing the truth?

Can you imagine if the SBC was a place where single women like Dorothy Scarborough and married women like Willie Dawson could flourish in their own right as teachers and preachers and convention leaders (even exercising authority over men), as they once did?

Can you imagine?

The Pastor's Wife Role Can Be Different

In 1976 Weptanomah W. Carter, the First Lady of New Shiloh Baptist Church in Baltimore, Maryland, wrote *The Black Minister's Wife: As a Participant in the Redemptive Ministry of Her Husband*. I confess that, out of all the pastor's wife books I have read, it is my favorite.

Let me tell you why.

Carter opens with a historical overview of the Black pastor's wife role that instantly clarified for me the cultural whiteness of the pastor's wife role in my evangelical world:

> The Black race has historically had a place for that person called "mother." During the years of slavery, mother meant . . . women who provided some continuing love, care, protection and affection for not only her children, but children and even adults who needed the warm hand of care. Thus "mother" meant one who provided food, care, healing and even stood as an image of the better things of life. Many times husbands were sold from one plantation to another or had to be away for weeks at a time. Thus, the place of "the mother" became strong and established. Moreover, the author's experience of study and lectures in West Africa during the summer of 1972 revealed the strong ancestral role of "mothers" in the West African communities. This ancestral trait did not

die with the passage of Black people from the Old World to the New World. The natural place for it to express itself would be the church, where the white man's overriding control would not be so strong and repressive of traditional West African behavior.[10]

I have been reading pastor's wife literature and archival material for over two years. White women, if they tell an origin story for the pastor's wife, usually turn to biblical exemplars, historical exemplars from the Reformation era, or cite Scripture about being a wife.

Carter does something different.

She roots the Black "mother of the church" and First Lady role in Black history, describing it as an ancestral tradition from West Africa that became a symbol of stability and hope for enslaved people. This female leadership role survived in the Black church because it was a space less affected by "the white man's overriding control."

Do you remember our conversation about the absence of Peter's wife? I dedicated a whole chapter to showing how the pastor's wife role, as perceived by my white evangelical world, is not in fact biblical. It is a product of church history.

Carter accepts that the pastor's wife role is historically created, and she tells a different origin story. Sure, similarities exist between a Black minister's wife and her white counterpart. Sure, Dorothy Patterson calls herself "First Lady" and emphasizes the importance of fancy clothes just as much as Carter does. Sure, Black authors talk about the man in patriarchal terms—such as Mary O. Ross's acknowledgment that "she enjoys looking 'up' to the man of her home" and Carter's reminder that a pastor's wife should "undergird" her husband instead of "destroying" him.[11]

But what if these nods to male headship are less about wives "submitting graciously" to their husbands and more about what Evelyn Higginbotham describes as the "politics of respectability"?[12] Candice Marie Benbow, in her smart and powerful book

*Red Lip Theology: For Church Girls Who've Considered Tithing
to the Beauty Supply Store When Sunday Morning Isn't Enough*,
explains Higginbotham's thesis: "Black church women would em-
ploy the 'politics of respectability' as a means of entering the cult
of true womanhood by proxy, thus being seen as Black women
worthy of respect. Today, 'respectability politics' is often short-
hand for ways Black people attempt to cater to Whiteness, but it
means so much more. The politics of respectability was a method
of survival in a world where Black women couldn't find safety
anywhere."[13]

Just think about it.

What if the Black First Lady supports male headship not because it is perceived as "biblical" but because it makes her husband
respectable in the world of white Christianity?

What if, instead of wearing hats as a symbol of female submission and modesty (as Dorothy Patterson does), the First Lady's
attention to fashion proclaims the worth of a Black woman in a
white world that once rejected her humanity? Beautiful clothing,
Carter writes, "has been a silent way the Black minister's wife has
been saying through the years that 'Black is beautiful.'"[14]

The politics of respectability helps explain why the Black minister's wife continues to wield more independent authority than her
white counterpart in conservative churches—even when lip service
is given to submission. I found that Black ministers' wives often
preach, serve as co-pastors, and exercise considerable (and visible)
independent leadership. This is exactly the type of minister's wife
envisioned by Carter. She argues that a minister's wife firm in her
individuality and independence serves as the best "compliment"
to her husband's "mission" and "work." The most effective Black
minister's wife "is fully in control of herself and not playing out
some image-role assigned to her by her husband, her church, or
her community." As the first woman to receive a master of divinity
from Virginia Seminary, Carter lived up to her description. She
also served as dean at the Maryland Baptist School of Religion,

taught as a visiting professor at Virginia Seminary, and preached widely—both in person and through her radio ministry.[15]

While it is true that I noted an increase in the presence of submission language in Black-authored books published after 2005, I wonder if the politics of respectability is still at play—especially since this increase follows the same pattern in white-authored books. Perhaps as white pastors courted Black pastors during the racial reconciliation movement of the 1990s and early 2000s, inviting them into their churches and platforms, Black pastors' wives used the politics of respectability just as Benbow describes: as a method of survival. Adapting the language of biblical submission made Black women and their pastor husbands more acceptable to the white evangelical world increasingly dominated by complementarian theology.

But what if it doesn't have to be this way?

What if, instead of white evangelicalism influencing the Black pastor's wife role, the Black church—which has historically been much more welcoming of women's leadership—could influence the white pastor's wife role?

The more I read from white evangelical women, the more Carter became a symbol of hope for me that a pastor's wife does not have to be bound by complementarian theology. I almost dropped Carter's book when I first read her chapter on engaging in redemptive ministry. Listen to what she writes: "Many Black ministers' wives who feel no particular need to be involved in Christian service in the local church, might wish to express themselves through some form of community Christian service."[16]

Did you hear that?

Giving teeth to her recognition that sometimes the Black pastor's wife complements her husband's ministry and sometimes she ministers independently from him, Carter does not expect all ministers' wives to be involved in service in their local church. And it is okay.

Can you imagine?

Instead of confusing historical context with biblical truth, Carter embraces the historical roots of the minister's wife role and offers a more expansive path. As she concludes, "no longer can the Black minister's wife be relegated behind the mask of her husband. She has served a role that identifies her responsibilities as being, at times, separate and unique, and, at other times, complementary. . . . She knows that when she joins the church, her loyalty is to Christ, not to her relationship to her husband. She will not permit domestic issues to color her commitment to Christ or in serving the needs of others."[17]

Can you imagine if this vision of the pastor's wife role prevailed instead of that presented by Dorothy Patterson?

The Church Mother served as a symbol of hope for enslaved Africans. Maybe the Black minister's wife can serve as a symbol of hope for the pastor's wife too. Benbow reminds us that "we are on a constant journey of getting it wrong and getting it right." God loves us regardless, but when we get it wrong, the "hope" is we will "course-correct."[18]

What if we course-corrected the pastor's wife role?

What if we recognize how much of what we perceive as a biblical role for pastors' wives has been created by culture (especially white Southern culture)?

What if we recognize that a woman married to a minister can have a calling separate from her husband, that her domestic role does not define her identity in Christ?

What if we recognize that the only true "biblical" role for a woman is to do whatever God has called her to do?

Can you imagine?

Together for the Gospel

I have been a pastor's wife for more than twenty-five years. I no longer worry about what I should and shouldn't do. I no longer worry about how I dress. I no longer worry about what the congregation thinks of me. I just do what I can, what I feel God calls me to do. I teach Sunday school because I love it. I tell my husband when I can help and when I can't. I try to fill in the gaps where the church needs me—not because I have to but because I want to.

History shows me that the pastor's wife role has a deep, rich, and complicated history. I have told only a small part of the story, stemming from my experience as a white evangelical woman who became a pastor's wife in the Southern Baptist world. There is so much more I wish I could say. I wish I could write more about the role of the pastor's wife in the Black church; I wish I could write more about co-pastors and Pentecostal churches; I wish I had more time to consider pastors' wives in the global church. I wish I could share more women's stories.

I know from my experience as a pastor's wife how important the role is. I know the difference I have made in the lives of so many people. For better and for worse, pastors' wives like me have faithfully served the church, we have taught the gospel, and we have served alongside our husbands.

At the same time, I know that my white evangelical and Southern Baptist tradition has used the pastor's wife role to enshrine biblical womanhood as the only godly role for women. Because the pastor's wife role provides an acceptable way in complementarian theology for women to serve in ministry, it has been weaponized to condemn women's ordination and exclude women from pastoral positions.

But what if it doesn't have to be this way?

What if the white evangelical church could follow the example more prevalent in Black churches where women married to ministers can serve as co-pastors alongside their husbands?

What if women married to ministers did not feel pressure to assume ministry roles to which they feel no calling?

What if, instead of fighting against one another, women encouraged one another in their callings—whatever those callings may be?

What if our churches made room for both pastors' wives and female pastors, for those who happened to marry pastors and those who chose not to marry at all?

What if we built a new evangelical coalition that could stand together for the gospel in reality as well as in name, recognizing the full equality of women and their value as ministerial leaders?

What if we welcomed the pastoral leadership of women like Milburga, supported women called to ministry like Sarah Lee, helped women like Maria Acacia, and learned from women like Weptanomah Carter?

Can you imagine?

I can.

History shows me how women like me became the pastor's wife.

History shows me how the pastor's wife role has been used to push women out of ordained ministry.

But history also shows me that it doesn't have to be this way.

History has taught me that women, including the wives of pastors, can change the church.

I think it is time that we change it.

Acknowledgments

It took a village to write this book. As I stand here, at the end, I can tell you that I would not have finished this journey without the great number of people who supported and helped me along the way.

I owe so much to Brazos Press, especially those I have worked closely with for so long: Katelyn Beaty, Eric Salo, Erin Smith, Shelly MacNaughton, Paula Gibson, and Jeremy Wells: you have transformed my research and writing into a beautiful book (with a beautiful cover!), of which I am so proud. Thank you for making me better, for encouraging me, for patiently waiting on my drafts and forgiving me for adding so many footnotes, for being honest about what I need to change, and for making the marketing and publicity fun and easy (at least on my end). I am especially grateful for the care Brazos has shown me as a person. Thank you for trusting me to write this book. It is my honor to be a Brazos author.

To Giles Anderson and Jim Chaffee, I never dreamed I would be working with both a literary agent and a speaking agent. But you both have done so much to help me. Giles, you walked me through the contract process and provided me with so much advice about the book publishing process. Jim, you have patiently waited on my emails and helped me make good decisions about speaking engagements. I am so grateful for my chance to work alongside you both.

It goes without saying that this book is only possible because of the research support I received from the Southern Baptist Historical Library and Archives in Nashville, Tennessee, the Texas Collection at

Baylor University in Waco, Texas, and the archives at Southwestern Baptist Theological Seminary in Fort Worth, Texas. Taffey Hall, the director of the Southern Baptist Historical Library and Archives, welcomed me on three different occasions. She and her staff went above and beyond in providing access to the archival material I needed, even providing financial assistance through the Lynn E. May study grants. Taffey answered numerous emails from me with patience and precision. I could not have written this book without her guidance. Likewise, I am so grateful to Jill Botticelli Cabal, director of libraries and archivist at Southwestern Baptist Theological Seminary. SWBTS was the first archive I visited for both this project and my next, and the kindness and generosity shown me was so encouraging. The Texas Collection at Baylor University has become a longtime friend to me. My favorite thing to do at the end of a long week is spend a few hours in the peaceful reading room learning more about women like Dorothy Scarborough. University archivist Elizabeth Rivera and all the staff, especially Benna Vaughan, have made possible my ability to draw connections between my work as a medievalist and the local history of my town and university. Finally, I cannot say thank you enough to archivist Adam McCulloch and director Gordon Heath at Canadian Baptist Archives at McMaster Divinity College. I am overwhelmed by the amount of time you spent with me, helping locate documents and even helping me read through the documents to find what I needed. I owe you much more than a pub lunch.

To the scholars who read chapter drafts and chapter sections and gave me much-needed advice—Scot McKnight, Nijay Gupta, Todd Still, David Whitford, Lynneth Renberg, Katherine Goodwin Lindgren, Elizabeth Marvel, Elesha Coffman, Mandy McMichael, Taylor Sims, and Betsy Flowers—this book is infinitely better because of your generosity and knowledge. Scot, it is because of a conversation I had with you that I decided to write this book in the first place. You have never stopped encouraging me, and I thank God for bringing you and Kris into my life. Betsy, you walked with me through some difficult research moments and shared the wealth of your own research and knowledge to help me write this book. What I owe you is immeasurable. Katherine, Lynneth, Liz, and David, you helped me find the right path in my medieval and reformation chapters. Katherine, thanks especially for lending me your expertise on Katherine Zell too.

To the scholars who answered last-minute questions by phone and email and generously helped me make connections in the Baptist world, thank you Benjamin Cole (the Baptist Blogger) and Melody Maxwell. You helped me pull the pieces together for my research. I owe thanks to Bob Smietana at Religion News Service, too, as he gave me advice and help at a critical moment. Thanks also to my anonymous SBC friends who talked with me about seminary course work and Baptist politics. It is my honor to know you.

To my friends Leanne and Dallas Friesen, what can I say? You welcomed a stranger into your home, shared with me the ins and outs of Canadian Baptist history, and even took me to see Niagara Falls. I came to Toronto in search of history; I found kindred spirits who blessed my life. To Leanne, who is also the executive minister of CBOQ, the executive staff—especially Koon Wah Leung and Ken Foo—and CBOQ board who cared more about truth than protecting a difficult past. If only the SBC had chosen a path more like CBOQ, our Baptist world would be a better place. I am grateful also to my anonymous friends who shared their knowledge about a difficult chapter of their lives. Thank you for trusting me with your story. As you wrote to me, may this book provide "healing to some people and correction for others." From your lips to God's ears, may it be so.

To Baylor University, it continues to amaze me how much support and care I receive from my workplace. My colleagues in the history department, especially my chair Julie deGraffenried and former chair Barry Hankins, welcomed me back from my years in the graduate school, even allowing me to hold the James Vardaman Endowed Professorship, and supported me in finding the resources I needed to finish this project. To Betsy Vardaman, I can never say enough how much holding the Vardaman Professorship means to me. The endowment has made researching this book so much easier, and I am humbled every time I see the Vardaman name alongside mine. To my colleagues in religion and English, David Whitford and Greg Garrett—I am so grateful for the encouragement you give me as well as your academic expertise. To my colleague in modern languages and culture, Karol Hardin, your friendship (especially dragging me out into the sunshine for frequent walks) keeps me grounded and reminds me of what is most important in my life. You and Mike have walked with Jeb and me through some of our most difficult hours; you have also helped us keep smiling. To Larry Lyon—you are still my favorite boss, you gave me the space I needed to write as an associate dean, and you helped me navigate my way back to a full-time research and teaching job so that I could keep writing.

I would also like to thank Linda Livingstone, the president of Baylor University, and Nancy Brickhouse, the provost of Baylor University. I am grateful for your incredible leadership and support, both professionally and personally. Thank you for fostering a research culture at Baylor that empowers women like me and encourages public scholarship.

Every project that I have completed since 2011 is because of the support of my writing group. Kara Poe Alexander, Leslie Hahner, and Theresa Kennedy, thank you for reading my work even at the roughest stage. Your wise comments helped me start this book in the right direction, and your friendship encouraged me to finish strong. Both this book and *The Making of Biblical Womanhood* owe some sections to research that began on the *Anxious Bench* blog. A piece of me will always be writing on that bench.

I cannot say thank you enough to three people who worked with me on the research for this book. Katie Heatherly started this journey with me as a master's student at Baylor. She accompanied me to two archives and was with me when I began to untangle the story I tell in chapter 8. She also tracked down scholarship on the IRS clergy tax credit and helped me make sense of it. Brooke

LeFevre read so many pastor's wife books (more than you probably ever wanted to), helped make sure my drafted chapters had proper citation, and even lent her voice to the section about Marion Grant and the pastor's wife award. Savannah Locke joined me on my final research trip. It is her vision that has given birth to the accompanying podcast miniseries with *The Bible for Normal People*. Thank you, all of you, for believing in my research and joining me for the journey.

The final people I must thank are those who walked with me every step of the way. Kristin Du Mez and Kristie Wahlquist, you listened when I needed to talk, gave me reasons to laugh even when I was writing the hardest parts, and lent me the strength I needed to finish this book stronger than I ever imagined. My parents, Kathy and Crawford Allison, have done more than I could ever thank you for. You have always believed in me; you gave me the foundations for the strong faith I have today; and you have never failed to pick a child up from volleyball practice or bring us a meal when we needed it. I have to also thank our family friend Martha Bumpas who was the first Baptist woman I ever saw preach and gave me some valuable insight into the lives of missionary women. I am also grateful to my siblings, Jennifer Sternberg who housed and fed me for all my Nashville trips, Michael Allison who helped check my childhood memories, and Amy Kaszak who gave me even more reason to admire her as she fought and beat breast cancer this past year.

Last but not least, this book is for my husband and children. Stephen and Elena, I am so proud to be your mother. You have seen the worst of Christianity yet come through with faith stronger than mine was at your age. I thank God every day for the privilege of raising you. Jeb, this is the third book you have lived with me through. You are the only one who really knows my writing struggles. Thank you for believing in me, for putting up with me, for picking up the slack I drop, and for being not only an amazing husband and father but also the best pastor I have ever known. You are a man after God's own heart and I am proud to walk beside you.

Chronological List
of Pastor's Wife Books

Below is the list of 150 pastor's wife books examined as part of the research for this book. To compile this list, we (Brooke LeFevre and Katie Heatherly and I) began by searching WorldCat and Amazon for books with variations of "pastor's wife" and "minister's wife" in the title. We expanded the initial list by adding books cited and/or referenced by other authors, examining syllabi of courses designed for ministry wives, and searching websites either focused on equipping ministry wives or directing some material toward them. With a few exceptions, we mostly focused on books intended as guides or helps for women that were published in North America during the last one hundred years (1923–present). I plan to continue expanding this research in future academic work.

Shelhamer, Julia A. *Trials and Triumphs of a Minister's Wife*. Repairer, 1923.

Elson, Frances Sandys. *Quiet Hints to Ministers' Wives*. Stratford, 1934.

Bader, Golda Maude Elam, ed. *I Married a Minister*. Abingdon-Cokesbury, 1942.

McDaniel, Douglass Scarborough. *The Pastor's Helpmate*. Broadman, 1942.

Hewitt, Arthur Wentworth. *The Shepherdess*. Willett, Clark, 1943.

Ross, Mary O. *The Minister's Wife*. Arbora, 1946. Reprinted, Harlo, 1983.

Fisher, Welthy Honsinger. *Handbook for Ministers' Wives*. Woman's Press, 1951.

Williams, Loyd Elmo. *Queen without a Crown: The Preacher's Wife*. Naylor, 1952.

Parrot, Lora Lee. *How to Be a Preacher's Wife and Like It*. Zondervan, 1956.

Stark, Phyllis. *I Chose a Parson*. Oxford University Press, 1956.

Raley, Helen Thames. *As the Years Go By*. Oklahoma Baptist University Standard Press, 1959.

Nyberg, Kathleen Neil. *The Care and Feeding of Ministers*. Abingdon, 1961.

Denton, Wallace. *The Role of the Minister's Wife*. Westminster, 1962.

Pentecost, Dorothy. *The Pastor's Wife and the Church*. Moody, 1964.

Douglas, William. *Ministers' Wives*. Harper and Row, 1965.

Brown, Marilyn Oden. *The Minister's Wife: Person or Position?* Abingdon, 1966.

Keable, Gladys. *Such as We Are: Parsons' Wives and Parsons' Families*. Darton, Longman, & Todd, 1967.

Taylor, Alice. *How to Be a Minister's Wife and Love It: Life in a Goldfish Bowl*. Zondervan, 1968.

Lewis, Esther Lambert. *We Also Build: The Role of the Minister's Wife*. Beacon Hill, 1969.

Nordland, Frances. *Unprivate Life of a Pastor's Wife*. Moody, 1972.

Truman, Ruth. *Underground Manual for Ministers' Wives*. Abingdon, 1974.

Carter, Weptanomah. *The Black Minister's Wife: As a Participant in the Redemptive Ministry of Her Husband*. Progressive National Baptist Publishing House, Gateway, 1976.

Nelson, Martha. *This Call We Share*. Broadman, 1977.

Rich, Marion K., ed. *Rejoice, You're a Minister's Wife*. Compiled by the Ministers' Wives Leadership Conferences. Beacon Hill, 1978.

Bailey, Mary Frances, and Robert Bailey. *Coping with Stress in the Minister's Home*. Broadman, 1979.

Senter, Ruth. *So You're the Pastor's Wife*. Zondervan, 1979.

Ross, Charlotte. *Who Is the Minister's Wife? A Search for Personal Fulfillment*. Westminster, 1980.

Coble (Lawther), Betty. *The Private Life of the Minister's Wife*. Broadman, 1981.

MacDonald, Gail. *High Call, High Privilege*. Tyndale, 1981.

Sinclair, Donna. *The Pastor's Wife Today*. Abingdon, 1981.

Turner, Denise. *Home Sweet Fishbowl: Confessions of a Minister's Wife*. Word, 1982.

Montgomery, Shirley E. *A Growth Guide for Ministers' Wives*. Broadman, 1984.

Truman, Ruth. *Spaghetti from the Chandelier: And Other Humorous Adventures of a Minister's Family*. Abingdon, 1984.

Buckingham, Michele, ed. *Help! I'm a Pastor's Wife*. Charisma Media, 1986.

Peck, Terry. *Minister's Mate: Two for the Price of One?* Convention, 1986.

White, Ruthe. *What Every Pastor's Wife Should Know*. Tyndale, 1986.

Bess, Mary E. *Tips for Ministers and Mates*. Broadman, 1987.

Daughtery, Sharon. *Called by His Side: The Role of the Minister's Wife*. Victory Christian Center, 1987.

Gilbert, Barbara G. *Who Ministers to Ministers? A Study of Support Systems for Clergy and Spouses*. Alban Institute, 1987.

Montgomery, Shirley E. *Winning Ways for Ministers' Wives*. Broadman, 1987.

Langberg, Diane, and Ruth Senter. *Counsel for Pastors' Wives*. Zondervan, 1988.

Tucker, Ruth. *First Ladies of the Parish: Historical Portraits of Pastors' Wives*. Ministry Resources Library, 1988.

Lee, Cameron, and Jack Balswick. *Life in a Glass House: The Minister's Family in Its Unique Social Context.* Zondervan, 1989.

Eppinger, Paul, and Sybil Eppinger. *Every Minister Needs a Lover.* Baker, 1990.

Hunt, Harley, ed. *The Stained Glass Fishbowl: Strengthening Clergy Marriages.* Ministers Council, 1990.

Hyles, Beverly. *Life, as Viewed from the Goldfish Bowl.* Sword of the Lord, 1990.

Leavell, Jo Ann Pairs, and Rhonda Kelley. *Don't Miss the Blessing.* Pelican, 1990.

Senter, Ruth Hollinger. *The Guilt-Free Book for Pastors' Wives.* Victor Books, 1990.

Garrett, Yvonne. *The Stained Glass House: A Handbook for Ministers' Wives.* Vernon, 1991.

Greenbacker, Liz, and Sherry Taylor. *Private Lives of Ministers' Wives.* New Horizon, 1991.

Harbour, Brian. *Marriage in the Minister's Home.* Convention, 1992.

Randall, Robert L. *The Eternal Triangle: Pastor, Spouse, and Congregation.* Fortress, 1992.

Tucker, Ruth. *Private Lives of Pastor's Wives.* Zondervan, 1992.

Pannell, Nancy. *Being a Minister's Wife and Being Yourself.* B&H, 1993.

Dugan, Lynne, ed. *Heart to Heart with Pastors' Wives: Twelve Women Share the Wisdom They've Gained as Partners in Ministry.* Regal, 1994.

Dobson, Lorna. *I'm More Than the Pastor's Wife.* Zondervan, 1995.

Wilson, Virginia. *Lose the Halo, Keep the Wings: Great Advice for Ministers' Wives.* New Hope/Women's Missionary Union, 1996.

London, H. B., and Neil B. Wiseman. *Married to a Pastor: How to Stay Happily Married in the Ministry.* Regal, 1999.

Heim, Pamela Hoover. *The Pastor's Wife Balancing Her Multiple Relationships.* Harvest, 2001.

Paulk, Norma. *Stand by Your Man: The Story of a Preacher's Wife.* Cathedral of the Holy Spirit, 2001.

Harvey, Donald, and Gene Williams. *Living in a Glass House: Surviving the Scrutiny of Ministry and Marriage.* Beacon Hill, 2002.

Hughes, Barbara, ed. *Devotions for Ministry Wives: Encouragement from Those Who've Been There.* Zondervan, 2002.

Patterson, Dorothy. *A Handbook for Ministers' Wives: Sharing the Blessing of Your Marriage, Family, and Home.* B&H, 2002.

Slamp, Kathy. *You Might Be a Pastor's Wife If . . .* Vessel Ministries, 2002.

DeLisle, Susan Rice. *The View From the Parsonage.* Warner Press, Church of God Ministries, 2003.

Lodholz, Lois Koenig. *Parsonage Pitfalls.* Heins, 2003.

Phillips, Nancy H. *Confessions of a Preacher's Wife: You Need More Than a "12-Step Program."* 1stBooks, 2003.

Haggard, Gayle. *A Life Embraced: A Hopeful Guide for the Pastor's Wife.* WaterBrook, 2004.

Musgrove, Peggy. *Musings of a Maraschino Cherry: Reflections on the Role of a Minister's Wife.* ACW, 2004.

Briscoe, Jill. *Renewal on the Run: Embracing the Privileges and Expectations of a Ministry Wife.* New Hope, 2005.

Evans, Lois, Vonette Bright, Serita Jakes, Anna Hayford, Bobbie Houston, Dianna Hagee, Gayle Haggard, Carol Kent, Beverly LaHaye, Donna Mullins, Kay Arthur, and Lisa Bevere. *Free to Soar: Global Pastor's Wives Network.* Bethany House, 2005.

Sommerville, Mary. *One with a Shepherd: The Tears and Triumphs of a Ministry Marriage.* Kress Christian, 2005.

Trotman, Gloria Lindsey. *By Her Side: A Pastor's Guide to Supporting His Wife.* General Conference of Seventh-Day Adventists, Ministerial Association, 2005.

Williams, Joyce. *She Can't Even Play the Piano! Insights for Ministry Wives.* Beacon Hill, 2005.

Harrington, Paula. *A Sunday Afternoon with the Preachers' Wives.* Lulu, 2006.

Scheyder, Susie. *The Other Side of the Pulpit.* Xulon, 2006.

Williams, Joyce. *Quiet Moments for Ministry Wives: Scriptures, Meditations, and Prayers.* Beacon Hill, 2006.

York, Elaine. *The ABC's and 123's of Being a Pastor's Wife.* BookSurge, 2006.

Clifford, Laurie Berry, and Margie Berry Fogal. *Tales of a Crazy Pastor's Wife: Okay, So I've Got Some 'Splainin' to Do!* Sister-Friend, 2007.

Ellison, Judy. *Touching the Heart of Pastors' Wives and Women in Ministry.* Armour of Light, 2007.

Flint-Borden, Teresa. *Women Married to Men in Ministry: Breaking the Sound Barrier Together.* Abingdon, 2007.

Kyles, Ysidra. *The Hunt Is Over! Memoirs of an Ex-Preacher's Wife.* Xak Xak, 2007.

Bryant, Cecelia Williams. *Letters of Light for First Ladies.* Judson, 2008.

Miles-Howard, Donnie. *Open Diary of a Pastor's Wife.* Tate, 2008.

Siefert, Kimberly. *Tales from a Pastor's Wife: What the Pastor's Wife Is Really Thinking.* Tate, 2008.

Valimont, Jelly. *I Have Issues.* Ministry Solutions, 2008.

Bromell, Poiette McGill. *Saved and Sexual: A Survival Guide for Pastors' Wives.* Lulu, 2009.

Hawkins, Susie. *From One Ministry Wife to Another: Honest Conversations about Ministry Connections.* Moody, 2009.

Lovingood, Rachel, and Jennifer Landrith. *In Our Shoes: Real Life Issues for Ministers' Wives by Ministers' Wives.* Lifeway, 2009.

Molina, Clara E. *The Pastor's Wife: Missionary to the World: The Do's and Don'ts of a Pastor's Wife.* Crossbooks, 2009.

Trotman, Gloria Lindsey. *What No One Tells the Pastor's Wife.* General Conference Ministerial, 2009.

Cocklin, Kay. *Nobody Told Me: A Guide for Pastors' Wives.* Xulon, 2010.

Floyd, Jeana. *10 Things Every Minister's Wife Needs to Know.* New Leaf, 2010.

Leavell, Jo Ann Paris, with Rhonda Harrington Kelley. *Don't Miss the Blessing.* Pelican, Gretna, 2010.

McKay, Lisa. *You Can Still Wear Cute Shoes: And Other Great Advice from an Unlikely Preacher's Wife.* David C. Cook, 2010.

Thorne, Deloise C. *The Cross Bearing of a Pastor's Wife.* Xulon, 2010.

Alder, Donna Bordelon. *When the Pastor Is Your Husband: The Joy and Pain of Ministry Wives.* Beacon Hill, 2011.

Benton, Ann, with Val Archer, Julia Jones, Rachel Lawrence, Jane McNabb, Kath Paterson, Ruth Shaw and Lizzy Smallwood. *The Minister's Wife: Privileges, Pressures and Pitfalls.* IVP, 2011.

Rodda, Jane. *How to Be a Pastor's Wife: Your Step by Step Guide.* HowExpert, 2011.

Stephen, Yolanda King. *The Upside of the Down Low: A Pastor's Wife's Memoir.* No Ordinary Rose, 2011.

Areogun, Oyenike. *Godly Wisdom for a Pastor's Wife.* Xlibris, 2012.

Claypool, JoEllen. *A Realist Guide to Being a Pastor's Wife.* Valley Walker, 2012.

Hylton, Judith S. *The Faith of the Pastor's Wife: Surviving in Ministry Yet Remaining in Love with God and His People.* WestBow, 2012.

Croft, Brian, and Cara Croft. *The Pastor's Family: Shepherding Your Family through the Challenges of Pastoral Ministry.* Zondervan, 2013.

Hoover, Christine. *The Church Planting Wife: Help and Hope for Her Heart.* Moody, 2013.

Martin, Albert N. *Encouragement for Pastors' Wives.* Chapel Library, 2013.

Richey, K. T. *Sunday Morning Blues.* Urban Books LLC, 2013.

Rogers, Joyce. *Chosen to Be a Minister's Wife.* Innovo, 2013.

Stewart, Catherine J., ed. *Letters to Pastors' Wives: When Seminary Ends and Ministry Begins.* P&R, 2013.

Wilhite, Lori, and Brandi Wilson. *Leading and Loving It: Encouragement for Pastors' Wives and Women in Leadership.* FaithWorks, 2013.

Wilson, Nancy. *True Companion: Thoughts on Being a Pastor's Wife.* Cannon, 2013.

Rhea, Rhonda. *Join the Insanity Crazy-Fun Life in the Pastors' Wives Club.* New Hope, 2014.

Clark, Theresa Ann. *Tell the Truth and Shame the Devil: The Untold Story of a Pastor's Wife.* Trinity and Talbot, 2015.

Furman, Gloria. *The Pastor's Wife: Strengthened by Grace for a Life of Love.* Crossway, 2015.

Hoover, Christine. *Partners in Planting: Help and Encouragement for Church Planting Wives.* Self-published, 2015.

Jones, Nan. *The Perils of a Pastor's Wife.* Straight Street, 2015.

McCurley, Chris. *Girl, We Need to Talk: The Minister's Wife and Her Struggles.* Start2FinishBooks, 2015.

Thrasher, Joyce. *A Crazy Pastor's Wife: Wit and Wisdom from Saints and Scoundrels.* Self-published, 2015.

Ellison, Judy. *Touching the Heart of Pastors' Wives: A Conversation.* Leeds, 2016.

Molina, Clara E. *Oh No! I Married the Pastor! The Do's and Don'ts of a Pastor's Wife.* Westbow, 2016.

Sigler, Latheira. *Secrets of a Minister's Wife.* Christian Faith, 2016.

Butler, Yolanda. *The Heart of a First Lady: A Practical Guide for the Pastor's Wife.* Revised edition. First Lady Butler Ministries, BookPatch LLC, 2017.

White, Shauntae Brown. *The First Lady: African American Pastors' Wives in Their Own Voices.* Self-published, 2017.

Barba, Claudia. *The Monday Morning Club: You're Not Alone—Encouragement for Ministry.* Press On! Ministries, 2018.

Moyo, Daisy. *A Handbook for the Pastor's Wife.* Self-published, 2018.

Veal, Elisa. *Somebody Tell the Truth . . . About Being a Pastor's Wife.* Self-published, 2018.

Warren, Kay. *Sacred Privilege: Your Life and Ministry as a Pastor's Wife.* Revell, 2018.

Harris, Pasha. *Behind the Pulpit: The Memoir of a Pastor's Wife.* Lulu, 2019.

Hildreth, Janice. *What Would the Pastor's Wife Say? Answers to Everyday Questions from a Pastor's Wife.* Brynwood, 2019.

Kinney, Barbara. *The Life of a Pastor's Wife: "Why Didn't Someone Tell Me?"* Covenant, 2019.

Oyedepo, Faith. *The Effective Minister's Wife.* Dominion, 2019.

Meadows, Kate. *Faith to Follow the Journey of Becoming a Pastor's Wife*. Westbow, 2020.

Sheppard, Meredith R. *Letters to Pastors' Wives*. Xulon, 2020.

Stiller, Karen. *The Minister's Wife: A Memoir of Faith, Doubt, Friendship, Loneliness, Forgiveness, and More*. Zondervan, 2020.

Williams, Eleanor L. *Diary of a Pastor's Wife*. Shallaywa Hinds, 2020.

Hill, Megan. *Partners in the Gospel: 50 Meditations for Pastors' and Elders' Wives*. P&R, 2021.

Hosmer, Lori. *Pastor's Wife and the Many Lessons God Has Taught Me along This Journey*. Christian Faith, 2021.

Kelsey, Suzanne. *Skipping Church: Notes from an Accidental Minister's Wife*. Shanti Arts, 2021.

Myers, Patricia Jackson. *A Pastor's Wife: God, What Were You Thinking?* Christian Faith, 2021.

Ortlund, Jani. *Help! I'm Married to My Pastor*. Crossway, 2021.

Thompson, Kelly, and Terry Thompson. *Pastor's Wife Survival Playbook: A Thriving Marriage and Ministry in the Mayhem*. Rainer, 2021.

Ellison, Judy. *Touching the Heart of Pastors' Wives*. Leeds, 2022.

Hoover, Christine. *How to Thrive as a Pastor's Wife*. Baker Books, 2022.

Johnson, Deloris Penny. *Secrets of a Pastor's Wife: The Good, the Bad, and the Pastor's Wife*. Self-published, 2022.

Bagby, Velma, et al. *All the Preacher's Wives, An Anthology: A Peek Behind the Curtain of a Preacher's Wife*. MADDCity Media, 2023.

Burgess, Lori. *Someone Should've Told Me*. Relentless, 2023.

Kimber, Shevalle T. *FirstLadyDom in the Black Church*. BookBaby, 2023.

Wynn-Johnson, Leisa. *First Ladies, Can We Talk? Walking in Your Calling and Purpose*. Christian Living, 2023.

Aladekoba, Patricia. *Solace: Empowering Pastors' Wives to Prevent and Overcome Burnout*. Paradise Restored, 2024.

Gilbert, Stephanie, Jessica Taylor, and Jenna Allen. *Pastor's Wives Tell All: Navigating Real Church Life with Honesty and Humor*. Baker Books, 2024.

Notes

Introduction

1. I agree with Kristin Du Mez that "evangelical" is a cultural descriptor "intertwined with white racial identity." "For conservative white evangelicals, the 'good news' of the Christian gospel has become inextricably linked to a staunch commitment to patriarchal authority, gender difference, and Christian nationalism, and all of these are intertwined with white racial identity." Kristin Du Mez, *Jesus and John Wayne: How White Evangelicals Corrupted a Faith and Fractured a Nation* (Liveright, 2020), 6–7. Elizabeth Flowers provides a historical overview of evangelicals: "Historically, evangelicals were born of the great revivals that swept the country during the second Great Awakening. They emphasized belief in the Bible as the inspired word of God, the experience of individual conversion, the assurance of salvation through the work of Jesus Christ, and the ongoing cultivation of a personal relationship with God within the community of the church. . . . After the 1970s, many evangelical traditions splintered, though almost all claimed a heritage shaped by these earlier events, beliefs, and practices." Flowers, *Into the Pulpit: Southern Baptist Women and Power since World War II* (University of North Carolina Press, 2012), 8–9. For a recent assessment of evangelical identity that roots the movement firmly within the cultural context of the post–World War II era, see Matthew Avery Sutton, "Redefining the History and Historiography on American Evangelicalism in the Era of the Religious Right," *Journal of the American Academy of Religion* (August 13, 2024), https://doi.org/10.1093/jaarel/lfae063.

2. Mary O. Ross, *The Minister's Wife* (1946; repr., Harlo Press, 1983), 115, 25–26.

3. Dorothy Pentecost, *The Pastor's Wife and the Church* (Moody, 1964), 144, 171.

4. Dorothy Kelley Patterson, *A Handbook for Ministers' Wives: Sharing the Blessings of Your Marriage, Family, and Home* (Broadman & Holman, 2002; repr., Northeastern Baptist Press, 2021), 61, 58.

5. Marilyn Brown Oden, *The Minister's Wife: Person or Position?* (Abingdon, 1966), 34.

6. I recognize and celebrate the husbands of pastors. This book focuses on the wives of ministers because, historically, it is women whose identity has been more likely to be subsumed into their husbands' vocations. Also, unlike women, Protestant

men have had access to ordination/clerical offices whereas women have faced varying restrictions, making the role of pastor's wife more significant to women (as they have fewer options) than the role of pastor's husband for men.

7. Nancy Wilson, *True Companion: Thoughts on Being a Pastor's Wife* (Canon, 2013), 63–64.

8. Gail E. Murphy-Geiss, "Married to the Minister: The Status of the Clergy Spouse as Part of a Two-Person Single Career," *Journal of Family Issues* 32, no. 7 (2011): 950, 933.

9. Tamika L. Ledbetter, "No-Choice Volunteer Leader: A Hermeneutic Phenomenological Inquiry of the Lived Experiences of Pastors' Wives" (PhD diss., University of Phoenix, 2018). These phrases are used throughout the dissertation, but see especially the conclusion, 144–47.

10. Murphy-Geiss, "Married to the Minister," 933.

11. "How Healthy Are Pastors' Relationships?," Barna Group, February 15, 2017, https://www.barna.com/research/healthy-pastors-relationships.

12. Weptanomah W. Carter, *The Black Minister's Wife: As a Participant in the Redemptive Ministry of Her Husband* (Progressive National Baptist, 1976), 27–28.

13. Yolanda G. Butler, *The Heart of a First Lady: A Practical Guide for the Pastor's Wife*, rev. ed. (First Lady Butler Ministries, 2017), chap. 2.

14. Journalist Rachel Zoll accurately described ministers' wives as "unpaid volunteers at their husband's churches." Zoll, "Behind Every Good Minister . . . Is a Wife Who Doesn't Get Paid to Help Minister to a Flock," *Statesville Record & Landmark*, June 10, 2001, 8A, archived in Women in Baptist Life Collection, AR 160, at Southern Baptist Historical Library and Archives (SBHLA), Nashville, Tennessee.

15. David Bebbington, *Evangelicalism in Modern Britain: A History from the 1730s to the 1980s* (Unwin Hyman, 1989), 2–3; and Du Mez, *Jesus and John Wayne*, 6–7. Flowers describes how the Reformed and Wesleyan traditions are "evangelicalism's two theological sides." Flowers, *Into the Pulpit*, 6–9.

16. Flowers, *Into the Pulpit*, 10–11.

17. Benjamin R. Knoll and Cammie Jo Bolin, *She Preached the Word: Women's Ordination in Modern America* (Oxford University Press, 2018), 21.

18. H. Leon McBeth, "Role of Women in Southern Baptist History," *Baptist History and Heritage* 12 (January 1977): 18, 23, quoted in Barry Hankins, *Uneasy in Babylon: Southern Baptist Conservatives and American Culture* (University of Alabama Press, 2002), 203–4.

19. The entire Kansas City Resolution of 1984 can be found at "Resolution on Ordination and the Role of Women in Ministry," Southern Baptist Convention, June 1, 1984, https://www.sbc.net/resource-library/resolutions/resolution-on-ordination-and-the-role -of-women-in-ministry, in Women in Baptist Life Collection, AR 160, SBHLA, Nashville, Tennessee. See also W. A. Reed and Tom Mulgrew, "Baptist Group Hits Resolution on Ordination: Starts Nucleus of Move Supporting Women's Role," *Tennessean*, August 29, 1984, in Women in Baptist Life Collection, AR 160, SBHLA, Nashville, Tennessee. As pivotal as the 1984 resolution was, it began to be seen as too harsh. Indeed, Elizabeth Flowers shows how Dorothy Patterson was instrumental in "softening" it. Instead of women's subjugation being a product of the fall (as the 1984 resolution states), it began to be seen as a product of creation. Flowers, *Into the Pulpit*, 134–35.

20. Hankins, *Uneasy in Babylon*, 204. I worked with two Baylor University graduate students, Katie Heatherly and Brooke LeFevre, analyzing books by and for pastors' wives. We compiled an initial list of around 180 books ranging from the eighteenth to twenty-first century. For this study, we analyzed 150 books written mostly in the US

as guides for the pastor's wife role between 1923 and 2023. Of these, we closely read ninety, examining changes in language used to describe the role of the pastor's wife (especially concerning male headship, female submission, and women's ordination). Mostly I have used the pastor's wife literature within this book as textual evidence about how pastor's wives perceive the role and teach it to others. However, I do provide a preliminary analysis of my findings in chap. 6. I plan to continue honing the evidence for academic publication as a journal article. In the meantime, I include a list of the pastor's wife books consulted for this study so others may evaluate these findings.

21. Betty J. Coble, *The Private Life of the Minister's Wife* (Broadman, 1981), 53–57.

22. For a succinct summary of the theological and historical debates over female ordination and a history of the practice, see Gary Macy, *The Hidden History of Women's Ordination: Female Clergy in the Medieval West* (Oxford University Press, 2008).

23. I am adapting the words of Judith Bennett: "Patriarchy might be everywhere, but it is not everywhere the same." Bennett, *History Matters: Patriarchy and the Challenge of Feminism* (University of Pennsylvania Press, 2006), 54.

24. Kate Bowler, *The Preacher's Wife: The Precarious Power of Evangelical Women Celebrities* (Princeton University Press, 2019), 6.

25. Today, Black Protestants report the greatest familiarity with female pastors and women serving as congregational leaders (Knoll and Bolin, *She Preached the Word*, 127). Yet women's ordination has also been contested in the Black church. See the example of Jarena Lee, discussed in Elesha J. Coffman, *Turning Points in American Church History: How Pivotal Events Shaped a Nation and a Faith* (Baker Academic, 2024), 101.

26. Flowers confirms this sentiment as predominating within the SBC: "The concept of call in twentieth-century Southern Baptist life was second in significance to salvation only and part of the Southern Baptist emphasis on personal piety. . . . The specific language of call, however, was most often reserved for those who felt God's stirring in the direction of vocational ministry or a career in missions. For a Southern Baptist girl or woman who heard or felt a call from God, this usually predicted that she would serve as a missionary or a pastor's wife." Flowers, *Into the Pulpit*, 211n33.

Chapter 1 Where Is Peter's Wife?

1. Complementarian churches argue that they support women in ministry because women in their churches serve in a variety of nonpastoral roles under male authority. This is not how I am using the phrase "women in ministry." I am referencing women's ability to serve in authoritative and ordained ministerial roles including, but not limited to, that of senior pastor. For further research, I recommend Elizabeth Flowers's forthcoming book on the history of complementarianism, contracted with Oxford University Press for publication in 2026.

2. For more about Baylor's history as a Baptist university, see Donald D. Schmeltekopf, *Baylor at the Crossroads: Memoirs of a Provost* (Cascade, 2015), 6–7; Schmeltekopf, "A Christian University in the Baptist Tradition: History of a Vision," in *The Baptist and Christian Character of Baylor*, ed. Donald D. Schmeltekopf, Dianna Vitanza, and Bradley J. B. Toben (Baylor University Press, 2003), 1–20; and Marv Knox, "Waco Church Believed First in Texas to Call Woman Pastor," *Baptist Press*, June 5, 1998, https://www.baptistpress.com/resource-library/news/waco-church-believed-first -in-texas-to-call-woman-pastor.

3. See Blake Beattie, "Catherine of Siena and the Papacy," in *A Companion to Catherine of Siena*, ed. Carolyn Muessig, George Ferzoco, and Beverly Mayne Kienzle (Brill, 2012), 73–98.

4. For a starting place for scholarship on women's preaching and pastoral authority, see Beverly Mayne Kienzle and Pamela J. Walker, eds., *Women Preachers and Prophets through Two Millennia of Christianity* (University of California Press, 1998).

5. Carolyn Muessig, Susan Hylen, Anthea Butler, Catherine Brekus, and Bettye Collier-Thomas are some of my favorite scholars whose work demonstrates both women exercising religious authority and resistance to women's authority. I challenge you to read their work (as well as Kienzle and Walker's edited volume, *Women Preachers and Prophets through Two Millennia of Christianity*) and compare it with the history presented in John Piper and Wayne Grudem's *Recovering Biblical Manhood and Womanhood: A Response to Evangelical Feminism* (Crossway, 1991). See Carolyn Muessig, "Women as Performers of the Bible: Female Preaching in Premodern Europe," in *Performing the Sacred: Christian Representation and the Arts*, ed. Carla M. Bino and Corinna Ricasoli (Brill, 2023), 116–39; Susan Hylen, *Women in the New Testament World* (Oxford University Press, 2018); Anthea Butler, *Women in the Church of God in Christ: Making a Sanctified World* (University of North Carolina Press, 2018); Catherine Brekus, *Strangers and Pilgrims: Female Preaching in America 1740–1845* (University of North Carolina Press, 1998); and Bettye Collier-Thomas, *Daughters of Thunder: Black Women Preachers and Their Sermons, 1850–1979* (Jossey-Bass, 1997).

6. Nancy Wilson, *True Companion: Thoughts on Being a Pastor's Wife* (Canon, 2013), 12, 23.

7. See the 1983 correspondence between Sarah Wood Lee and Irwin Dawson as well as the Department of Missionary Personnel Candidate Fact Sheets for William Sean Lee, Sarah Wood Lee, Merlin Jeffrey Hoppe, and Kathy Jo Bynum Hoppe. Home Mission Board Executive Office Files, AR 631-3, Southern Baptist Historical Library and Archives (SBHLA), Nashville, Tennessee. Kathy Hoppe's candidate sheet (dated September 14, 1982) states that she is "to be ordained 12/82." This means the Home Mission Board knew of her ordination before they appointed her.

8. Home Mission Board Executive Office Files, AR 631-3, SBHLA, Nashville, Tennessee. More information on the Lee/Hoppe ordination controversy can be found in the Wilmer C. Fields Papers, AR 627-5, SBHLA, Nashville, Tennessee; and James T. Draper Papers, AR 607-2, SBHLA, Nashville, Tennessee.

9. Home Mission Board Executive Office Files, AR 631-3, SBHLA, Nashville, Tennessee. Kathy Hoppe and Sarah Lee were both listed on a confidential "Report on Ordained Women Serving as Missions Personnel." It was emphasized that both were categorized "home and church," as is "true with most missionary wives." It also was emphasized that Lee was "ordained after appointment."

10. Home Mission Board Executive Office Files, AR 631-3, SBHLA, Nashville, Tennessee.

11. Lifeway Research, "State of Ministry to Women," https://research.lifeway.com/state-of-ministry-to-women.

12. Jen Wilkin, "Honor Thy Church Mothers—with Wages," *Christianity Today*, September 11, 2023, https://www.christianitytoday.com/ct/2023/october/wilkin-women-ministry-leaders-church-staff-wages-lifeway.html.

13. Nijay K. Gupta, *Tell Her Story: How Women Led, Taught, and Ministered in the Early Church* (InterVarsity, 2023), 135.

14. "Proposed Statement to HMB Directors by William Tanner," in Home Mission Board Executive Office Files, AR 631-3, SBHLA, Nashville, Tennessee.

15. Luis Josué Salés, "Galatians 3:28 and the Ordination of Women in Second-Century Pauline Churches," in *Women and Ordination in the Orthodox Church:*

Explorations in Theology and Practice, ed. Gabrielle Thomas and Elena Narinskaya (Cascade, 2020), 77.

16. Lisa M. Bowens, *African American Readings of Paul: Reception, Resistance, and Transformation* (Eerdmans, 2020), 240.

17. R. Albert Mohler Jr., "Biblical Pattern of Male Leadership Limits Pastorate to Men," *Albert Mohler* (blog), July 15, 2004, https://albertmohler.com/2004/07/15/biblical -pattern-of-male-leadership-limits-pastorate-to-men. Al Mohler made this same claim in defense of the Baptist Faith and Message 2000 (a Baptist statement of faith): "For nearly 2,000 years, Christian churches unanimously understood the preaching office as restricted to men." Mark Wingfield, "Saddleback and Fern Creek Churches Face Off Against Al Mohler at SBC Meeting," *Baptist News Global*, June 14, 2023, https://baptistnews.com/article/saddleback-and-fern-creek-churches-face-off-against -al-mohler-at-sbc-meeting.

18. Mohler, "Biblical Patterns of Male Leadership."

19. Jesse T. Jackson, "Al Mohler Clarifies 'Pastor' Title in Baptist Faith and Message," *Ministry Watch*, August 3, 2022, https://ministrywatch.com/al-mohler-clarifies -pastor-title-in-baptist-faith-and-message; and R. Albert Mohler Jr., "Women Pastors, Women Preachers, and the Looming Test of the Southern Baptist Convention," *Albert Mohler* (blog), May 10, 2021, https://albertmohler.com/2021/05/10/women-pastors -women-preachers-and-the-looming-test-of-the-southern-baptist-convention.

20. Or at least the word we translate as *pastor*. The word also appears in Eph. 4:11, Acts 20:28, and 1 Pet. 5:2. Much conversation exists about how to translate biblical leadership roles into modern church positions. See Bob Smietana's article about the word *pastor* in the wake of the Southern Baptist Convention 2023: Bob Smietana, "What Does the Bible Say a Pastor Is? It's Complicated," *Baptist Standard*, June 28, 2023, https://www.baptiststandard.com/news/baptists/what-does-the-bible-say-a-pastor- is-its-complicated.

21. As I will discuss in chap. 4, hierarchy began to be more regularly inserted into differences in clerical function in the central Middle Ages (eleventh to thirteenth centuries).

22. "At Southern Seminary we recognize the vital role that women play in God's Kingdom. To that end, we've created a variety of academic programs and gender-specific ministries to address the issues and giftedness of women. . . . If you've been called by God to work with other women, whether in the local church or on the mission field, Southern Seminary is the place for you." This is a description from an advertisement for women's ministry at The Southern Baptist Theological Seminary in the conference program for the forty-ninth annual Ministers' Wives Conference of the Southern Baptist Convention (June 15, 2004). Conference of Southern Baptist Ministers' Wives Collection, AR 369, SBHLA, Nashville, Tennessee.

23. Dorothy Kelley Patterson "describes herself as first and foremost a homemaker." This is the description of Patterson in her short bio included in the 2005 President's Notebook for the fiftieth annual Ministers' Wives Conference of the Southern Baptist Convention. Conference of Southern Baptist Ministers' Wives Collection, AR 369, SBHLA, Nashville, Tennessee.

24. Dorothy Kelley Patterson, *A Handbook for Ministers' Wives: Sharing the Blessings of Your Marriage, Family, and Home* (Northeastern Baptist Press, 2021), 71 and 176.

25. Patterson, *Handbook for Ministers' Wives*, 195.

26. Julia Foote, *A Brand Plucked from the Fire: An Autobiographical Sketch by Mrs. Julia A. J. Foote* (W. F. Schneider, 1879), reprinted in William L. Andrews, ed.,

Sisters of the Spirit: Three Black Women's Autobiographies of the Nineteenth Century (Indiana University Press, 1986), 207–9, quoted in Lisa M. Bowens, *African American Readings of Paul: Reception, Resistance, and Transformation* (Eerdmans, 2020), 237.

27. "Resolution on Ordination and the Role of Women in Ministry," Southern Baptist Convention, June 1, 1984, https://www.sbc.net/resource-library/resolutions/resolution-on-ordination-and-the-role-of-women-in-ministry; and W. A. Reed and Tom Mulgrew, "Baptist Group to Fight for Ordination," *Tennessean*, August 29, 1984, in Women in Baptist Life Collection, AR 160, SBHLA, Nashville, Tennessee.

28. Draper, letter to Mrs. Delos L. Ray, March 16, 1983. James T. Draper Papers, AR 607, SBHLA, Nashville, Tennessee.

29. "Marriage would appear to have been the normal state of life for church leaders in the late first or early second century, according to the Pastoral Epistles." David G. Hunter, "Married Clergy in Eastern and Western Christianity," in *A Companion to Priesthood and Holy Orders in the Middle Ages*, ed. Greg Peters and C. Colt Anderson (Brill, 2015), 96–97.

30. Clement of Alexandria, *Stromata* 3.6.53, in *Alexandrian Christianity: Selected Translations of Clement and Origen*, Library of Christian Classics 2, ed. John Ernest Leonard Oulton and Henry Chadwick (Westminster, 1954), 65, available at https://www.earlychristianwritings.com/text/clement-stromata-book3-english.html.

31. Marg Mowczko, "Believing Wives and Female Co-workers of the Apostles," *Marg Mowczko* (blog), February 14, 2014, https://margmowczko.com/believing-wives-female-co-workers-of-the-apostles.

32. Some of the "pastor's wife" books reference Peter's wife as a biblical exemplar of the role. Jill Briscoe suggests that the letters of Peter can be used to glean possible information about her, even while recognizing that very little direct information about her exists. Briscoe, *Renewal on the Run: Encouragement for Wives Who Are Partners in Ministry* (Harold Shaw, 1992), 24–26.

33. Lynn Cohick, *Women in the World of the Earliest Christians: Illuminating Ancient Ways of Life* (Baker Academic, 2009), 241.

34. There is one extrabiblical reference to her that suggests she was martyred alongside Peter. "They say, accordingly, that when the blessed Peter saw his own wife led out to die, he rejoiced because of her summons and her return home, and called to her very encouragingly and comfortingly, addressing her by name and saying, 'Oh thou, remember the Lord.' Such was the marriage of the blessed and their perfect disposition toward those dearest to them." Clement, *Stromata* 7.11, quoted in Eusebius Pamphilus, *Church History* 3.30.2, in *A Select Library of Nicene and Post-Nicene Fathers of the Christian Church*, series 2, vol. 1, ed. Philip Schaff and Henry Wace (Christian Literature, 1890–1900; repr., Hendrickson, 1994), 162. I am grateful to Nijay Gupta for pointing me to this source.

35. Jaime Clark-Soles, *Women in the Bible: Interpretation Resources for the Use of Scripture in the Church* (Westminster John Knox, 2020), 231, 254.

36. Gloria C. Furman, *The Pastor's Wife: Strengthened by Grace for a Life of Love* (Crossway, 2015), 20; Patterson, *Handbook for Ministers' Wives*, back cover.

37. Karen Jo Torjesen, *When Women Were Priests: Women's Leadership in the Early Church and the Scandal of their Subordination in the Rise of Christianity* (Harper-One, 1995).

38. See Meghan J. DiLuzio, *A Place at the Altar: Priestesses in Republican Rome* (Princeton University Press, 2016); and Wilda C. Gafney, *Daughters of Miriam: Women Prophets in Ancient Israel* (Fortress, 2008).

39. DiLuzio, *Place at the Altar*, 240.

40. DiLuzio, *Place at the Altar*, 143.

41. Gafney, *Daughters of Miriam*, 1.

42. Susan E. Hylen, *Finding Phoebe: What New Testament Women Were Really Like* (Eerdmans, 2023), 144.

43. Just for clarification, I do not identify as charismatic.

44. Sarah Coakley, *Powers and Submissions: Spirituality, Philosophy, and Gender* (Wiley & Sons, 2008).

45. Original proponents of complementarianism attempted to diminish the significance of praying and prophesying, especially divorcing both from teaching. Dorothy Patterson drew from Wayne Grudem to argue that the teaching of male apostles "provided the doctrinal and ethical norms by which the early church was regulated," arguing that prophecy is only "a human reporting of a divine revelation given to encourage, build up, comfort, and inspire." Because they considered teaching the more authoritative role (inserting hierarchy into spiritual gifting), preachers and teachers (who they argued are men) trump prophets (which includes women who might otherwise counter male authority). Dorothy Patterson, "Why I Believe Southern Baptists Should Not Ordain Women," paper delivered at the 1988 Southern Baptist Historical Society, later published in *Baptist History and Heritage* 23 (July 1988): 56–62, in Women in Baptist Life Collection, AR-160, SBHLA, Nashville, Tennessee.

46. Ruth S. Peale, *The Adventure of Being a Wife* (Prentice-Hall, 1971), 2, quoted in H. B. London Jr., foreword to Joyce Williams, *She Can't Even Play the Piano! Insights for Ministry Wives* (Beacon Hill, 2005), 9–10.

47. Alex Murashko, "John Piper: God Gave Christianity a 'Masculine Feel,'" *Christian Post*, February 1, 2012, https://www.christianpost.com/news/john-piper-god-gave -christianity-a-masculine-feel.html.

48. Here are some recommendations to begin this journey: Candice Marie Benbow, *Red Lip Theology: For Church Girls Who've Considered Tithing to the Beauty Supply Store When Sunday Morning Isn't Enough* (Convergent, 2022); Butler, *Women in the Church of God in Christ*; Wilda C. Gafney, *Womanist Midrash: A Reintroduction to the Women of the Torah and the Throne* (Westminster John Knox, 2017); Evelyn Brooks Higginbotham, *Righteous Discontent: The Women's Movement in the Black Baptist Church, 1880–1920* (Harvard University Press, 1993); Jemar Tisby, *The Color of Compromise: The Truth about the American Church's Complicity in Racism* (Zondervan, 2019).

49. Gail MacDonald, *High Call, High Privilege: A Pastor's Wife Speaks to Every Woman in a Place of Responsibility* (Hendrickson, 2000), 11–12.

50. MacDonald, *High Call, High Privilege*, 11–12.

51. Weptanomah W. Carter, *The Black Minister's Wife: As a Participant in the Redemptive Ministry of Her Husband* (Progressive National Baptist, 1976), 19.

52. Carter, *Black Minister's Wife*, 20. I am grateful to Brooke LeFevre for drawing my attention to this passage.

53. Patterson, *Handbook for Ministers' Wives*, 36.

54. Patterson, *Handbook for Ministers' Wives*, 39.

55. Patterson, *Handbook for Ministers' Wives*, 293.

56. Tommy French, quoted in Benjamin Hawkins, "SWBTS Honors Tommy French and Family for 'Tremendous Contribution,' Scholarship Gift," *Baptist Press*, April 13, 2009, https://www.baptistpress.com/resource-library/news/swbts-honors-tommy -french-family-for-tremendous-contribution-scholarship-gift (emphasis added).

57. Christine Hoover, *The Church Planting Wife: Help and Hope for Her Heart* (Moody, 2013), 99.

58. We surveyed 150 books written by and for the wives of ministers mostly within the United States. The dates ranged across a century, from 1923 to 2023, with the bulk

of these types of books published between 1985 and 2024. The decades with the highest production of pastor's wife books are between 2000 and 2020. Most of these texts were published and written by white authors; however, Black authors have had a consistent presence since the 1946 publication of Mary O. Ross's *The Minister's Wife*. Diversity in authorship has increased significantly in the twenty-first century.

59. Furman, *Pastor's Wife*, 20–21.

60. Furman, *Pastor's Wife*, 74, 86.

61. Furman, *Pastor's Wife*, 68.

62. The 2022 course descriptions for asynchronous classes at the Seminary Wives Institute at The Southern Baptist Theological Seminary includes this course listing:

SW704 Essentials I and II SW705 (*Required Classes—must be taken together*)

Instructors: Team taught by faculty wives (and one session taught by a seminary professor)

Texts: *The Pastor's Wife* by Gloria Furman (Crossway, 2015)

Help! I am Married to My Pastor by Jani Ortlund (Crossway, 2021)

63. Patterson, *Handbook for Ministers' Wives*, 3.

64. Hoover, *Church Planting Wife*, 31.

65. Hoover, *Church Planting Wife*, 52.

66. Shevalle T. Kimber, *First Ladydom in the Black Church* (Book Baby, 2023), introduction.

Chapter 2 When Women Were Priests

1. Facts Overlooked on Women Pastors," *Clarion Ledger*, July 3, 2000, in Christian Life Commission Resource Files, AR 138-2, Southern Baptist Historical Library and Archives (SBHLA), Nashville, Tennessee.

2. Christine Schenk, *Crispina and Her Sisters: Women and Authority in Early Christianity* (Fortress, 2017), 45.

3. Schenk, *Crispina and Her Sisters*, 147–48.

4. Nicola Denzey, *The Bone Gatherers: The Lost Worlds of Early Christian Women* (Beacon, 2007), 121–24.

5. Schenk, *Crispina and Her Sisters*, 45.

6. Carolyn Osiek and Margaret Y. MacDonald, *A Woman's Place: House Churches in Early Christianity* (Fortress, 2006), 163.

7. Osiek and MacDonald, *Woman's Place*, 132.

8. Schenk, *Crispina and Her Sisters*, 48–49.

9. Susan E. Hylen, *Finding Phoebe: What New Testament Women Were Really Like* (Eerdmans, 2023), 174.

10. Pliny the Younger, *Letter to Trajan*, letter 97, available at https://www.gutenberg .org/files/2811/2811-h/2811-h.htm.

11. Elizabeth Flowers, *Into the Pulpit: Southern Baptist Women and Power since World War II* (University of North Carolina Press, 2012), 104.

12. See Karen K. Seat, "From Molly Marshall to Sarah Palin: Southern Baptist Gender Battles and the Politics of Complementarianism," in *A Marginal Majority: Women, Gender, and a Reimagining of Southern Baptists*, ed. Elizabeth H. Flowers and Karen K. Seat (University of Tennessee Press, 2020), 201–6. Paige Patterson delivered a paper in 1994 at the Evangelical Theological Society on the success of the conservative takeover of the SBC: L. Paige Patterson, "Anatomy of a Reformation: The Southern Baptist Convention 1978–1994," *Faith and Mission* 16, no. 3 (Summer 1999), paper presented at the National Meeting of the Evangelical Theological Society,

Chicago, Illinois, November 17, 1994. Dorothy Patterson served on the board of the CBMW. See Kate Shellnutt, "Divorce after Abuse: How Paige Patterson's Counsel Compares to Other Pastors," *Christianity Today*, April 30, 2018, https://www.christianity today.com/news/2018/april/paige-patterson-divorce-domestic-abuse-swbts-cbmw.html; "Women's Leadership Consultation with CBMW-Affiliated Speakers Draws Women from Nine States," February 24, 2005, Council on Biblical Manhood and Womanhood, https://cbmw.org/2005/02/24/womens-leadership-consultation-with-cbmw-affiliated -speakers-draws-women-from-nine-states; Mark Wingfield, "There's a New Religious Advocacy Group with Ties to Patterson and Conservative Baptist Network," *Baptist News Global*, March 12, 2024, https://baptistnews.com/article/theres-a-new-dobson -endorsed-religious-advocacy-group-with-ties-to-patterson-and-conservative-baptist -network; Pat Ennis, "How to Practice Biblical Hospitality," The Gospel Coalition, December 12, 2015, https://www.thegospelcoalition.org/article/how-do-we-practice -biblical-hospitality. See also Barry Hankins's oral history interview with Dorothy Patterson, in which she discusses her role in crafting the 1998 amendment to the Baptist Faith and Message: Dorothy Kelley Patterson, interview by Barry Hankins, June 8, 1999, transcript, Baylor University Institute for Oral History, Waco, Texas, https:// digitalcollections-baylor.quartexcollections.com/documents/detail/1671392; and the Fall 1998 edition of *Southwestern News* 67, no. 1, which contains an interview with Dorothy Patterson, https://issuu.com/swnews/docs/fall2008.

13. Dorothy Patterson, "Biblical Womanhood," March 1998, pp. 26, 7. Christian Life Commission / Ethics and Religious Liberty Commission Seminar Proceedings Collection, AR 138-6, box 15, SBHLA, Nashville, Tennessee.

14. Dorothy Patterson, "Why I Believe Southern Baptists Should Not Ordain Women," paper delivered at the 1988 Southern Baptist Historical Society, later published in *Baptist History and Heritage* 23 (July 1988): 56–62, in Women in Baptist Life Collection, AR-160, SBHLA, Nashville, Tennessee.

15. Dorothy Patterson, "Biblical Womanhood," March 1998, p. 7. Christian Life Commission / Ethics and Religious Liberty Commission Seminar Proceedings Collection, AR 138-6, SBHLA, Nashville, Tennessee.

16. Amy Peeler, *Women and the Gender of God* (Eerdmans, 2022), 141–42.

17. I submitted the summaries of these conversations with participants in Patterson's courses to Brazos Press. When possible, I corroborated their descriptions of material within these courses with textual evidence. For references about what she taught in her classes, see also Patterson, *Handbook for Ministers' Wives*, esp. 61, 224. Women who participated in these classes also sent me, through social media, copies of material, including diagrams for packing suitcases. Many of these messages, often unsolicited, include testimonials.

18. Denzey, *Bone Gatherers*, 113, quoted in Schenk, *Crispina and Her Sisters*, 156.

19. Schenk, *Crispina and Her Sisters*, 156. Schenk notes that both Osiek and Denzey "agree" that "a woman or women probably made the decisions about which frescoes would fill the space."

20. Karen Jo Torjesen, "The Early Christian Orans: An Artistic Representation of Women's Liturgical Prayer and Prophecy," in *Women Preachers and Prophets through Two Millennia of Christianity*, ed. Beverly Mayne Kienzle and Pamela J. Walker (University of California Press, 1998), 46, 53.

21. Schenk, *Crispina and Her Sisters*, 436–37.

22. Schenk, *Crispina and Her Sisters*, 447.

23. Schenk, *Crispina and Her Sisters*, 281–83.

24. Christine Schenk, "Women's Prophetic Leadership Changed the Face of the Roman Empire," *Vatican News*, February 2, 2024, https://www.vaticannews.va /en/church/news/2024-02/sisters-project-story-consecrated-life-early-christian-church .html.

25. Sandra L. Glahn, *Nobody's Mother: Artemis of the Ephesians in Antiquity in the New Testament* (IVP Academic, 2023); and Bonnie Bowman Thurston, *The Widows: A Women's Ministry in the Early Church* (Fortress, 1989).

26. Kevin Madigan and Carolyn Osiek, eds., *Ordained Women in the Early Church: A Documentary History* (Johns Hopkins University Press, 2005), 21–22.

27. Madigan and Osiek, *Ordained Women in the Early Church*, 22; Thurston, *The Widows*, 104.

28. Schenk, *Crispina and Her Sisters*, 162.

29. Denzey, *Bone Gatherers*, 84, 86, see also 74–86.

30. This is how the official guidebook to the catacombs presents the veiled woman. Raffaella Giuliani, *The Catacombs of Priscilla: With an Essay about the Museum by Barbara Mazzei*, trans. Raffaella Bucolo (Pontifical Commission for Sacred Archaeology, 2016), 20–28.

31. Schenk, *Crispina and Her Sisters*, 159.

32. Gary Macy, endorsement of *Crispina and Her Sisters* by Christine Schenk, https://www.fortresspress.com/store/product/9781506411880.

33. Joan Taylor and Helen Bond, *Women Remembered: Jesus' Female Disciples* (Hodder & Stoughton, 2022), 214–15.

34. Gabrielle Thomas and Elena Narinskaya, eds., *Women and Ordination in the Orthodox Church: Explorations in Theology and Practice* (Cascade, 2020), xvii; Luis Josué Salés, "Galatians 3:28 and the Ordination of Women in Second-Century Pauline Churches," in Thomas and Narinskaya, *Women and Ordination in the Orthodox Church*, 67–85; and Madigan and Osiek, *Ordained Women in the Early Church*, 3, 9.

35. Leonard I. Sweet, *The Minister's Wife: Her Role in Nineteenth-Century American Evangelicalism* (Temple University Press, 1983), 12.

36. Jane Tibbetts Schulenburg, review of *The Hidden History of Women's Ordination: Female Clergy in the Medieval West*, by Gary Macy, *Speculum* 85, no. 4 (2010): 994–96.

37. R. Albert Mohler Jr., "Biblical Pattern of Male Leadership Limits Pastorate to Men," *Albert Mohler* (blog), July 15, 2004, https://albertmohler.com/2004/07/15/biblical -pattern-of-male-leadership-limits-pastorate-to-men. See also Mohler's comment about the Baptist Faith and Message 2000: "For nearly 2,000 years, Christian churches unanimously understood the preaching office as restricted to men." Quoted in Mark Wingfield, "Saddleback and Fern Creek Churches Face Off Against Al Mohler at SBC Meeting," *Baptist News Global*, June 14, 2023, https://baptistnews.com/article/saddle back-and-fern-creek-churches-face-off-against-al-mohler-at-sbc-meeting.

38. Gary Macy, *The Hidden History of Women's Ordination: Female Clergy in the Medieval West* (Oxford University Press, 2008), vii, 4.

39. Nijay K. Gupta, *Tell Her Story: How Women Led, Taught, and Ministered in the Early Church* (InterVarsity, 2023), 80–93.

40. Madigan and Osiek, *Ordained Women*, 207–18.

41. Kevin J. Madigan, "The Meaning of *Presbytera* in Byzantine and Early Medieval Christianity," in *Patterns of Women's Leadership in Early Christianity*, ed. Joan E. Taylor and Ilaria L. E. Ramelli (Oxford University Press, 2021), 261.

42. Macy, *Hidden History of Women's Ordination*, 59–60, 75.

43. Macy, *Hidden History of Women's Ordination*, 59–60, 62.

44. Macy, *Hidden History of Women's Ordination*, 75–76.

45. Macy, *Hidden History of Women's Ordination*, 76.

46. Andrew Bartlett, *Men and Women in Christ: Fresh Light from the Biblical Texts* (IVP, 2019).

47. For information about the Canterbury UNESCO World Heritage site, see https://www.canterburyunescotour.co.uk. For more information about Bertha, see Lisa Bitel, *Women in Early Medieval Europe 400–1100* (Cambridge University Press, 2002), 117. See also "Queen Bertha: A Historical Enigma," English Heritage, accessed September 11, 2024, https://www.english-heritage.org.uk/learn/histories/women-in -history/queen-bertha-historical-enigma.

48. Lisa Bitel relates that Bertha and her priest probably knew of the missionaries' journey in advance and persuaded Ethelbert to give the missionaries a fair hearing; Ethelberth only agreed to be baptized after Bertha began attending regular church services conducted by Augustine and his monks. Bitel, *Women in Early Medieval Europe*, 117.

49. For more information about the church, including a virtual tour in which you can see the niche of Bertha's door and the stained-glass window discussed above, see "The Story of St. Martin's," https://www.martinpaul.org/the-story-of-st-martins.

50. John Piper, "A Vision of Biblical Complementarity: Manhood and Womanhood Defined according to the Bible," in *Recovering Biblical Manhood and Womanhood: A Response to Evangelical Feminism*, ed. John Piper and Wayne Grudem (Crossway, 1991), 60–61.

Chapter 3 The Not-So-Hidden History of Medieval Women's Ordination

1. For more information about Mirk and *Festial*, see my published dissertation, Beth Allison Barr, *The Pastoral Care of Women in Late Medieval England* (Boydell, 2008).

2. For evidence of Milburga's story (including discussions of the primary sources above), see Simon Yarrow, "The Invention of St. Mildburg of Wenlock: Community and Cult in an Anglo-Norman Shropshire Town," *Midland History* 38, no. 1 (Spring 2013): 4; Angela Josephine Mary Edwards, "Odo of Ostia's History of the Translation of St. Milburga and Its Connection with the Early History of Wenlock Abbey" (unpublished dissertation, University of London, 1960); Rose Lagram-Taylor, "From Minster to Priory: St. Milburga's, Wenlock," *Transactions of the Shropshire Archaeological and Historical Society* 89 (2015): 1–14; and John McNeill, "Wenlock Priory," *English Heritage Guidebook* (English Heritage, 2020). See also "St. Milburga," English Heritage, accessed September 11, 2024, https://www.english-heritage.org.uk/visit /places/wenlock-priory/history/st-milburga.

3. David W. Rollason, *The Mildrith Legend: A Study in Early Medieval Hagiography in England* (Leicester University Press, 1982), 69.

4. For the account of Milburga's relics, see Yarrow, "Invention of St. Mildburg of Wenlock."

5. Al Mohler, quoted in Jesse T. Jackson, "Al Mohler Clarifies 'Pastor' Title in Baptist Faith and Message," Church Leaders, August 2, 2022, https://churchleaders.com/news /430958-sbc-seminary-president-theologian-dr-albert-mohler-clarifies-pastor-title-in -baptist-faith-and-message.html/2. Since the 2023 convention decision, this amendment has been updated to describe the scriptural office of "pastor" as "pastor/elder/overseer." Baptist Faith and Message 2000, "VI. The Church," https://bfm.sbc.net/bfm2000/#vi.

6. For a succinct history of the founding of Wimnicas, see Lagram-Taylor, "From Minster to Priory"; and McNeill, "Wenlock Priory."

7. Catherine Peyroux and Sarah Foot, "Double Monasteries," Routledge Resources Online, June 18, 2023, https://doi.org/10.4324/9780415791182-RMEO161-1.

8. McNeill, "Wenlock Priory," 27.

9. Rose Lagram-Taylor, "From Minster to Priory," 1. See also A. J. M. Edwards, "An Early Twelfth-Century Account of the Translation of St. Milburga of Much Wenlock," *Transactions of the Shropshire Archaeological Society* 57 (1961–64), 134–51.

10. Jennifer Edwards, *Superior Women: Medieval Female Authority in Poitiers' Abbey of Sainte-Croix* (Oxford University Press, 2019), 147–52.

11. Edwards, *Superior Women*, 147–52; Jean LeClercq, "Eucharist Celebrations without Priests in the Middle Ages," in *Living Bread, Saving Cup: Readings on the Eucharist* (Liturgical Press, 1982), 222–41.

12. Sarah Foot, *Veiled Women: The Disappearance of Nuns from Anglo-Saxon England* (Routledge, 2000), 86. See also Foot, "Bede's Abbesses," in *Women Intellectuals and Leaders in the Middle Ages*, ed. Katherine Kerby-Fulton, Katie Ann-Marie Bugyis, and John Van Engen (D. S. Brewer, 2020), 261–76.

13. Foot, "Bede's Abbesses," 266.

14. Foot, *Veiled Women*, 95.

15. Gary Macy, *The Hidden History of Women's Ordination: Female Clergy in the Medieval West* (Oxford University Press, 2008), 41.

16. Nijay K. Gupta, *Tell Her Story: How Women Led, Taught, and Ministered in the Early Church* (InterVarsity, 2023), 81–82.

17. Gupta, *Tell Her Story*, 84.

18. Edwards, *Superior Women*, 1.

19. William T. Ditewig, "From Function to Ontology: The Shifting Diaconate of the Middle Ages," in *A Companion to Priesthood and Holy Orders in the Middle Ages*, ed. Greg Peters and C. Colt Anderson (Brill, 2015).

20. Macy, *Hidden History of Medieval Women's Ordination*, 33.

21. Denny Burk, "Albert Mohler Offers 10 Points on Complementarianism in the SBC," *Denny Burk* (blog), October 15, 2019, https://www.dennyburk.com/albert -mohler-offers-10-points-on-complementarianism-in-the-sbc.

22. See the Latin transcription of her words: Angela Josephine Mary Edwards, "Odo of Ostia's History of the Translation of St. Milburga and Its Connection with the Early History of Wenlock Abbey" (PhD dissertation, unpublished, University of London, 1960), 86–87.

23. Macy, *Hidden History of Medieval Women's Ordination*, 28.

24. John F. Romano, "Priests and the Eucharist in the Middle Ages," in *A Companion to Priesthood and Holy Orders in the Middle Ages*, ed. Greg Peters and C. Colt Anderson (Brill, 2015), 188–216.

25. Macy, *Hidden History of Medieval Women's Ordination*, 46.

26. The first article adopted by Pope Innocent III at Fourth Lateran Council of 1215 includes this description of transubstantiation, quoted in Macy, *Hidden History of Women's Ordination*, 46.

27. See especially Lagram-Taylor, "From Minster to Priory," 1–14.

28. Vivien Bellamy, *A History of Much Wenlock* (Shropshire, 2001), 13.

29. Edwards, *Superior Women*, 151.

30. Personal correspondence with Kathy Hoppe that I include with her permission. I also was able to determine from documents in the SBHLA that the Home Mission Board had previous knowledge of her ordination. This suggests to me that the fact of her ordination became a problem because of the outcry of local SBC pastors. Before this outcry, the Home Mission Board had appointed and salaried her husband.

Kathy Hoppe's candidate sheet (dated September 14, 1982) states that she is "to be ordained 12/82." This means the Home Mission Board knew of her ordination before they appointed her. Home Mission Board Executive Office Files, AR 631-3, SBHLA, Nashville, Tennessee. See also Wilmer Clement Fields Papers, AR 627-5, SBHLA, Nashville, Tennessee.

31. For Bertha Smith's sermons, see https://www.sermonindex.net/modules /mydownloads/viewcat.php?cid=768 and https://vimeo.com/channels/1280783. For her influence on SBC leaders, see Michael Foust, "Adrian Rogers, Longtime Bellevue Pastor and Leader in Conservative Resurgence Dies," *Baptist Press*, November 15, 2005, https://www.baptistpress.com/resource-library/news/adrian-rogers-longtime-bellevue -pastor-and-leader-in-conservative-resurgence-dies; and Susie Hawkins, "Bertha Smith: Women in Church History," Lifeway Research, March 3, 2023, https://research.lifeway .com/2023/03/03/bertha-smith-women-in-church-history. For Daniel Akin's sermon, see Akin, "Galatians 2:20 and Bertha Smith, A Soul-Winning Missionary—Galatians 2:20," *Danny Akin* (blog), August 19, 2014, https://www.danielakin.com/galatians-220 -bertha-smith-a-soul-winning-missionary. See also Olive Bertha Smith Collection, AR 856, SBHLA, Nashville, Tennessee.

32. Akin, "Galatians 2:20 and Bertha Smith."

33. Elizabeth Marvel, "The Ordination of Women: A Global Perspective," in a forthcoming title edited by David Bebbington (Baylor University Press, forthcoming).

Chapter 4 The Rise of the Pastor's Wife

1. Nonnberg Abbey, https://www.salzburg.info/en/sights/churches-cemeteries /stift-nonnberg, accessed May 30, 2024. See also the "Nonnberg (Nunberg, Nonberg) Abbey," Monastic Matrix, accessed May 30, 2024, https://arts.st-andrews.ac.uk/mo nasticmatrix/monasticon/nonnberg-nunberg-nonberg-abbey.

2. Elizabeth Makowski, *Canon Law and Cloistered Women: Periculoso and Its Commentators, 1298–1545* (Catholic University of America Press, 1999), 3. I'm grateful for the scholarship of Elizabeth Marvel introducing me to Makowski's work. I had the privilege of directing Marvel's dissertation, "Precarity and Pastoral Care: Nuns and Bishops in the Fifteenth-Century Diocese of Lincoln," in which I learned quite a bit about the enactment of *Periculoso*.

3. Janina Ramriez, *Femina: A New History of the Middle Ages, through the Women Written Out of It* (Hanover Square, 2023), 179, 183.

4. Jennifer Edwards, *Superior Women: Medieval Female Authority in Poitiers' Abbey of Sainte-Croix* (Oxford University Press, 2019), 6.

5. John Van Engen, "Religious Women in Leadership, Ministry, and Latin Ecclesi-astical Culture," in *Women Intellectuals and Leaders in the Middle Ages*, ed. Katherine Kerby-Fulton, Katie Ann-Marie Bugyis, and John Van Engen (D. S. Brewer, 2020), 253.

6. David G. Hunter, "Married Clergy in Eastern and Western Christianity," in *A Companion to Priesthood and Holy Orders in the Middle Ages*, ed. Greg Peters and C. Colt Anderson (Brill, 2015), 97–100.

7. Robert Swanson, "Apostolic Successors: Priests and Priesthood, Bishops, and Episcopacy in Medieval Western Europe," in *A Companion to Priesthood and Holy Orders in the Middle Ages*, ed. Greg Peters and C. Colt Anderson (Brill, 2016), 41.

8. This title is in reference to Jennifer Thibodeaux, *The Manly Priest: Clerical Celibacy, Masculinity, and Reform in England and Normandy, 1066–1300* (University of Pennsylvania Press, 2015).

9. John F. Romano, "Priests and the Eucharist in the Middle Ages," in *A Companion to Priesthood and Holy Orders in the Middle Ages*, ed. Greg Peters and C. Colt Anderson (Brill, 2015), 190–92.

10. Romano, "Priests and the Eucharist in the Middle Ages," 203–4.

11. Romano, "Priests and the Eucharist in the Middle Ages," 209.

12. William T. Ditewig, "From Function to Ontology: The Shifting Diaconate of the Middle Ages," in *A Companion to Priesthood and Holy Orders in the Middle Ages*, ed. Greg Peters and C. Colt Anderson (Brill, 2015), 350–51.

13. Ditewig, "From Function to Ontology," 350.

14. Thibodeaux, *Manly Priest*, 5, 12.

15. For an excellent article on the failure of the medieval celibacy campaign, see Janelle Werner, "Living in Suspicion: Priests and Female Servants in Late Medieval England," *Journal of British Studies* 55, no. 4 (October 2016): 660–65.

16. "Dr. Jerry Falwell—Biography," Liberty University website, accessed May 30, 2024, https://www.liberty.edu/about/founder-jerry-falwell-senior.

17. Associated Press, "Jerry Falwell Jr. Sued by Liberty University for Millions over Sex, Extortion Scandal," NBC News, April 16, 2021, https://www.nbcnews.com/news/us-news/jerry-falwell-jr-sued-liberty-university-millions-over-sex-extortion-n1264319; and Liz Lykins, "Liberty University Broke Safety Laws for Years, Leaked Government Investigation Finds: Report," Roys Report, October 3, 2023, https://julieroys.com/liberty-university-broke-safety-laws-years-leaked-government-investigation-finds.

18. "Who Was Jack Hyles?," Jack Hyles Library, accessed May 30, 2024, https://www.jackhyleslibrary.com/about-jack-hyles.

19. "Pastor Denies Adultery, 2 Other Charges," *Chicago Tribune*, May 25, 1989, https://www.chicagotribune.com/1989/05/25/pastor-denies-adultery-2-other-charges; Steve Rabey, "Hammond Pastor Serving Time for Sex Crimes Again Seeks Release," Ministry Watch, February 12, 2021, https://ministrywatch.com/hammond-pastor-serving-time-for-sex-crimes-again-seeks-release; Kate Shellnutt, "Hundreds Accuse Independent Baptist Pastors of Abuse," *Christianity Today*, December 12, 2018, https://www.christianitytoday.com/news/2018/december/independent-fundamentalist-baptist-church-abuse-scandal.html.

20. Thibodeaux, *Manly Priest*, 3.

21. Beth Allison Barr, *The Making of Biblical Womanhood: How the Subjugation of Women Became Gospel Truth* (Brazos, 2021), 95.

22. Lynneth Miller Renberg, *Women, Dance, and Parish Religion in England, 1300–1640* (Boydell & Brewer, 2022), 70.

23. Werner, "Living in Suspicion," 662.

24. Papal control of benefices throughout Western Europe took three centuries to be successful, and it was still only a partial success. Joseph Lynch, *The Medieval Church: A Brief History* (Taylor & Francis, 2013), 176.

25. I am simplifying. For a more comprehensive discussion of the different types of clergy, see Nicholas Orme, *Going to Church in Medieval England* (Yale, 2021); and Gary Macy, "The Treatment of Ordination in Recent Scholarship on Religious Women in the Early Middle Ages," in *Women Intellectuals and Leaders in the Middle Ages*, ed. Kathryn Kerby-Fulton, Katie Ann-Marie Bugyis, and John Van Engen (Boydell & Brewer, 2020), 299.

26. Technically, those who received ordination were required to hold a benefice. C. Colt Anderson, "Reforming Priests and the Diverse Rhetoric of Ordination and Office from 1123–1418," in *A Companion to Priesthood and Holy Orders in the Middle Ages*, ed. Greg Peters and C. Colt Anderson (Brill, 2015), 304. But gaining a benefice

required the petitioner to prove "he had the required age, education, and good character to be granted a benefice" as well as the ordained status.

27. Hugh M. Thomas, *The Secular Clergy in England, 1066–1216* (Oxford University Press, 2014), 17–36.

28. Thibodeaux, *Manly Priest*, 7, 14, see also 1–14.

29. "Though the history of ordination and women is complex, by this time women had been excluded from any hope of membership in the clergy, partly on the basis of pollution fears." Thomas, *Secular Clergy in England*, 9–10.

30. John Stow, *A Survey of London: Containing the Original Antiquity, Increase, Modern Estate, and Description of that City, Written in the Year 1598*, ed. Henry Morley (G. Routledge and Sons, 1890), 371.

31. Claire Nally, "Cross Bones Graveyard: Excavating the Prostitute in Neo-Victorian Popular Culture," *Journal of Victorian Culture* 23, no. 2 (April 2018): 247–61, https://doi.org/10.1093/jvc/vcx006; and Megan B. Brickley, ed., *The Cross Bones Burial Ground, Redcross Way, Southwark, London: Archaeological Excavations (1991–1998) for the London Underground Limited Jubilee Line Extension Project* (Museum of London Archaeology, 1999).

32. For scholarship on the Bankside stews (brothels), see Henry Angsar Kelly, "Bishop, Prioress, and Bawd in the Stews of Southward," *Speculum* 77 (2000): 342–88; Martha Carlin, *Medieval Southwark* (Hambledon, 1996); Ruth Mazo Karras, *Common Women: Prostitution and Sexuality in Medieval England* (Oxford University Press, 1996); and P. J. P. Goldberg, "Pigs and Prostitutes: Streetwalking in Comparative Perspective," in *Young Medieval Women*, ed. Katherine J. Lewis, Noël James Menuge, and Kim M. Phillips (Sutton, 1999), 172–93. See also Ben Johnson, "Cross Bones Graveyard," Historic UK, https://www.historic-uk.com/HistoryMagazine/DestinationsUK/Cross-Bones-Graveyard.

33. Sondra L. Hausner, *The Spirits of Crossbones Graveyard: Time, Ritual, and Sexual Commerce in London* (Indiana University Press, 2016), 87.

34. Hausner, *Spirits of Crossbones Graveyard*, 62.

35. Karras, *Common Women*, 41–42, 104. See also Carlin, *Medieval Southwark*, 209–29.

36. Hausner, *Spirits of Crossbones Graveyard*, 38. The quotation is often ascribed to Augustine as quoted by Aquinas; it is actually from Aquinas's student Ptolemy of Lucca. István Bejczy, "*Tolerantia*: A Medieval Concept," *Journal of the History of Ideas* 58, no. 3 (July 1997): 373. But medieval people thought Aquinas said it.

37. Marjorie Elizabeth Plummer, *From Priest's Whore to Pastor's Wife: Clerical Marriage and the Process of Reform in the Early German Reformation* (Ashgate, 2012).

38. Plummer, *From Priest's Whore to Pastor's Wife*, 23.

39. Plummer, *From Priest's Whore to Pastor's Wife*, 291.

40. Plummer, *From Priest's Whore to Pastor's Wife*, 214.

41. Plummer, *From Priest's Whore to Pastor's Wife*, 215–17.

42. Plummer, *From Priest's Whore to Pastor's Wife*, 218, 228.

43. Plummer, *From Priest's Whore to Pastor's Wife*, 282.

Chapter 5 Two for the Price of One

1. Dorothy Kelley Patterson, *A Handbook for Ministers' Wives: Sharing the Blessings of Your Marriage, Family, and Home* (Northeastern Baptist Press, 2021), 133–34.

2. Patterson, *Handbook for Ministers' Wives*, 133, 135.

3. Patterson, *Handbook for Ministers' Wives*, 61.

4. Patterson, *Handbook for Ministers' Wives*, 144.

5. Patterson, *Handbook for Ministers' Wives*, 68.

6. Patterson, *Handbook for Ministers' Wives*, 93.

7. Lisa McKay, *You Can Still Wear Cute Shoes: And Other Great Advice from an Unlikely Preacher's Wife* (David C. Cook, 2010), 17.

8. McKay, *You Can Still Wear Cute Shoes*, 19.

9. McKay, *You Can Still Wear Cute Shoes*, 42.

10. Shevalle T. Kimber, *First Ladydom in the Black Church* (Book Baby, 2023), introduction.

11. McKay, *You Can Still Wear Cute Shoes*, 39.

12. McKay, *You Can Still Wear Cute Shoes*, 40.

13. Yvonne Garrett, *The Stained Glass House: A Handbook for Ministers' Wives* (Vernon, 1991), 5–6.

14. McKay, *You Can Still Wear Cute Shoes*, 143–44 (emphasis added).

15. Patterson, *Handbook for Ministers' Wives*, 130.

16. Kate Bowler, *The Preacher's Wife: The Precarious Power of Evangelical Women Celebrities* (Princeton University Press, 2019), 116.

17. Gayle Haggard, *A Life Embraced: A Hopeful Guide for the Pastor's Wife* (Waterbrook, 2004), chap. 7, Kindle.

18. "Why Gayle Haggard Stayed," Oprah.com, January 26, 2010, https://www .oprah.com/oprahshow/why-gayle-haggard-stayed/all.

19. Haggard uses this phrase to describe Evelyn Roberts, the wife of college president Oral Roberts. Evelyn was a "leader" who used her leadership to "strengthen and support her husband's ministry." Haggard approves this attitude, describing it as using influence "wisely." Haggard, *A Life Embraced*, chap. 9, Kindle.

20. Margaret H. Watt, *The History of the Parson's Wife* (Religious Book Club, 1945), 173–74.

21. Marjorie Elizabeth Plummer, *From Priest's Whore to Pastor's Wife: Clerical Marriage and the Process of Reform in the Early German Reformation* (Ashgate, 2012), 243.

22. David Whitford, *The Making of a Godly Man: Martin Luther and the Reformation of Masculine Identity* (Routledge, forthcoming).

23. Ruth A. Tucker, *Private Lives of Pastors' Wives* (Zondervan, 1993), 16.

24. Leonard Sweet, *The Minister's Wife: Her Role in Nineteenth-Century American Evangelicalism* (Temple University Press, 1983), 3.

25. Whitford, *Making of a Godly Man*.

26. Katherine Goodwin Lindgren, "From Spiritual Guide to Church Mother: The Performative and Printed Preaching of Two Strasbourg Women," *Church History and Religious Culture* 103, nos. 3–4, special issue "Regendering the Narrative: Women in the History of Christianity," ed. Beth Allison Barr, Allison M. Brown, Katherine Goodwin Lindgren, and David M. Whitford (December 2023): 239–58. Apart from her article, I am also grateful for Katherine's advice and input in writing this section.

27. Katharina Schütz Zell, "Lament and Exhortation of Katharina Zell to the People at the Grave of Master Matthew Zell," in Elsie McKee, ed. and trans., *Church Mother: The Writings of a Protestant Reformer in Sixteenth-Century Germany* (University of Chicago Press, 2006), 114–15.

28. Tucker, *Private Life of Pastors' Wives*, 36.

29. Lindgren, "From Spiritual Guide to Church Mother," 240.

30. I find it interesting to compare Lindgren's assessment of Zell with Anthea Butler's assessment of the Church Mother role in Black Protestant denominations like

the Church of God in Christ. These women, writes Butler, "carved a niche of spiritual and temporal power for themselves within a black patriarchy that continues to assert its leadership and authority over women by denying them ordination, yet allows them to have tremendous power and authority." Butler, *Women in the Church of God in Christ: Making a Sanctified World* (University of North Carolina Press, 2007), 1.

31. Patterson, *Handbook for Ministers' Wives*, 118.

32. Watt, *History of the Parson's Wife*, 53–54.

33. Beth Allison Barr, *The Making of Biblical Womanhood: How the Subjugation of Women Became Gospel Truth* (Brazos, 2021), esp. chaps. 4 and 6.

34. Sweet, *The Minister's Wife*, 14.

35. Katherine L. French, *Household Goods and Good Households in Late Medieval London: Consumption and Domesticity After the Plague* (University of Pennsylvania Press, 2021), 15.

36. French, *Household Goods and Good Households*, 100.

37. French, *Household Goods and Good Households*, 16.

38. Merry E. Wiesner-Hanks, *Gender in History: Global Perspectives*, 2nd ed. (Wiley-Blackwell, 2011), 68–69.

39. Conference on Southern Baptist Ministers' Wives Collection, AR 369-3, SBHLA, Nashville, Tennessee. Andy and Joan Horner, the founders of Premier Designs jewelry company, "gave a generous gift to the seminary for the purpose of constructing a building conducive for instruction in homemaking." Keith Collier, "Building the Next Generation of Homemakers," *Southwestern News: A Publication of Southwestern Baptist Theological Seminary* 67, no. 1 (Fall 2008): 18–19. Premier Designs contributed to the Southern Baptist Ministers' Wives Conference and advertised in the conference programs during the early 2000s.

40. The Holy Household references the "theology of gender" ushered in by the Protestant Reformation that placed women more firmly under the household authority of their husbands. The term *Holy Household* draws from Lyndal Roper, *The Holy Household: Women and Morals in Reformation Augsburg* (Oxford University Press, 1991). For a discussion of the Holy Household, see Barr, *Making of Biblical Womanhood*, chap. 4.

41. Jill Fehleison, "Nurturing and Caring? Francis de Sale's Views on Women, Family, and Spirituality," *Church History and Religious Culture* 103, nos. 3–4, special issue "Regendering the Narrative: Women in the History of Christianity," ed. Beth Allison Barr, Allison M. Brown, Katherine Goodwin Lindgren, and David M. Whitford (December 2023): 305–21.

42. Sweet, *The Minister's Wife*, 18.

43. Wiesner-Hanks, *Gender in History*, 66–68.

44. "Little River Baptist Church and Cemetery," Milam County Historical Commission, accessed May 30, 2024, http://www.milamcountyhistoricalcommission.org /markers_little_river_baptist_church_cemetery.php.

45. "Delilah Morrell," Find a Grave, accessed May 30, 2024, https://www.finda grave.com/memorial/25681549/delilah-morrell; "Z. N. Morrell," Texas State Cemetery, https://cemetery.tspb.texas.gov/pub/user_form.asp?pers_id=119.

46. In addition to my own exploration of Little River Baptist Church and cemetery, as well as my conversations with current church members, I used the following sources for Delilah Morrell and her marriage: Steve Sadler, "The Life and Ministry of Zachariah N. Morrell" (MA thesis, Baylor University, 1980); Samuel Hesler, "Zachariah Morrell," *Southern Baptist Quarterly Review* 31 (October 1971); James Milton Carroll, *A History of Texas Baptists* (Baptist Standard, 1923); Steve Sadler, "Morrell,

Z. N. (1803–1883)," Texas State Historical Association Handbook of Texas, https://www.tshaonline.org/handbook/entries/morrell-z-n.

47. Z. N. Morrell, *Flowers and Fruits in the Wilderness, or Forty-Six Years in Texas and Two Winters in Honduras* (Gould and Lincoln, 1872; repr., Griffin Graphic Arts, 1966).

48. Rufus B. Spain, *At Ease in Zion: Social History of Southern Baptists, 1865–1900* (University of Alabama Press, 2003), 205.

49. B. F. Fuller, *A History of Texas Baptists* (Baptist Book Concern, 1900), 380, 287–88.

Chapter 6 The Best Pastor's Wife

1. Ryan Gosling, "I'm Just Ken," written by Mark Ronson and Andrew Wyatt, track 8 on *Barbie the Album*, 2023, Atlantic Records, 2023, https://youtu.be/wwux9KiBMjE.

2. Allan G. Johnson, *The Gender Knot: Unraveling Our Patriarchal Legacy* (Temple University Press, 1997), 5–6.

3. Eyder Peralta, "'A Fire I Can't Put Out': Texas State Fair's 'Big Tex' Destroyed by Blaze," NPR, October 19, 2012, https://www.npr.org/sections/thetwo-way/2012/10/19/163247347/a-fire-i-cant-put-out-texas-state-fairs-big-tex-destroyed-by-blaze.

4. Southern Baptist Ministers' Wives Conference, AR 369-3, Southern Baptist Historical Library and Archives (SBHLA), Nashville, Tennessee.

5. The folder, "The Mrs. J. M. Dawson Award for Distinguished Minister's Wife," included a copy of the portrait of Willie Dawson that hangs in the lobby of Dawson Residence Hall at Baylor University. Southern Baptist Ministers' Wives Conference, AR 369-3, SBHLA, Nashville, Tennessee.

6. Conference of Southern Baptist Ministers' Wives Collection, AR 369, SBHLA, Nashville, Tennessee. The Willie Dawson biographical material, including copies of articles about her fundraising, can be found in several of the collection boxes.

7. Travis L. Summerlin, "Dawson, Willie Evelyn Turner (1888–1963)," Texas State Historical Association Handbook of Texas, December 1, 1994, updated August 12, 2015, https://www.tshaonline.org/handbook/entries/dawson-willie-evelyn-turner. This entry states that Dawson was nominated as president; she was actually nominated as vice president, per SBC 1923 program, digital resources of SBHLA, Nashville, Tennessee, http://media2.sbhla.org.s3.amazonaws.com/annuals/SBC_Annual_1923.pdf.

8. SBC 1933 program, digital resources of SBHLA, Nashville, Tennessee, http://media2.sbhla.org.s3.amazonaws.com/annuals/SBC_Annual_1933.pdf.
The 1937 SBC program contains an equally strong statement from the WMU about the leadership of women in Christian history: "In the conquest of the world Jesus chose women to be among those who should undertake the task. From the first 'Go tell,' woman has been in the vanguard of the heralds of the cross. . . . Just as Paul entreated his fellow-laborer to help those women associated with him in the gospel, so I exhort you, my fellow pastors to help ever and hinder never, the women whose vision and voice and venture bless our churches and the world." SBC 1937 program, digital resources of SBHLA, Nashville, Tennessee, http://media2.sbhla.org.s3.amazonaws.com/annuals/SBC_Annual_1937.pdf.

9. Southern Baptist Ministers' Wives Conference, AR 369-3, SBHLA, Nashville, Tennessee.

10. Southern Baptist Ministers' Wives Conference, AR 369-3, SBHLA, Nashville, Tennessee. This quote is used on many of the programs for the ministers' wives conference.

11. Letter from Mrs. H. A. Parker, May 6, 1983, in Southern Baptist Ministers' Wives Conference, AR 369-3, SBHLA, Nashville, Tennessee.

12. Instructions for the "Mrs. J. M. Dawson" Award as found throughout the collection, Conference of Southern Baptist Ministers' Wives Collection, AR 369, SBHLA, Nashville, Tennessee.

13. Alice Marshall, letter to "Marjorie," June 26, 1995, Conference of Southern Baptist Ministers' Wives Collection, AR 369, SBHLA, Nashville, Tennessee.

14. The 1959 newspaper accounts and letters estimate between 160 and 200 nominees (most report between 160 and 164) in 250 to 300 letters from 22 to 27 states. Someone confused letters with nominations at a later date and the conference programs began to report erroneously that it was 300 nominees. Conference of Southern Baptist Ministers' Wives Collection, AR 369, SBHLA, Nashville, Tennessee. I'm grateful for Brooke LeFevre's help in writing this section.

15. Marian Grant, letter to Loulie Owens, April 21, 1959, in Southern Baptist Ministers' Wives Conference, AR 369-3, SBHLA, Nashville, Tennessee.

16. Newspaper clipping from Thomasville, NC, Thursday March 26, 1959, article written by Mrs. J. Marse Grant (Marian Grant), in Southern Baptist Ministers' Wives Conference, AR 369-3, SBHLA, Nashville, Tennessee.

17. Jane Wooten, letter to Marian Grant, February 14, 1959, in Southern Baptist Ministers' Wives Conference, AR 369-3, SBHLA, Nashville, Tennessee.

18. James O. Duncan, letter to Marian Grant, April 27, 1959, in Southern Baptist Ministers' Wives Conference, AR 369-3, SBHLA, Nashville, Tennessee.

19. Dorothy Patterson, letter, June 15, 2005, unprocessed materials for the pastors' wives conference, in Southern Baptist Ministers' Wives Conference, AR 369-3, SBHLA, Nashville, Tennessee.

20. Southern Baptist Ministers' Wives Conference, AR 369-3, SBHLA, Nashville, Tennessee.

21. Dorothy Patterson, letter, June 15, 2005, unprocessed materials for the pastors' wives conference, in Southern Baptist Ministers' Wives Conference, AR 369-3, SBHLA, Nashville, Tennessee.

22. We also examined the earliest examples we could find of pastor's wife help books published in the US and UK between the seventeenth and nineteenth centuries, including George Herbert's description of a pastor's wife and Louise Lane Clark's *The Country Parson's Wife*. I hope this book will help generate more interest in the pastor's wife role. I plan to continue my academic research in this area to further hone my historical understanding of these women.

23. This description of O'Chester is from the 2004 Ministers' Wives Conference program, Conference of Southern Baptist Ministers' Wives Collection, AR 369, SBHLA, Nashville, Tennessee.

24. Elizabeth Flowers, *Into the Pulpit: Southern Baptist Women and Power since World War II* (University of North Carolina Press, 2012), 55–56.

25. Denise Turner, *Home Sweet Fishbowl: Confessions of a Minister's Wife* (Word, 1982), 132–37.

26. Turner, *Home Sweet Fishbowl*, 11.

27. Terry A. Peck, *The Minister's Mate—Two for the Price of One?* (Convention Press, 1986), 4.

28. Martha Nelson, *This Call We Share* (Broadman, 1977), 100–101.

29. Diane Langberg, *Counsel for Pastors' Wives* (Zondervan, 1988), 42.

30. Dorothy Kelley Patterson, *A Handbook for Ministers' Wives: Sharing the Blessing of Your Marriage, Family, and Home* (Broadman & Holman, 2002), 75.

31. This is a preliminary analysis. I was generous with my classification of submission language, categorizing a book as containing submission language only if it explicitly used such language. I have resisted citing percentages, as I have not submitted my findings for peer review in an academic journal and I do not want to feed the careless use of unverified percentages/statistics that so predominates in my evangelical world. I feel confident in my assessment of these books and have provided the list of books for those who want to check these sources. I will be submitting this research to an academic journal.

32. Melody Maxwell, *The Woman I Am: Southern Baptist Women's Writings, 1906–2006* (University of Alabama Press, 2014), 171. Maxwell also notes the role played by evangelical megachurches such as Willow Creek as well as the SBC in driving the growth of women's ministries (170–72).

33. Beverly Hyles, *Life as Viewed from the Goldfish Bowl* (Sword of the Lord, 1990), 118.

34. Hyles, *Life as Viewed from the Goldfish Bowl*, 39.

35. Seth Dowland, *Family Values and the Rise of the Christian Right* (University of Pennsylvania Press, 2015), chap. 5, Kindle.

36. "1992 Christianity Today Book Awards," *Christianity Today*, April 6, 1992, https://www.christianitytoday.com/1992/04/1992-book-awards.

37. Since the 2023 convention decision, this amendment has been updated to describe the scriptural office of "pastor" as "pastor/elder/overseer." Baptist Faith and Message 2000, "VI. The Church," https://bfm.sbc.net/bfm2000/#vi.

38. Kristin Du Mez, *Jesus and John Wayne: How White Evangelicals Corrupted a Faith and Fractured a Nation* (Liveright, 2020), 168–69.

39. Flowers, *Into the Pulpit*, 11; Maxwell, *Woman I Am*, 171–72.

40. "Resolution on Ordination and the Role of Women in Ministry," Southern Baptist Convention, June 1, 1984, https://www.sbc.net/resource-library/resolutions /resolution-on-ordination-and-the-role-of-women-in-ministry, in Women in Baptist Life Collection, AR 160, SBHLA, Nashville, Tennessee.

41. Lorna Dobson, *I'm More Than the Pastor's Wife: Authentic Living in a Fishbowl World* (Zondervan, 1995), 116.

42. Dobson, *I'm More Than the Pastor's Wife*, 23.

43. Benjamin R. Knoll and Cammie Jo Bolin, *She Preached the Word: Women's Ordination in Modern America* (Oxford University Press, 2018), 14.

44. Knoll and Bolin, *She Preached the Word*, 158.

45. Interview with an evangelical Protestant woman on the empowerment of women in lay leadership positions despite their exclusion from ordained roles. Knoll and Bolin, *She Preached the Word*, 174.

46. Knoll and Bolin, *She Preached the Word*, 157–59.

47. Lori Wilhite and Brandi Wilson, *Leading and Loving It: Encouragement for Pastors' Wives and Women in Leadership* (FaithWords, 2013), chap. 1, Kindle.

48. Kate Bowler, *The Preacher's Wife: The Precarious Power of Evangelical Women Celebrities* (Princeton University Press, 2019), 275.

49. The messaging from Southwestern Baptist Theological Seminary during the presidency of Paige Patterson, for example, emphasized that it was preparing women to do "whatever God calls a woman to do" while simultaneously combating "evangelical feminism in our culture." Women were to be prepared for global evangelism and theological conversations as long as they stayed within the confines of "biblical womanhood." One student, Emily Felts, remarked, "Although I believe being a homemaker is fulfilling God's created purpose for my life, it doesn't mean I have a comprehensive

innate knowledge of how to do it best. I still need to learn what my responsibilities include, to practice achieving them well and to get used to using the necessary tools." Addressing the "common question" of what sort of job a woman does who is trained by a seminary that will only sanction women in dependent ministry roles (as wives, subordinate church staff positions, etc.), the article leans into ambiguity. "The answer is both complex and simple. They serve in a thousand different contexts doing a thousand different things." They can do whatever they want as long as it isn't being a pastor and doesn't require ordination. Terri Stovall, "Our Heartbeat," *Southwestern News: A Publication of Southwestern Baptist Theological Seminary* 67, no. 1 (Fall 2008): 6–11.

50. Flowers, *Into the Pulpit*, 130.

Chapter 7 The (SBC) Road Less Traveled

1. *Designing Women*, season 2, episode 20, "How Great Thou Art," written by Linda Bloodworth-Thomason, directed by Harry Thomason, aired February 22, 1988, on CBS.

2. Leon McBeth, *Women in Baptist Life* (Broadman, 1979), 154.

3. See "Resolution on the Place of Women in Christian Service," Southern Baptist Convention, June 1, 1973, https://www.sbc.net/resource-library/resolutions/resolution -on-the-place-of-women-in-christian-service.

4. Robert O'Brien, "Women's Lib Resolution," June 14, 1973, http://media.sbhla .org.s3.amazonaws.com/3597,12-JUN-1973.pdf; and Russell Chandler, "Southern Baptists: Beside Still Waters," *Christianity Today*, July 6, 1973, https://www.christi anitytoday.com/1973/07/southern-baptists-beside-still-waters.

5. Elizabeth Flowers, *Into the Pulpit: Southern Baptist Women and Power since World War II* (University of North Carolina Press, 2012), 51–53.

6. Pamela R. Durso, "Baptists and the Turn toward Baptist Women in Ministry," in *Turning Points in Baptist History: A Festschrift in Honor of Harry Leon McBeth*, ed. Michael E. Williams and Walter B. Shurden (Mercer, 2008), 281, see also 275–87.

7. Flowers, *Into the Pulpit*, 51.

8. For more about the Equal Rights Amendment, see Christine Blackerby, "The Equal Rights Amendment: The Most Popular Never-Ratified Amendment," National Archives, Education Updates, December 5, 2013, https://education.blogs.archives.gov /2013/12/05/the-equal-rights-amendment. For more about the potential impact of the Equal Rights Amendment on women, see "ERA and Abortion Talking Points," Columbia Law School, Center for Gender and Sexuality Law, May 3, 2022, https://gender -sexuality.law.columbia.edu/content/era-and-abortion-talking-points. For more about current conversations on divorce and women's health, see Ayesha Rascoe, "Conservatives in Red States Turn Their Attention to Ending No-Fault Divorce Laws," *NPR*, July 7, 2024, https://www.npr.org/2024/07/07/nx-s1-5026948/conservatives-in-red-states -turn-their-attention-to-ending-no-fault-divorce-laws; Katia Riddle, "Pregnant Women in Missouri Can't Get Divorced. Critics Say It Fuels Domestic Violence," *NPR*, May 3, 2024, https://www.npr.org/2024/05/03/1247838036/divorce-pregnant-women-missouri -abortion-marriage-abuse; and Selena Simmons-Duffin, "In Post-Roe Texas, 2 Mothers with Traumatic Pregnancies Walk Very Different Paths," *NPR*, July 4, 2023, https:// www.npr.org/sections/health-shots/2023/07/04/1185904719/texas-abortion-bans-dobbs -fetal-anomaly.

9. Flowers, *Into the Pulpit*, 53–58.

10. Resolutions from the Southern Baptist Convention on May 20, 1959, in "Statement Concerning the Status of 'Commissioned' Ministers of the Gospel Under the

Social Security and Rental Allowance Provisions of the Internal Revenue Code," in Southern Baptist Convention, Executive Committee Administrative and Program Planning Files, AR 627-1, Southern Baptist Historical Library and Archives (SBHLA), Nashville, Tennessee. I am indebted to Katie Heatherly for helping me with this section.

11. "Statement Concerning the Status of 'Commissioned' Ministers," in Southern Baptist Convention, Executive Committee Administrative and Program Planning Files, AR 627-1, SBHLA, Nashville, Tennessee.

12. Revenue Bill of 1921, House of Representatives, 67th Congress, 1st Session, Report No. 486, Amendment No. 153, p. 23; Samuel D. Brunson, "God Is My Roommate? Tax Exemptions for Parsonages Yesterday, Today, and (if Constitutional) Tomorrow," *Indiana Law Journal* 96 (2021): 527; Internal Revenue Code of 1954, "Section 107. Rental Value of Parsonages," p. 32; Adam Chodorow, "The Parsonage Exemption," *UC Davis Law Review* 51 (2018): 858; Bridget J. Crawford and Emily Gold Waldman, "Ministerial Magic: Tax-Free Housing and Religious Employers," *Journal of Constitutional Law* 22 (2019): 101–2.

13. "Tom Reynolds moved that the following be added to Article IX of the Constitution under the "Missionary Qualifications": "All appointments, endorsements, etc. (including the military and industrial chaplaincy) whose function will be that of a pastor, which is restricted to males by Scripture, must meet those requirements as outlined in the New Testament." Proceedings of Southern Baptist Convention, Dallas, Texas, June 11–13, 1974, https://cdn.sbhla.org/wp-content/uploads/20211228152111/sbc_proceedings_1974.pdf, SBHLA, Nashville, Tennessee.

14. The *Fort Worth Star-Telegram* ran an article on October 10, 1986, reporting on the SBC Home Mission Board voting "to stop paying salaries for women pastors. The 3–1 vote prevents women from assuming any of an estimated 1,000 pastorships in small churches under the board's financial control." Home Mission Board Executive Office Files, AR 631-3, SBHLA, Nashville, Tennessee. "In the wake of a decision by the Southern Baptist North American Mission Board to no longer endorse ordained women as chaplains, the Cooperative Baptist Fellowship endorsed six of them." James Dotson, "NAMB Will No Longer Endorse Ordained Female Chaplains," *Baptist Press*, February 8, 2002, https://www.baptistpress.com/resource-library/news/namb-will-no-longer-endorse-ordained-female-chaplains.

15. Elgee Bentley, "Women of the Southern Baptist Convention," AR 160, SBHLA, Nashville, Tennessee.

16. Susan Lockwood, interview by Mandy McMichael, April 17, 2023, audio, Baylor University Institute for Oral History, Waco, Texas.

17. "James Bartley Autobiography," in Peggy and James Bartley papers, accession #3952, box 1, folder 31, Texas Collection, Baylor University.

18. See Melody Maxwell's discussion of the use of "home and family" (home and church) to discuss missionary women's ministry. The official category was "church and family" for Sarah Lee and Kathy Hoppe in the 1980s. I am unsure if Peggy Bartley was officially categorized as "church and family," as Lee and Hoppe were, so I have used the "home and family" terminology that was visible with the "missionary homemaker" role at the time the Bartleys became SBC missionaries. Maxwell, *The Woman I Am: Southern Baptist Women's Writings, 1906–2006* (University of Alabama Press, 2014), 102–17.

19. "Annual Report of Peggy Bartley, 1968–1969," in Peggy and James Bartley papers, accession #3952, box 1, folder 37, Texas Collection, Baylor University.

20. "Annual Report of Peggy Bartley, 1971–1972," in Peggy and James Bartley papers, accession #3952, box 1, folder 38, Texas Collection, Baylor University.

21. "Annual Report of Peggy Bartley, 1954–1955," in Peggy and James Bartley papers, accession #3952, box 1, folder 32, Texas Collection, Baylor University.

22. "Annual Report of Peggy Bartley, 1955–1956," in Peggy and James Bartley papers, accession #3952, box 1, folder 32, Texas Collection, Baylor University.

23. "Annual Report of Peggy Bartley, 1960–1961," in Peggy and James Bartley papers, accession #3952, box 1, folder 34, Texas Collection, Baylor University.

24. "Annual Report of Peggy Bartley, 1971–1972," in Peggy and James Bartley papers, accession #3952, box 1, folder 38, Texas Collection, Baylor University.

25. "Annual Report of Peggy Bartley, 1982," in Peggy and James Bartley papers, accession #3952, box 1, folder 40, Texas Collection, Baylor University.

26. "Annual Report to the Uruguayan Baptist Mission, James Bartley—July 6, 1982," in Peggy and James Bartley papers, accession #3952, box 1, folder 40, Texas Collection, Baylor University.

27. Nancy Gatlin and Joe Gatlin, "Our Calling and Life in Christian Community," February 2018, https://static1.squarespace.com/static/5ad1392aa9e0287aecf2f7fa /t/5e48129883fe885c77ff46b0/1581781657232/Our+Calling+and+Life+in+Commu nity.pdf.

28. Cyrus Schleifer and Amy D. Miller, "Occupational Gender Inequality among American Clergy, 1976–2016: Revisiting the Stained-Glass Ceiling," *Sociology of Religion* 78, no. 4 (2017): 406.

29. Crawford and Waldman, "Ministerial Magic," 101–2.

30. Flowers, *Into the Pulpit*, 138, 184–87.

31. Southern Baptist Theological Seminary, Seminary Wives Institute, "Course Descriptions for Asynchronous Classes," accessed May 30, 2024, https://cf.sbts.edu /sbts2023/uploads/2023/09/swi.async_.course.descrpit23-1.pdf.

32. Southern Baptist Theological Seminary, "Course Descriptions for Asynchronous Classes."

33. "Lesson 14: Should Women Be Ordained? A Controversial Issue," Unit IV: Women in Baptist Churches Today, in "Women in the Church—Seminary Extensions," SBC Curriculum, 1979, in Women in Baptist Life Collection, AR 160, SBHLA, Nashville, Tennessee.

34. "Lesson 10: Women's Movements: Barriers or Bridges?" Unit III: Women in Contemporary Society, in "Women in the Church—Seminary Extension," SBC Curriculum, 1978, in Women in Baptist Life Collection, AR 160, SBHLA, Nashville, Tennessee.

35. "Resolution No. 3—On Ordination and the Role of Women in Ministry," Southern Baptist Convention, Kansas City, Missouri, 1984, in *FOLIO: A Newsletter for Southern Baptist Women in Ministry* 2, no. 2 (1984): 7, in Women in Baptist Life Collection, AR 160, SBHLA, Nashville, Tennessee, available at https://www.sbc .net/resource-library/resolutions/resolution-on-ordination-and-the-role-of-women-in -ministry.

36. George W. Cornell, "Despite Opposition from Church Leadership, the Ordination of Southern Baptist Women Soars," *Syracuse Herald-Journal*, Saturday, May 8, 1993, in Women in Baptist Life Collection, AR 160, SBHLA, Nashville, Tennessee.

37. H. H. Hobbs, "Ordination," in *Encyclopedia of Southern Baptists* (Broadman, 1958), 2:1057.

38. Marv Knox, "Women in Ministry 'Grieved' by HMB," *Baptist Press*, October 29, 1986, in Women in Baptist Life Collection, AR 160, SBHLA, Nashville, Tennessee.

39. Knox, "Women in Ministry 'Grieved' by HMB," in Women in Baptist Life Collection, AR 160, SBHLA, Nashville, Tennessee.

40. Nancy Hastings Sehested, "An Open Letter to the Home Mission Board, SBC, 1989," quoted in "Opening Doors: A Brief History of Women in Ministry in Southern Baptist Life, 1868–1993," pamphlet by *Southern Baptist Women in Ministry*, in Women in Baptist Life Collection, AR 160, SBHLA, Nashville, Tennessee.

41. Flowers, *Into the Pulpit*, 193. See also Maxwell, *Woman I Am*, chap. 6.

42. Flowers, *Into the Pulpit*, 193–94.

43. Kate Bowler, *The Preacher's Wife: The Precarious Power of Evangelical Women Celebrities* (Princeton University Press, 2019), 15.

Chapter 8   The Cost of Dorothy's Hats

1. Linda Barnes Popham, quoted in Greg Garrison, "Pastor Linda Barnes Popham Found Faith as an Alabama Child, Fights to Preach in Southern Baptist Church," AL.com, June 14, 2023, https://www.al.com/news/2023/06/pastor-linda-barnes -popham-found-faith-as-an-alabama-child-fights-to-preach-in-southern-baptist -church.html.

2. Bob Allen, "Newspaper Story on Sexual Abuse in SBC Was a Long Time Coming for Activist Christa Brown," *Baptist News Global*, February 11, 2019, https://baptist news.com/article/newspaper-story-on-sexual-abuse-in-sbc-was-a-long-time-coming -for-activist-christa-brown.

3. Beth Allison Barr, "The Irony of Rick Warren Being the Main Character in the Fight for Women Pastors," MSNBC, June 15, 2023, https://www.msnbc.com/opinion /msnbc-opinion/rick-warren-southern-baptists-women-rcna88964.

4. All of the SBC documents concerning this case can be found in James T. Draper Jr. Papers, AR 607, Southern Baptist Historical Library and Archives (SBHLA), Nashville, Tennessee.

5. Tom Edwards, letter to William G. Tanner, December 27, 1983, in James T. Draper Papers, AR 607, SBHLA, Nashville, Tennessee.

6. James T. Draper Papers, AR 607, SBHLA, Nashville, Tennessee.

7. William G. Tanner, letter to Tom Edwards, December 21, 1983, in James T. Draper Papers, AR 607, SBHLA, Nashville, Tennessee.

8. James T. Draper, letter to Mr. H. P. Wu, March 1, 1983, in James T. Draper Papers, AR 607, SBHLA, Nashville, Tennessee.

9. I thought long and hard about whether to use the names of those involved in this case. I decided to use Maria's name because she is dead and because I received permission through the proper channels of the CBOQ (including a conversation with a family member), but I have omitted the name of the other victim.

10. Lynneth Miller Renberg made a similar statement to me after reading the section I wrote about the Winchester Geese in the third chapter. I adapted her statement to Maria as it fit so well.

11. "Resolution on Ordination and the Role of Women in Ministry," Southern Baptist Convention, June 1, 1984, https://www.sbc.net/resource-library/resolutions /resolution-on-ordination-and-the-role-of-women-in-ministry, in Women in Baptist Life Collection, AR 160, SBHLA, Nashville, Tennessee.

12. Susan Lockwood, interview by Mandy McMichael, April 17, 2023, audio, Baylor University Institute for Oral History, Waco, Texas.

13. Records regarding Mario and Maria's life can be found in Canadian Baptist Archives, Historical Collection Baptist Convention of Ontario and Quebec, McMaster Divinity College, Hamilton, Ontario, https://mcmasterdivinity.ca/canadian-baptist -archives. For this specific source, see "Induction Service of the Reverend Mario Acacia,

BA, BC, in the College Street Baptist Church, Toronto, Ontario, April 18, 1961," in Canadian Baptist Archives, Historical Collection Baptist Convention of Ontario and Quebec, file: ACACIA, Mario, no. 05412. I am deeply grateful for the assistance of Gordon Heath (director) and Adam McCulloch (archivist).

14. "Sixty Years of Witness, 1906–1966," booklet commemorating the sixtieth anniversary of Dufferin Street Baptist Church, file: Dufferin Baptist, Toronto, CA, Canadian Baptist Archives.

15. There are contradictory notes about her education in the SBC and CBOQ archives, as well as in various Baptist newspaper announcements. What I can say is that she attended three colleges: Northwest Bible (College), Nazareth College (Michigan), and Southern Baptist Theological Seminary. She received a BA in theology with honors from either Northwest Bible or Nazareth College.

16. "The Globe and Mail, Saturday, April 15, 1961," in Canadian Baptist Archives, Historical Collection Baptist Convention of Ontario and Quebec.

17. Broadway Baptist Church originally stood between Southern Baptist Theological Seminary and the WMU training school; it relocated between 1948 and 1950. It was an SBC church when Mario Acacia received ordination but today affiliates with the Cooperative Baptist Fellowship. "Broadway Baptist Church," accessed May 30, 2024, http://www.broadwaybaptist.org/history.

18. "Induction Service of the Reverend Mario Acacia, BA, BD," in the College Street Baptist Church, Toronto, Ontario, April 18, 1961, in Canadian Baptist Archives, Historical Collection Baptist Convention of Ontario and Quebec, file: ACACIA, Mario, no. 05412.

19. "Induction Service of the Reverend Mario Acacia, BA, BD," in the College Street Baptist Church, Toronto, Ontario, April 18, 1961, in Canadian Baptist Archives, Historical Collection Baptist Convention of Ontario and Quebec, file: ACACIA, Mario, no. 05412.

20. Joyce Rogers, *Chosen to Be a Minister's Wife* (Innovo, 2013), 10–11.

21. There are many reasons for this decline. I am not suggesting that the pastor is always at fault for declining membership. My point is the contrast between Joyce Rogers's life as a pastor's wife at continuously growing churches and the continuing challenges faced by Maria Acacia during her life as a pastor's wife.

22. Rogers, *Chosen to Be a Minister's Wife*, 22, 34, 41.

23. Paul Pressler, *A Hill on which to Die: One Southern Baptist's Journey* (Broadman & Holman, 1999), 101.

24. Katherine Burgess, "This Memphis Pastor Helped Chart the Conservative Course of the Southern Baptist Convention," *Memphis Commercial Appeal*, July 9, 2019, https://www.commercialappeal.com/story/news/2019/07/09/memphis-pastor-adrian-rogers-helped-chart-conservative-course-southern-baptist-convention/1633087001.

25. Rogers, *Chosen to Be a Minister's Wife*, 66.

26. Interviews with former church members at CBOQ office, January 2024. Both CBOQ and Brazos Press have copies of the interview notes. The names of the interviewees have been redacted from publication at their request.

27. *Baptist Advance*, February 1964, p. 3, in Canadian Baptist Archives, Historical Collection Baptist Convention of Ontario and Quebec.

28. Dorothy Kelley Patterson, *A Handbook for Ministers' Wives: Sharing the Blessings of Your Marriage, Family, and Home* (Northeastern Baptist Press, 2021), 68.

29. "Annual Report, Year of 1977, Dufferin Baptist Church," January 27, 1978, in Canadian Baptist Archives, Historical Collection Baptist Convention of Ontario and Quebec, File: Dufferin Baptist Church, Toronto, CA.

30. For more on clergy sex abuse, especially the impact on victims, see David Kenneth Pooler and Liza Barros-Lane, "A National Study of Adult Women Sexually Abused by Clergy: Insights for Social Workers," *Social Work* 67, no. 2 (March 14, 2022): 123–33; and a forthcoming article by Sandra Moncrief-Stuart and David K. Pooler, "Adult Clergy Sexual Abuse Survivors, Post Traumatic Stress Disorder and Institutional Betrayal Trauma," cited in Rebecca Hopkins, "Some Churches Call Clergy Sexual Misconduct an 'Affair': Survivors Are Fighting to Make It against the Law," *Christianity Today*, June 10, 2024, https://www.christianitytoday.com/2024/06/clergy-sex-abuse-consent-law-crime.

31. Kenneth W. Morrison, February 9, 1978, in Canadian Baptist Archives, Historical Collection Baptist Convention of Ontario and Quebec, File: ACACIA, Mario, No. 0512.

32. Kenneth W. Morrison, February 9, 1978, in Canadian Baptist Archives, Historical Collection Baptist Convention of Ontario and Quebec, File: ACACIA, Mario, No. 0512.

33. Jerome, "Letter 77. To Oceanus," in *A Select Library of Nicene and Post-Nicene Fathers of the Christian Church*, series 2, vol. 6, ed. Philip Schaff and Henry Wace (Christian Literature, 1890–1900; repr., Hendrickson, 1994), 157–63.

34. Merry E. Wiesner-Hanks, *Gender in History: Global Perspectives*, 3rd ed. (Wiley-Blackwell, 2022), 47.

35. Wiesner-Hanks, *Gender in History*, 74.

36. Kate Bowler, *The Preacher's Wife: The Precarious Power of Evangelical Women Celebrities* (Princeton University Press, 2019), 37.

37. Elesha J. Coffman, *Turning Points in American Church History: How Pivotal Events Shaped a Nation and a Faith* (Baker Academic, 2024), 264.

38. The Equal Rights Amendment passed in Congress in 1972; it failed to gain ratification from enough states to be adopted as a Constitutional Amendment.

39. Rogers, quoted in Coffman, *Turning Points in American Church History*, 265, citing Elizabeth Flowers, *Into the Pulpit: Southern Baptist Women and Power since World War II* (University of North Carolina Press, 2012), 86.

40. Flowers, *Into the Pulpit*, 76–78.

41. Findings Report of the 1978 Convocation on Women in Church-Related Vocations, "The Psychological Impact of Women in Ministry," by Andrew D. Lester, in Women in Baptist Life Collection, AR 160, SBHLA, Nashville, Tennessee; Bob Allen, "Lawsuit Accuses Once-Admired Evangelical Family Expert of Sexual Abuse," *Baptist News Global*, January 15, 2016, https://baptistnews.com/article/lawsuit-accuses-once-admired-evangelical-family-expert-of-sexual-abuse; Rachel T. Keeney, "Inclusive Language—Reform or Revolution?," *Folio: A Newsletter for Baptist Women in Ministry* 17, no. 3 (Winter 1999–2000): 9, in SBHLA, Nashville, Tennessee.

42. "Resolution No. 3—On Ordination and the Role of Women in Ministry," Southern Baptist Convention, Kansas City, Missouri, 1984, in *FOLIO: A Newsletter for Southern Baptist Women in Ministry* 2, no. 2 (1984): 7, in Women in Baptist Life Collection, AR 160, SBHLA, Nashville, Tennessee, available at https://www.sbc.net/resource-library/resolutions/resolution-on-ordination-and-the-role-of-women-in-ministry.

43. Susan Lockwood, interview by Mandy McMichael.

44. H. P. Wu, letter to James T. Draper, February 20, 1983, in James T. Draper Papers, AR 607, SBHLA, Nashville, Tennessee.

45. William G. Tanner, letter to James T. Draper, March 7, 1983, in James T. Draper Papers, AR 607, box 2, SBHLA, Nashville, Tennessee.

46. Oscar I. Romo, letter to James T. Draper, March 11, 1983, in James T. Draper Papers, AR 607, SBHLA, Nashville, Tennessee.

47. Oscar I. Romo, letter to James T. Draper, March 11, 1983, in James T. Draper Papers, AR 607, SBHLA, Nashville, Tennessee.

48. Per interviews with former members of Dufferin Street Baptist Church. Maria's hospitalization, and the reasons for it, were well known.

49. James T. Draper, letter to Oscar Romo, March 16, 1983, in James T. Draper Papers, AR 607, SBHLA, Nashville, Tennessee.

50. I strongly recommend reading Christa Brown's *Baptistland: A Memoir of Abuse, Betrayal, and Transformation* (Lake Drive Books, 2024). See also Megan Lively's story reported in Michelle Boorstein, "A Rape Survivor's Careful Activism in a Place Where #MeToo Feels Taboo," *Washington Post*, December 13, 2022, https://www .washingtonpost.com/religion/2022/12/13/sbc-megan-lively-evangelical-metoo.

Chapter 9 Together for the Gospel

1. *Doctor Who*, season 5, episode 10, "Vincent and the Doctor," written by Richard Curtis, directed by Jonny Campbell, aired June 25, 2010, on BBC, https://www.bbc.co .uk/programmes/b00spgsf.

2. Susan Lockwood, interview by Mandy McMichael, April 17, 2023, audio, Baylor University Institute for Oral History, Waco, Texas.

3. Casey Schumacher, "Dorothy Scarborough," May 8, 2015, Texas Collection, https://blogs.baylor.edu/texascollection/category/baylor/dorothy-scarborough. See also Dorothy Scarborough papers, accession #153, Texas Collection, Baylor University. For previous scholarship as well as pedagogical instruction, I have worked through much of the Scarborough collection.

4. Mark Andrew Olsen, interview by Robert Darden, "Dorothy Scarborough," episode 11, *Treasures of the Texas Collection* (radio show), December 4, 2011, https://www.pod casts-online.org/the-treasures-of-the-texas-collection-431775032, transcript available at https://studylib.net/doc/17810477/treasures-of-the-texas-collection-dorothy-scarborough.

5. Mark Andrew Olsen, interview by Robert Darden.

6. Mandy McMichael, "A 1984 Prediction Comes True for the SBC," *Baptist News Global*, June 15, 2023, https://baptistnews.com/article/a-1984-prediction-comes-true -for-the-sbc.

7. "Resolution on Women," Southern Baptist Convention, June 1, 1983, https:// www.sbc.net/resource-library/resolutions/resolution-on-women-3.

8. McMichael, "1984 Prediction Comes True."

9. "Resolution on Women," Southern Baptist Convention, June 1, 1983, https:// www.sbc.net/resource-library/resolutions/resolution-on-women-3.

10. Weptanomah W. Carter, *The Black Minister's Wife: As a Participant in the Redemptive Ministry of Her Husband* (Progressive National Baptist, 1976), 30–31.

11. Mary O. Ross, *The Minister's Wife* (1946; repr., Harlo Press, 1983), 49.

12. Evelyn Brooks Higginbotham, *Righteous Discontent: The Women's Movement in the Black Baptist Church, 1880–1920* (Harvard University Press, 1993).

13. Candice Marie Benbow, *Red Lip Theology: For Church Girls Who've Considered Tithing to the Beauty Supply Store When Sunday Morning Isn't Enough* (Convergent, 2022), 13–15.

14. Carter, *Black Minister's Wife*, 40.

15. Carter, *Black Minister's Wife*, 18, 105.

16. Carter, *Black Minister's Wife*, 76–77.

17. Carter, *Black Minister's Wife*, 87, 91.

18. Benbow, *Red Lip Theology*, 54.

BETH ALLISON BARR (PhD, University of North Carolina at Chapel Hill) is the James Vardaman Endowed Professor of History at Baylor University in Waco, Texas, where she specializes in medieval history, women's history, and church history. She is the author of *USA Today* bestseller *The Making of Biblical Womanhood: How the Subjugation of Women Became Gospel Truth*. Her work has  been featured by NPR and the *New Yorker*, and she has written for *Christianity Today*, the *Washington Post*, the *Dallas Morning News*, *Sojourners*, and *Baptist News Global*. Barr lives in Texas with her husband, a Baptist pastor, and their two children.

─────────────── Connect with Dr. Barr ───────────────

bethallisonbarr.com

bethallisonbarr.substack.com

bethallisonbarr

@bethallisonbarr

@bethallisonbarr

@bethallisonbarr1